SAMUEL

"One Armed"

BERRY

SAMUEL
"One Armed"
BERRY

Shaker, Teacher, Ruthless Civil War Guerilla

BRYAN BUSH

Acclaim Press
MORLEY, MISSOURI

P.O. Box 238
Morley, MO 63767
(573) 472-9800
www.acclaimpress.com

Book layout and design: Steward&Wise Graphic Design
Cover design: Frene Melton

ISBN: 978-1-956027-92-1 | 1-956027-92-0
Library of Congress Control Number: 2024941647

First Printing: 2024
Printed in the United States of America
10 9 8 7 6 5 4 3 2 1

This publication was produced using available information.
The publisher regrets it cannot assume responsibility for errors or omissions.

Contents

Introduction 7

Chapter 1: The Early Years 16

Chapter 2: The Murder of Sam Berry's Sister Susan 19

Chapter 3: Revenge 23

Chapter 4: Sam Berry Joins General John Hunt Morgan's Command 30

Chapter 5: The 1862 Confederate Invasion of Kentucky 36

Chapter 6: Confederate General John Hunt Morgan Captures
            Gallatin, Tennessee 38

Chapter 7: The Battle of Castalian Springs and Hartsville, Tennessee 41

Chapter 8: Confederate General John Hunt Morgan's Christmas Raid
            in Kentucky 45

Chapter 9: Confederate General John Hunt Morgan's Great Raid 49

Chapter 10: Union Authorities Cracks Down on Guerillas in Kentucky ... 56

Chapter 11: Confederate General Morgan's Attack of Mt. Sterling 62

Chapter 12: Battle of Cynthiana, Kentucky 68

Chapter 13: Union General Stephen Gano Burbridge's Order No. 59 73

Chapter 14: September 1864: Berry Fights Union Captain Harvey
            Buckley and the Robbing of the Lebanon Train. 81

Chapter 15: October 1864: The Robbery of Harrodsburg and
            Perryville, Kentucky 86

Chapter 16: November 1864: Berry Gang Rampage of Murder and
            Robbery 96

Chapter 17: December 1864: The Killing of African Americans 104

Chapter 18: January 1865: The Simpsonville Massacre 117

Chapter 19: February 1865: Berry Encounters Captain Edwin Terrell
            and Captain James Bridgewater, Union Guerilla Hunters 130

Chapter 20: Henry Magruder and Marcellus Jerome Clarke aka
            Sue Mundy is Captured 138

Chapter 21: April 1865: The Civil War Comes to an End 145

Chapter 22: Captain Sam Berry Surrenders 149

Chapter 23: Conclusion 159

Endnotes 168

Bibliography 183

About the Author 185

Index 186

Introduction

Samuel Berry was born in 1840. In 1858, Sam left home and attended Kentucky State Normal School in Lexington, Kentucky and was a schoolmate of Judge Robert J. Breckinridge, of Danville, who remembered him as a diligent student and a bright mischievous child. After graduating from Kentucky State Normal School, Samuel Berry taught at Laurel Hill and at Martin's School House near Dixville. He served with Confederate General John Hunt Morgan for two years and after Morgan was captured, Berry, along with Jerome Clarke, Henry Magruder, Bill Marion (Stanley Young), formed a guerilla band and began a reign of terror in Kentucky. What circumstances drove Samuel Berry and his brother Thomas into becoming guerillas?

Before describing how Berry became a guerilla, the definition of the different types of guerillas has to be defined and what category of guerilla that Berry had become during the Civil War and after the cessation of the War. As Brian McKnight stated that "one of the most pervasive elements in the study of the American Civil War guerillas is the necessary but frustrating need of classifying them within the context of their peers and their roles in the larger conflict." Contrary to the traditional popular perception, Civil War irregulars were complex figures in multifaceted groups. ... They also moved fluidly between various roles." Sam Berry, Henry Magruder, and Marcellus Jerome Clarke moved between these various roles throughout the war. Daniel Sutherland in his book *A Savage Conflict* defined guerillas by distinguishing them between independent and official figures. Early in the war, guerillas used the name "partisan" and were interchangeable. The Confederate government sanctioned partisans who operated in the military margins with government sanction. Partisans were "generally mounted and organized in company-or battalion sized units, they operated on "detached service" to provide reconnaissance, conduct raids, and attack small groups of enemy soldiers."[1] He saw the common guerilla as someone who operated when, where, and however he saw fit, and that the partisan was a loosely connected member of the army and expected to behave as a soldier in exchange for his operational independence and the protection of military law. Sutherland stated that guerillas came in many forms. He categorized bushwhackers as anyone who were outside the military law, such as outlaws, deserters, and ruffians, people who settled a vendetta, killed people, or destroyed property for sport, or out of meanness. As Sutherland pointed out, Union soldiers referred to all guerillas as bushwhackers. Sutherland stated that two things clearly defined nearly all "guerillas." "First, there was a "irregular" way they attacked, harassed, or worried their foe, quite unlike the methods used by regular soldiers in conventional armies. Second, their responsibility, their very reason for being in most cases, was local defense, protection of their families or communities against both internal and external foes."[2] According to James Martin, there were three different types of guerillas: partisan rangers, war-rebels, and outlaws. The first group fell under the Confederate Partisan Ranger Act of 1862. The Act authorized partisan rangers to conduct the war against Union soldiers with hit and run tactics and guerilla type tactics. The Confederacy authorized certain cavalry units to operate independently in irregular warfare. Some of the more notable Partisan Rangers were Confederate General John S. Mosby, General Adam Rankin "Stovepipe" Johnson, who commanded the 10th Kentucky Cavalry, and rode with Confederate General John Hunt Morgan. The Confederate soldiers who rode with Mosby, Johnson, and Morgan were legitimate Confederate soldiers on an authorized mission, but Union authorities and civilians treated the partisan rangers as guerillas when they were captured and punished them accordingly.[3] The partisan rangers were not viewed as legitimate Confederate soldiers by Union authorities but were placed in the general category of guerillas. The rangers were treated by Union authorities as outlaws. Many of Morgan's men returned to Kentucky to recruit Southern sympathizers and returned Confederate soldiers in order to raise a regiment that would carry raids into Union occupied areas of Kentucky. In September 1864, the Confederate government issued Order Number 211 which gave Adam Rankin Johnson authority to "inspect, muster in, and organize recruits, and conscripts... [and to] organize new regiments of cavalry and infantry, and new companies of artillery."[4]

The second group were known as "war-rebels," who were a large number of Confederate soldiers who returned to Kentucky during 1863 to 1865. They were soldiers who fought in the war as soldiers, but when they returned to their homes, they found the state under martial law. Their leaders held a valid commission in the Confederate army, and they all claimed to be members of the Confederate army.[5] The Confederate soldiers or Southern sympathizers decided to take the war to Union authorities and citizens. Most of these units were made up between ten to fifty men, although sometimes the groups could be as large as a couple hundred men. War-rebels were not authorized to operate in Kentucky, such as Johnson or Morgan. They were treated under Article 82 of General Order Number 100. The men believed themselves to be to be legitimate Confederate soldiers, dedicated to the Southern cause. Many of these soldiers fought under Morgan, such as Samuel Berry, his brother Thomas Berry, Henry Magruder, and Marcellus Jerome Clarke aka Sue Mundy. They continued to carry the war to their sworn enemies in the Union army. They were supported by members of the community in Kentucky that had Southern sympathies and provided the war rebels with supplies and medical care. War Rebels made up the majority of the guerillas in Kentucky. The big difference between partisans and war rebels was that partisans had authorization from the Confederate government to carry out raids, where war rebels carried their brand of war to the Union authorities on their own terms without authorization or orders from the Confederate government. The war rebels for the most part directed their activities against Union authorities or Union sympathizers who were their sworn enemies. They considered themselves patriots of the Confederacy and not outlaws.

Sue Mundy, Sam and Tom Berry, Henry Magruder entered Kentucky with Morgan on his last raid in Kentucky and remained with Morgan's division until Morgan was captured and finally killed in Greeneville, Tennessee in September of 1864. As James Martin in his article on guerilla warfare in Kentucky, referred to

Confederate General John Hunt Morgan. When Morgan was killed in 1864, several of his men followed Morgan's playbook on how to conduct raids, which led to Marcellus Jerome Clarke, Henry Magruder, Sam "One-Armed" Berry, and many others. (Library of Congress)

Morgan as "the father of guerilla warfare in Kentucky. Morgan was a teacher, and his organization spawned tens of smaller groups who sought to combat the Unionists in the same way Morgan had fought earlier."[6] Although Sue Mundy, Sam Berry, Henry Magruder, and members of their gang were no longer connected with the main Confederate army, Sam Berry, Jerome Clarke (Sue Mundy), and Magruder decided to take the war to the Union people of Kentucky. They were judge and jury and decided who were their enemies were, not the Confederate government. Jerome Clarke (Sue Mundy) along with Sam and Thomas Berry, stated that they had Confederate commissions and they considered themselves Confederate soldiers and entitled to be treated as prisoners of war, not murders or brigands.

The last group of guerillas were outlaws. During 1864, 1865, and 1866, a group of ex Confederate soldiers held no value for human life. James Martin referred to the outlaws as men who "used the war as an excuse either to settle old debts or to seek personal gain." As the war came to an end, the partisans and war rebels surrendered and petitioned for an amnesty oath, but the outlaws ignored the Confederate surrender and continued to raid, rob, rape, and murder, in Kentucky. Sam Berry became an outlaw towards the end of the war.

Guerillas had been categorized by historians, Union authorities, and Union civilians in Civil War Kentucky as murders and outlaws, who had a minimal effect on the outcome of the larger conflict, which was fought on battlefields, such as Gettysburg, Chickamauga, and Vicksburg. But guerilla warfare was an extension of the war, which brought the conflict literally into the homes of Union sympathizers and Southern sympathizers in Kentucky. The violence of guerilla warfare brought the Civil War to the forefront of Kentucky families. Guerilla warfare increased the tension between families, when the relatives either fought for the Union or the Confederacy. When the Civil War erupted on the American landscape, Kentucky decided to declare neutrality. Some of the families in Kentucky had sons who fought both for the Union and the Confederate armies. As James Martin stated in his article on guerilla warfare in Kentucky wrote: "The irregular warfare in Kentucky was not an accident of nature nor a simple outbreak of social violence. It was a part of the war effort of the South and had more impact on the populace of the Bluegrass State than any battle." Daniel Sutherland stated: "Guerillas helped check invading armies at every turn. They distracted the Federals from their primary objectives, causing them to alter strategies, injured the morale of Union troops, and forced the reassignment of men and resources to counter threats to railroads, river traffic, and foraging parties. They shielded communities, stymied Union efforts to occupy the South, and spread panic throughout the lower Midwest."[7] Guerillas played a large part in the Civil War history of Kentucky.

Union authorities dealt with Albert "Stovepipe" Johnson and Morgan's men under Article 82, of General Order Number 100, which treated their men as highway robbers and pirates, instead of Article 81, which Johnson's men were entitled to be treated as prisoners of war. According to Union authorities, anyone found wearing a Confederate uniform in Kentucky was considered a guerilla.

Morgan led raids into Kentucky to secure supplies and to deny the supplies to the Union army. Morgan destroyed bridges and railroads to stop the supply of arms, equipment, food to the Union armies fighting in the South, such as Tennessee.

Samuel Berry's brother, Thomas, joined the Confederate army under General John Hunt Morgan and eventually gained a rank of captain. Samuel was a Confederate sympathizer and tried to stay out of the war and raise his family. The defining moment that changed Samuel and his brother's Thomas, to becoming Confederate guerillas, was the murder of their sister Minnie, when a Union soldier bayonetted their sister, when she tried to save a family sword from being stolen by the Union soldiers. Samuel and his brother swore revenge on the Union soldiers who killed their sister. After Samuel and his brother Thomas killed the culprits who killed their sister, Thomas persuaded his brother to join Morgan's cavalry. Samuel became a member of the 6th Kentucky Confederate Cavalry and fought alongside his brother with Morgan. Samuel rose to the rank of sergeant. When Samuel rode with Morgan on his Great Raid in July of 1863, and Morgan was captured, Samuel, along with other members of Morgan's old command, such as Jerome Clarke aka Sue Mundy, Henry Magruder, formed their own band of war rebels and took the war to the Union army in Kentucky. Sam and Thomas recruited Southern sympathizers for the Confederate army and recruited men who had been wronged by the Union army for their own group. If you asked Samuel Berry, he would testify that he was a legitimate Confederate soldier who fought for the Confederacy and should be treated as a prisoner of war.

But Samuel Berry changed from being a war rebel to outlaw when he decided to form his own gang when Henry Magruder and Sue Mundy were captured and hung. Although the war was over, he continued to rob, kill, and rape. He no longer robbed Union soldiers but robbed stagecoaches with ordinary citizens.

He robbed civilians in the streets and robbed toll gates. When he surrendered to Union authorities, he thought he would be treated as a legitimate prisoner of war, but Union authorities treated him as an outlaw to be hung. Luckily, he was not hung as many of his fellow gang members, but committed to a prison, with the sentence of ten years hard labor.

Many of those who joined the Berry's in their revenge also had injustices performed on them by either having livestock stolen, or harassment because they were Confederate sympathizers, or had their crops stolen. Henry Magruder was plowing his field when Union soldiers wanted his horse and when he refused to let the Union soldiers have his horse, they beat him almost to death. He swore to never take another Yankee alive. As stated earlier, Sam, his brother Tom, Jerome Clarke, Henry Magruder, and others rode with General Morgan and learned his guerillas tactics. Many books have showed Jerome Clarke as the leader of the guerilla band, but as eyewitness testimony in Federal courts point out that all of them were captains. Jerome Clarke, Henry Magruder, Sam and Tom Berry, Bill Marion (Stanley Young), banded together in a lose band of guerillas who were dedicated to bring the war to the Union soldiers, not on a battlefield, but in small groups.

Guerilla warfare had a major impact in Kentucky both psychologically and monetarily to the Federal government. The area were the guerillas fought was literally in areas where they grew up. The people they robbed, killed, and pillaged, were relatives, friends, and town acquaintances who knew them. The Union soldiers they killed were many times fellow Kentuckians, who lived in their communities. When the guerillas wore red, meaning they took no quarter, they terrorized local communities. The war was no longer in some distant battlefield, but in their own communities as the guerillas killed, robbed, burned courthouses, and carried out terrorist acts on the local community. The local citizens lived in fear, never knowing when their home or their community would be next in the reign of terror. When a community member was pro Union and their son returned from the war and was shot and killed for no other reason than returning home, the war became real in the worst way. The Federal government had to spend time and money tracking down the guerillas. District Military Commander for Kentucky Union General Stephen Gano Burbridge passed Order No. 59 in which he stated that for every Union soldier or sympathizer killed by a Confederate guerilla he would select four Confederate guerillas in prison and execute them on the spot of the killing. The order only made matters worse and forced the guerillas to raise the black flag. After Burbridge was replaced with Union General John Palmer, Palmer hired and paid Union guerillas such as Captain Edwin Terrell and Captain James Bridgewater to hunt down and kill Confederate guerillas. Terrell was almost worse than the Confederate guerillas. The action would have immense repercussions after the war, when Kentuckians decided to turn away from Union authorities and embrace the Lost Cause, electing many ex-Confederate officers into positions of authority, such as Governor Simon Buckner.

SAMUEL
"One Armed"
BERRY

Shaker, Teacher, Ruthless Civil War Guerilla

CHAPTER ONE

The Early Years

According to Thomas Berry, Sam Berry's brother, their great-great-grandfather was a soldier under Marlborough and was in all the battles in the Netherlands and the Levant under Iron Duke. In 1702, he immigrated to America with six sons and three daughters. He settled in near Williamsburg, Virginia and later to Westmoreland, County. His grandfather was born in 1724. When the American Revolution broke out, his grandfather joined the army under General George Washington. During the war, his grandfather reached the rank of captain. He married Miss McGraw, who was the daughter of a distinguished Revolutionary soldier. After the American Revolution, his grandfather and his soldier friends moved to Kentucky.[8]

Berry's grandfather settled in Woodford County, Kentucky, and later Boyle County. Thomas Berry stated that his grandfather fought against the Native Americans and was seriously wounded at the Battle of French Lick Springs, Indiana. He was saved from a scalping by a comrade. His father was Samuel Oscar Berry, who was born in Westmoreland County, Virginia in 1760 and died in Lexington, Kentucky in 1869. He married Miss Elizabeth McGraw of Boyle County, daughter of Major John McGraw, a Revolutionary soldier. He had six children: Samuel Oscar, William W., Susan, Minnie, Thomas F., and Alex Berry. Susan died in infancy. All his children were born in Woodford County. Samuel was born in Liberty County, Missouri in 1840. Samuel Berry lost his mother who died in 1836. His father was miserable over the loss of his wife. To make matters worse, his father received a letter stating that his brother, William Berry, had been seriously wounded in the Battle at San Antonio, Texas and on that day same day Colonel John Milam, his brother-in-law, had been killed. His father Samuel moved Uncle William to New Orleans and left him in the care of surgeons.[9]

Before he left home to head for Texas he placed all his children with his brothers and sisters. Thomas was left with his grandfather John McGraw of

Boyle County. His brothers Sam and William were left with Uncle Jim and Uncle Younger near Lexington, Kentucky. Samuel's sister was placed with Uncle Lewis Berry. His father left his business affairs in the hands of his brother Younger. His father fought with Sam Houston and was present at the battle of San Jacinto. At the time, Thomas Berry was living in Lexington when the Mexican War broke out and his father joined Captain Perry Beard's company, under Humphrey Marshall's regiment. John Hunt Morgan was a lieutenant in Captain Beard's company. Thomas had a best friend, James Campbell, who was older than him, and joined Captain Scarce's company of the same regiment. Thomas wanted to be with his friend, so his friend smuggled him aboard a ship and hid him from the officers, especially his father. The men disembarked at Pointe Isabel. His father was surprised when he saw his son disembarking with the soldiers and threatened to whip him, but all the soldiers in the company begged his father not to whip him. At the time, Thomas was fourteen years old. After the battle of Chapultepec, Thomas was sent with James Campbell, who was seriously wounded to a military hospital. Both Thomas and James stayed at a hospital in Vera Cruz. Thomas was in six battles. After the Mexican War, Thomas returned to Lexington. He joined Captain John Hunt Morgan's Lexington Rifles and attended school.[10]

Sam and Thomas' father married for a second time and settled at Versailles, Kentucky and later moved to Lexington. He resumed his business. Samuel, his brother Thomas, and William had reached manhood and were making their own way in the world. Thomas stayed with his grandfather. He later moved in with his uncle John McGraw, who was professor of geology and stayed with him for two years. Both Thomas and his uncle took a trip to South America, visiting Peru, Bolivia, Columbia, Paraguay, Brazil, Yucatan, Mexico, and Guatemala. When they returned from their trip, they lived with Uncle John, who was a professor of geology at Transylvania University.[11]

In 1858, Sam left home and attended Kentucky State Normal School in Lexington, Kentucky and was a schoolmate of Judge Robert J. Breckinridge, of Danville, who remembered him as a diligent student and a bright mischievous child. After graduating from Kentucky State Normal School, Samuel Berry taught at Laurel Hill and at Martin's School House near Dixville.[12] Many of Berry's students in Perryville stated that he was a splendid teacher and disciplinarian. He was also kind and affectionate towards his pupils. D. C. Claunch, who lived a mile from Perryville, stated that while attending Berry's school at Martin's, he frequently engaged in playing the game of marbles with him. According to David Vanderipe, son of James Vanderipe, Berry lost his arm while operating a cider mill or possibly a hemp machine, while living at the Shaker community, at Pleasant Hill, although some reports stated that Berry lost his arm in Lexington. Berry was married and had one daughter. His wife was Miss Rose, of the Rose Hill neighborhood in Mercer County. Berry continued to teach school in the different districts.

Sam Berry was described as "medium height, with broad shoulders and heavy body, dark hair and beard, and a brutal face, backed with the courage of a lion. He was a dangerous man to tamper with under any circumstances. When sober, however, he was inclined to be quiet as long as let alone, but when intoxicated he knew no reason or hesitated to perform no deed.[13]

Sketch portraying a scene that was carried out across Kentucky. As the Union army carried out raids on local homesteads, the male members of the family would avenge the wrongs by joining the Confederate cavalry or the guerillas. (Library of Congress)

CHAPTER TWO

The Murder of Sam Berry's Sister Susan

Sam Berry's brother Thomas Berry, at the age of twenty-seven, joined Company A, 2nd Kentucky Cavalry, "Dukes" Regiment, under Confederate General John Hunt Morgan. He rose to the rank of captain. Confederate General John Hunt Morgan was no stranger to Kentucky. Born in Huntsville, Alabama, on June 1, 1825, he became a member of a prominent Kentucky family. He attended Transylvania College in Lexington, Kentucky, but left the school after the college suspended him for an altercation with another student. Between 1846 and 1847 he served in the Mexican War as a first lieutenant with the 1st Kentucky. After the war, he bought a hemp factory and woolen mill and became a prominent member of society in Lexington. In 1857, he formed the Lexington Rifles, a local militia unit. When the war broke out, Morgan joined the Confederate army. He became a colonel of the 2nd Kentucky Cavalry. Morgan recruited at Camp Charity, located between Bardstown and Bloomfield, and recruited for the Confederacy.[14]

Captain Morgan, along with his force, including Thomas Berry moved to Bowling Green, Kentucky and were sworn into the Confederate service. While preparing to cross the Green River, Morgan's force was attacked by two companies of Home Guards and crossed the river under fire. When Morgan's men landed, they attacked the Home Guards. They encountered 179 Home Guards and managed to capture twelve prisoners and seventy horses, and twenty guns. In December 1861, Morgan was ordered to assist General Thomas Hindman, who commanded 3,500 men. His headquarters was at Bell's Tavern, twenty-five miles from Bowling Green. The Union army occupied Woodsonville, who advanced to the Green River. General Hindman moved out and sent two pieces of artillery and the 8th Texas Cavalry to scout the area. Hindman attacked the Union force. The battle became known as the Woodsonville. The commander of the 8th Texas Cavalry, Colonel Benjamin Terry was killed by members of the 32nd Indiana Infantry.

Morgan and his men burned the Bacon Creek Bridge. The Federal troops were camped three miles north. They dispersed a company of Home Guards. On January 25, 1862, Morgan rode into Lebanon. Several hundred Federal troops were camped near the town and a large amount of army stores were in two large buildings. Morgan set fire to the two buildings and captured thirty Federal soldiers. Morgan released most of the prisoners except nine men. They kept some of the blue uniforms to disguise themselves. They also captured their first flag.

Confederate General John Hunt Morgan. (Library of Congress)

Towards the end of January, Confederate General Albert Sidney Johnston, who was commander of the all the Confederate forces in the Western Theater, retreated after the devastating losses at Mill Springs and Fort Henry and Donelson. On February 14, 1862, Johnston evacuated his headquarters at Bowling Green, Kentucky and eventually fell back to Corinth, Mississippi. Morgan's men were the last to leave Nashville, Tennessee when the city was abandoned.

At the Battle of Shiloh, in April of 1862, Morgan's command was attached to General John Breckinridge's division. General Breckinridge had six thousand men and was the reserve. After the battle of Shiloh, Morgan's men passed through Springfield, and marched through Harrodsburg, Kentucky. Thomas Berry met his brother Sam who he had not seen in two years. Sam told his father and brother that that he had a hard time living as a Southerner in Kentucky. All Southerners were liable to arrest. Sam told his brother that he thought about joining Morgan's command. Thomas and his father tried to persuade Sam not to join the Confederate service because he had the duty to take care of his wife. Sam told his brother and father that the Union Home Guards were taunting him and had already arrested him three times. He was tired of the harassment. His wife's father was a strong Union man and was the source of his troubles. Sam owned a small piece of property and a nice home. His father-in-law wanted the land. According to Thomas, Sam Berry's wife's father could care less about her welfare or happiness and that her father was the reason why Sam had been arrested. Thomas begged his brother Sam Berry to stay home and protect his wife. Sam said he would stand the harassment as long as he could.

Thomas rejoined Morgan's command. While riding with Morgan, Thomas received a letter from his brother Sam. Sam stated that his life and surroundings were becoming unbearable, that he had been arrested and forced to give a heavy bond, with his father-in-law as surety. The Home Guard had stolen his two horses and three milk cows and five hogs and some sheep. When asked to pay for them, they told Sam to charge his losses to the Federal government, prove his loyalty, and then he might get paid for his losses. The Home Guard told Sam he better join the Union army or keep his "disloyal tongue in his head."

When Thomas Berry was recruiting a company for partisan service, he requested his brother Sam to write to Thomas under the nom de plume of Tom Henderson and enclose his letter in an envelope addressed to John Carter, Leesburg, Harrison County, Kentucky. While he was in Harrison County, Thomas received the daily paper giving him an account of an outrage perpetrated by some marauding bands of Union soldiers near a place called Foxtown, upon a defenseless family and the home was plundered. The paper stated that the Union soldiers did not stop plundering the home, they also killed a nineteen-year-old girl. After a few days, the paper confirmed the reports of the home being plundered of a house in the neighborhood of Foxtown between Nicholasville, Camp Dick Robinson, and Richmond.[15]

About this time, Thomas received a visitor who called himself John Carter, who was actually Henry Magruder. Carter pulled out a letter from Sam Berry. The letter described the assault on his sister, of the robbery and plundering of the house, trunks, drawers, etc. When Thomas Berry left his home in Lexington and joined Morgan's command, he had left his sister a chronometer watch and a sword presented to his grandfather McGraw at the time of his death. His grandfather was presented the sword after he had stormed Stony Point, under General Mad Anthony Wayne. The watch was presented to Thomas Berry by his father. He also left her his uniform.[16]

While trying to save the sword, one of the Union soldiers bayoneted Samuel's sister Minnie in the right side from behind. The bayonet passed through his sister's lower lobe of the liver and the bayonet ended up coming out the front. She lived for five days before dying. Sam wrote to his brother that she pleaded with him not to seek revenge upon her murderers. Sam wrote that he had written down the names of all of the Union soldiers in the party and saved them for future reference. Sam wrote to his brother that he would devote his entire life in trying to "wipe out the infamy thus perpetrated not only upon our sister, but upon the wives, daughters, and sisters of the state, in avenging his own wrongs as well. Now that sister was in her grave, this should be his life's business."[17]

CHAPTER THREE

Revenge

The young man that claimed he was John Carter was actually Henry Magruder. Thomas called Magruder into the room and informed him of the killing of his sister and that he must ride off immediately and take with him at least eighteen or twenty recruits. Thomas Berry told Magruder to ride to Georgetown and buy him forty Colt pistols and thousands of rounds of cartridges. Thomas gave Magruder a letter to give to a friend of his in Georgetown, asking for aid. Magruder was gone for two days, returning with the arms. In four days, Thomas rode out and was joined by two of his friends from Morgan's command. The party rode to Shakertown. They hid their horses and fed them. He told the new recruits about the brutal killing of his sister. He managed to recruit sixteen men, along with his two friends. The party passed through Shakertown, crossed Dick's River, and camped near Sam Berry's home. Magruder led Thomas Berry into a dense thicket and about a half mile from the edge, a picket halted them. Magruder gave the countersign and rode about three or four hundred yards. They were met by a man and Thomas asked him where his brother was located. The man led him to a log cabin hidden among the brush. Thomas entered the cabin and saw his brother, Samuel, sleeping. Sam woke to see his brother. Tears flowed down his eyes and threw his arms around his brother. He said: "Oh, Tom, tears are for women. The iron has entered my soul since I saw you last. We did not think then that it would be thus when we should meet again. "No, Sam, we did not; but war is a terrible thing, you know, and if you don't know it now you will soon learn." Sam told his brother he had buried his sister and Thomas said: "She is far better off now than we are. We have sacred duty to perform. Shall we perform it like men?" Sam said: "We shall."[18]

Sam had five men with him who had been forced from their homes by the Union Home Guard. George Enloe's home was burned and his horses, three wagons, and stock had been driven off by Union soldiers from Camp

Nelson in Jessamine County. He was the first person to tell Thomas Berry of the murder of his sister. Enloe met the Union party that killed the young woman and complained to Colonel Jacob but was beaten by the Union men that committed the crime. Enloe was not able to attend the funeral of Sam Berry's sister. He sought out Sam Berry's protection. The other three men that were with Sam all had the same experiences. There were forty Union soldiers present at the house where Sam's sister had been assaulted.[19]

Sam and his brother planned their revenge. They swore in the new recruits, shoed their horses, and took a solemn oath to stand by each other under all circumstances, to protect with their lives at all hazards any and every one, to carry away any wounded comrade who were unable to ride or to protect himself and in any case any comrade failed to protect the wounded it was the duty of all the others to report the fact, and if found guilty of such conduct or neglect of duty the offering party should be shot. Sam Berry decided to join the Confederate army.[20]

The plan was to keep watch over the Union camp on all roads leading from and to the camp. Sam and Thomas were divided into two or three squads. If any pickets or camp guards should leave their Union camps, Berry's men would follow them; watch for an opportunity to engage one or two stragglers in conversation when outside of the Union camp and shoot them in the forehead. All of Berry's men wore Union overcoats and trousers. They adopted the plan of quietly having twos, threes, or fours meet the unsuspecting Union soldiers on the roads outside their camps, with all of Berry's men dressed in blue, each squad had their own road, sometimes close to the Union camp and some far from the camp. Each squad had their chief, with signs all understood and all had a common place for meeting after a certain time of night, to report the day's activity to the captain and receive instructions for the next day. The men selected Sam Berry as captain, Thomas Berry, first lieutenant, Henry Magruder, second lieutenant; George Enloe has guide and scout.[21]

Henry Magruder was born in 1844 in Bullitt County. His mother was Amy Magruder. His father is unknown. His great-great grandfather was a Revolutionary War veteran, Archibald Magruder. His grandfather was Ezekiel Magruder. As a boy, he was bright, and active, and grew up to be one of the handsomest men in Nelson County. According to Tom Berry, Magruder was plowing a field of his widowed mother, when a band of marauding Federal soldiers on a foray saw Magruder in the field. The Union soldiers wanted the horse that Magruder was using to plow the field. They took the horse and because Magruder objected, they stripped and whipped him until the blood ran down his legs and kicked and cuffed him until he[22] was unconscious and left him for dead. Aroused by the rain falling on his face, he regained consciousness. He went home to his mother and told her of his brutal treatment by the Union soldiers. He bathed his many bruises, went to the stable, got another horse, and was determined to exact revenge on the Union soldiers. Until the Civil War, he was never known to do any acts of violence and was known for his mildness, except when roused, when he became "a perfect demon and never knew what fear was."[23] He followed the trail of his abusers. He had three pistols and double barrel shotgun. He caught up with the Federal soldiers near the Spencer County line. He rode into the Union soldiers. Of the sixteen men that abused him the day before, he killed ten, and the other six soldiers he chased for four miles, but they managed to escape Magruder. He later killed them all. He killed all who fell into his hands.[24] According to Tom Berry, Magruder's mother was also insulted and brutally treated by Union soldiers.

Confederate Major Jack Allen was recruiting for the Confederate army in Nelson County. Allen had selected a place for his organization near Bardstown and the Chaplin turnpike and gave the name of the recruiting station as Camp Charity. Magruder enlisted at Camp Charity. Magruder was assigned to Captain Ridley's Buckner Guards, which was an escort for General Simon Buckner. When Buckner left for Fort Donelson, he left the Bucker Guards in Bowling Green. When General Albert S. Johnston came to Bowling Green, he ordered the Buckner Guards to be transferred as his bodyguards and use them as spies, scouts, and guides. After the first day of battle at Shiloh, Magruder emptied pockets and watch fobs from the dead. He was sent during the night with dispatches for General John C. Breckinridge. As Magruder rode across the battlefield, he robbed $1,200 for the dead. Just before daylight, he came across an African American boy, who belonged to General Johnston's headquarters. The boy had $2,000 in gold, which he said he had taken from the dead General. Magruder stated that he shot the boy in the head and took the gold. He pulled off his boots and put the gold in the boots and tied them to his saddle and rode to his quarters. During the battle, Confederate General Albert Sidney Johnston was severely wounded and died from his injuries. Captain Riddle, Magruder, and four other men escorted Johnson's body to Corinth, Mississippi. After taking Johnston's body to Corinth, he returned to the battlefield and found the Confederate army retreating towards

Corinth. The Battle of Shiloh brought an end to the Buckner Guards and the men were told they were mustered out and should join another Confederate unit. After falling back with the Confederate army at Corinth, Magruder left Corinth, and he captured a Federal sutler and his mules. Magruder left his wagon with one of the Confederates and took the reins of the sutler wagon. Magruder was hoping to sell the wagon and mules. He sold the wagon and mules for $800. He joined the 2nd Kentucky (Duke's) Cavalry, under Major John Hunt Morgan.[25]

Berry's men moved closer to Camp Dick Robinson. Enloe guided them around the camp and showed them the various bridle paths and private roads. Enloe wore two pairs of blue trousers and two greatcoats. They rode the country in every direction, learning the topography and selecting the best places to meet, at springs and ravines. After familiarizing themselves with the area, the gang of vigilantes were ready to kill the Union soldiers that came in their path.

There were three roads that ran to or were centered close to their camps. They divided into three squads with eighteen men in each squad. All the men in each squad placed fourteen men in ambush and let two men patrol the road in the opposite directions, keeping a lookout for Union soldiers. If the squad came across more than three or four men, they should let the Union soldiers pass. If there were only three or four soldiers, the squad should capture them without noise, take them into the thickets or ravines and shoot them or hang them.

On the second day of patrolling the Harrodsburg Pike, Sam Berry met six Union soldiers who were in the party that killed his sister. Enloe was with him and recognized the Union soldiers. They were disarmed, taken into the woods, and placed under guard. Later in the evening, Magruder took four more Union soldiers, three of the men had been involved in the murder of Berry's sister. Enloe beat one of the Union soldiers and burned his house. Thomas Berry was heading back to meet the whole party, when he came across a "villainous" man wearing a butternut suit. Thomas captured him. He asked Berry: "Why do you want to treat me this way? I am going to camp the nearest way." Berry told him to go his way, since the route was nearer to the camp. Berry took the man's weapons away. They moved rapidly through the woods until they reached their destination. The other two squads were waiting for them. They were two miles from the Kentucky River.

After discussing their next step, they agreed to take the prisoners near the river to a deep gorge in the cliff. Once they reached the spot, they halted. Enloe came up to Thomas Berry and told him that he had caught the man that killed his sister. Thomas Berry wanted to immediately kill the man, but Sam stopped him and told Thomas: "Wait for a few minutes. This is too important a matter to be done hastily. Let's be sure of this before we act." Thomas complied with his brother's request. All the prisoners were placed in a line and brought the man who had killed their sister before the other prisoners and asked them if they knew him. They all answered they did. All the prisoners were tied together. Thomas and Sam told the prisoners that they were not Federal soldiers, who were playing a practical joke on them, and they were avenging the death of Berry's sister. All the Union prisoners begged for their lives. The prisoners told Sam and Thomas that they should not kill them because of one man's actions. Thomas asked the prisoner if they were not in the company of the man who killed their sister? The prisoners said: "Yes, he was in our company, but we are not responsible for his crimes." All the prisoners stated that the man in the butternut suit was the guilty man. Thomas Berry faced the man in the butternut suit and asked him what he had to say. He said defiantly: "I did not mean to kill her but meant to scare her." Thomas asked the man: "You really did kill her, then. . .. Yes or no. Did you kill the woman?" The man replied: "I suppose I did-yes, I did. What are you going to do about it? Thomas replied: "We intend to shoot you like a dog and let the buzzards pick your bones." The vigilante party took the prisoners down the bluff to the bottom of the ravine and shot all the prisoners, leaving their bodies and left the scene.[26]

The next day the vigilante group captured three more Union soldiers and shot them. Sam and Thomas scouted the countryside and Thomas spotted a Union scouting party comprised of sixteen soldiers. Sam agreed with his brother to attack and capture the scouting party. They called together the vigilante group. All the vigilantes were armed with .44 Colt Army pistols. They devised a plan to allow the Union soldiers to meet them on the road, where Sam would salute their leader, while the vigilante's lines allowed the Union column to pass between them and when the signal was given each man was to face inwards, covering with his revolver on one of the Union soldiers.

Sam and Thomas, along with the other vigilantes, timed their movements so they could meet the scouts at a small stream in the road in a narrow lane. Sam and Thomas managed to capture the entire Union scouting party. According to Thomas, all of the Union scouting party belonged to the same company as the men they had killed. The vigilante group killed the entire Union scouting party. Within four days, Sam, Thomas, and the vigilante group killed thirty Union soldiers.

The next day Sam and Thomas met another seven Union soldiers. The Union soldiers asked the vigilantes what regiment they were with, and Sam replied they were with Colonel Thomas Bramlette's men. The leader of the Union group said he belonged to that regiment, and he did not recognize any of the vigilantes, but mentioned that he just recently joined the regiment. The officer of the Union scouting party asked Sam and Thomas if they had seen any smaller Union scouting parties because they had not returned to camp. The officer told Sam and Thomas they were ordered to look for the missing scouting parties. Sam asked the Union officer: "Did they belong to their company?" The Union lieutenant answered: "They did." Sam told the lieutenant to surrender, and he was their prisoner. Instantly, the seven Union soldiers had pistols aimed at them. Sam and Thomas informed the prisoners their mission. The officer was in command of the company when their sister was killed. The lieutenant told Sam and Thomas that he would have prevented the murder if he could, but the murder was done before he had time to interfere. Sam told the lieutenant: "But, you did not punish the man or friend who did the cowardly deed, and for this you deserve to die the death of a dog-the same death he had died." The vigilante group shot and killed all seven of the Union soldiers.

The killing of the Union soldiers brought out even more scouts patrolling the roads. Four days later, the vigilantes killed another twelve Union soldiers. On February 10, 1862, they met and charged a company, killing twenty-three men. On February 19, Sam, Thomas, and the vigilante group captured Union pickets while they were having dinner. They entered the house with pistols in each hand, killing sixteen Union soldiers out of seventeen. One of the Union soldiers jumped out the window. A few days later Sam and Thomas were surrounded by three companies under Union Colonel Richard Jacob's 9th Kentucky Cavalry. Sam and Thomas's pickets had been surprised and they fired a volley into Jacob's men. Sam and Thomas's pickets quickly mounted their horses. The Union cavalry followed Sam and Thomas's men. They gave the Union cavalry two volleys and then charged the Union soldiers with a Rebel yell, breaking through the Union lines. The Union cavalry fired over the heads of Sam and Thomas's men, while the vigilante group managed to dismount twenty of the Union soldiers. After the encounter with Jacob's men,

Sam and Thomas went into hiding into the Anderson County hills. Their mission was complete. Sam and Thomas killed all the Union soldiers that killed their sister.[27]

CHAPTER FOUR

Sam Berry Joins
General John Hunt Morgan's Command

Captain Sam Berry had thirty-five men and reorganized the company. Sam Berry was made captain, Thomas Berry was made first lieutenant, Henry Magruder was made second lieutenant, Tom Henry, first sergeant, Bob Taylor, second sergeant, "Texas", third sergeant, Jake Smith, first corporal, John Brothers, second corporal, Jim Toler, third corporal, Jerome Clarke, Sam Avery, Bill Marion, Rough Smith, Enloe, Jim David, Pat Calahan, Oscar Jones, Henry Johnson, Bill Johnson, John Cunningham, Henry Anderson, Billy Wilson, Herbert Spencer, James Trabue, Henry Todd, Burke Sanders, Frank Hawkins, Clarence Hutchinson, Ben Allen, James Conrad, John Hays, Ashbrook, Henry Sims, Jim Peyton, Silas Long, became privates.[28]

Jerome Clarke was born on August 25, 1845, in Simpson County. His mother was Mary Hail, wife of Brigadier General Hector M. Clarke, who was a prominent citizen and Postmaster at Franklin, Kentucky. His uncle, Branch Clarke, had a notorious career at Madisonville by committing two murders. Branch's son was Tandy, who was found guilty of robbing the mail and sent to prison. He chopped of his hand to avoid hard labor in prison. Clarke had another uncle by the name of Beverly Clarke, who represented the district once in Congress and afterwards sent by President James Buchanan as Minister of Nicaragua. He was the nephew to the wife of Confederate cavalry commander John S. Mosby, who was the sister of Beverly Clarke. By age ten, Jerome was an orphan. Clarke, along with his two older brothers, moved to McClean County, where he lived with his aunt Mrs. Mary Tibbs. His brothers married Mrs. Tibbs daughters. John Patterson also lived with Mrs. Tibbs. Mrs. Tibbs was his aunt. Clarke and Patterson were treated as brothers and belonged to the family. Clarke received a common education.[29]

When the Civil War broke out, Clarke joined the Confederate army with Patterson. According to his records, Clarke enlisted in the Kentucky Issaquena Artillery on September 7, 1861, but another record has Clarke enlisting on

August 26, 1861, in the 4th Kentucky Mounted Infantry C.S. at Camp Burnett, Tennessee. According to Thomas Berry, he first met Clarke at Woodsonville, Kentucky. He confirmed that Clarke was in the 4th Kentucky Infantry, Trabue's regiment. Clarke was captured after the fall of Fort Donelson in February 1862 and imprisoned at Camp Morton near Indianapolis, Indiana. Clarke and his sibling Patterson escaped back to Kentucky. When Clarke and Patterson arrived near Slaughterville, Kentucky, on their way to rejoin their command, they were joined by recruits and Patterson was in advance scouting the road. Suddenly, he saw a small troop of cavalry and thought they were friendly troops only to find out they were Federal cavalry. Patterson did not want to be recaptured, so he took the reins of his horse between his teeth, spurred his horse forward, and with a pistol in each hand, began to shoot his way through the small band of Union cavalry. His horse was captured, and Patterson surrendered. After giving his pistols to the Federal Cavalry, a man acting as a guide came up to him, put a pistol to the side of Patterson's head and fired. Both of Patterson's eyes were shot out and since the soldiers thought that Patterson was dead, they threw Patterson over the fence into a yard, where some ladies saw him. The ladies took Patterson inside their home and discovered he was still alive and nursed him. His brother survived the ordeal.[30] Clarke swore that he would never take a Union soldier alive. According to Captain Thomas Berry, Clarke's family was treated harshly. Berry described Clarke as a "brave man and one of a generous disposition. He was loyal to the cause he espoused, naturally impulsive, but always affectionate to his friends. He was a gentleman in all various relations of life and was unflinching to duty in a time of danger as a Roman." "He was a special favorite among the ladies and always polite, affable, and as gentle as a woman. With children he was a great favorite." Thomas Berry said that Clarke was a constant companion to his brother Sam Berry.[31]

George Prentice, the editor of the Louisville Journal referred to Jerome Clarke as "Sue Mundy,' because Clarke dressed in woman's clothing when he joined Henry Magruder. According to Captain Thomas Berry, the story is only partially true. On one of Clarke's raids, he met one of the most beautiful and charming young ladies he had ever met. She was Miss Sue Munday. She had a "mass of brown hair' that fell around her shoulders. Clarke was captivated by the young woman and when he visited Boston, Nelson County, Kentucky, he dismounted from his horse and picked up a lady's riding habit, which was lying in the road. Putting the habit over his head, he dashed off at a breakneck speed saying, "I am Sue Munday." He wore a broad brimmed hat, which was trimmed with flowers. He looked very much like a woman with his long black hair and smooth, boyish face, which gave him the appearance of a female.[32]

Bill Marion aka Al Catlin, aka John Oliver, was actually Stanley Young. He was a resident of Nelson County. He was born in 1831 and was the son of a Virginia native St. Clair Young and Kentucky resident Amelia Hammon. In 1840, St. Clair Young was killed at the dinner table by his brother-in-law William Marsh. He sought revenge for the death of his father. Nine years later he found Marsh talking to some other men on the street and he made his way to the second floor of a hotel and crawled out onto a porch directly above Marsh. He shot Marsh on the top of head. Young was arrested and served a term in prison for his revenge. After his release from prison, he had relatives in Louisville by the name of Marion so he changed his name to prevent embarrassment to his family.[33] According to one description, Marion was a handsome man, "but there was a kind of look in his eyes that would terrify anyone. He always rode a magnificent black horse and was never seen to smile."

The new organization heard that Union Colonel James Bridgewater was raiding the country between Samuel's Depot and Fairfield, in Nelson County. James Bridgewater was born in 1835 in Virginia. He was the son of Henry and Mary Hamlet Bridgewater. In the 1850's, James moved to Lincoln County, Kentucky. He married Susan Dawes on July 12, 1854, in Lincoln County. At the age of twenty-seven, on October 8, 1861, Bridgewater joined the 3rd Kentucky Infantry, under Captain King's Company, and was appointed 2nd Lieutenant of Company F. On January 17, 1862, he resigned his commission due his ill health and was at home sick when he turned in his resignation. On February 15, 1863, James Bridgewater was Chief of Police in Stanford, Kentucky and wrote a letter to the Federal army requesting his pay when he was a 2nd lieutenant of the 3rd Kentucky. During late 1863 or early 1864, Bridgewater organized a group of men referred to as "Bridgewater's Scouts." The unit was made up of his brother John and several of his wife's relatives. During 1864, the Scouts pursued guerillas throughout several counties in Kentucky. Numerous citizens complained of the Scouts taking horses, guns, and food while in pursuit of the Confederate guerillas. In October 1864, Bridgewater and fifty of his men had taken horses and guns from the homes in Spencer and Nelson Counties. According to James Wigginton, Bridgewater encouraged his two slaves Henry and Stephen, ages 22 and 20, to run away. Sarah Wells of Spencer County, who was a widow, stated that Bridgewater and about twenty to twenty-five of his men had spent the night in her home and had stolen clothing and a double barrel shotgun that belonged to her family. Most of the residents claimed that Bridgewater spread fear and terror throughout the two counties. In January 1865, Bridgewater's Scouts became the foundation of the Hall's Gap Battalion of Union Home Guard which included four companies of men from Lincoln, Boyle, Casey, Mercer, and Pulaski Counties. On March 1, 1865, Bridgewater was promoted to major. He had seventy-five men.

Captain Bridgewater was raiding the countryside between Samuel's Depot and Fairfield, Nelson County. Sam and his thirty-five men were also riding in the same direction as Bridgewater. Berry asked his men shall they "fight or a foot race?" All of his men said: "Fight." Sam shouted: "Then, close up form in fours, charge!" Sam Berry and his men charged Bridgewater's men. His men were loading corn and hay with no pickets. The haystacks and corn pens were in a large open field, and beyond the field was open woodlands with a grass pasture. They charged the Federal soldiers, firing one volley. Combat was hand to hand. Bridgewater tried to rally his men. After firing, the Union soldiers fled in every direction. Reaching Fairfield, the Union soldiers tried to rally. Enloe and Clarke killed six; Toler killed five men, Texas killed five, Clarence Hutchinson killed four, Jones killed four and others killed three and two each. Captain Sam Berry pushed the Federals to Bardstown, where there were three hundred Union soldiers. Sam Berry lost three men: Herbert, Bell, and Spencer. Four men were wounded. The Federals lost twenty-seven killed and twelve wounded.[34]

Captain Berry and his men rode off with two hundred Federal soldiers following him. Berry's scouts encountered a wagon train with supplies for the garrison at Bardstown, escorted by thirty soldiers. Captain Berry called in his rear guards and gave the order to charge the wagon train. Berry's men rode into the Union ranks and killed thirteen and wounded six. After burning six wagons, Lieutenant Magruder galloped up to Captain Berry. Sam said: Mac, this is fine day's work, being the first for two weeks. We shall now go into the river hills and camp."

The Union army tracked Captain Sam Berry's men and while his men were eating their breakfast, shots rang out in Berry's camp. The Salt River was in front of Berry's men. Berry's men mounted their horses. Captain Berry was surrounded by three or four hundred Union soldiers. Captain Berry received a flag of truce, demanding his men to surrender. The Union soldiers were behind trees and logs. Captain Berry ordered his men to make two charges. Captain Berry withdrew to an area near the river. The Union force approached Captain Berry's force. He ordered his force into two squads and was determined to hold back the Union force. While one squad crossed the river, the other would protect them until they reached the other side of the river. Captain Berry was completely hemmed in, and he was quickly running out of ammunition. The three hundred Federals soldiers attacked Captain Berry on three sides. The banks of the river were twenty feet high and perpendicular. Sam ordered Thomas to take fifteen men across the river. Captain Berry's men formed on the other side of the river, taking shelter behind trees and shouted for the other men to follow. Thomas and his men poured volley after volley into the Union soldiers. All of Captain Berry's men made their way across the river, except five of his men who were killed and seven wounded, including Captain Sam Berry. The Federals lost nineteen killed and twenty-eight wounded.[35]

After the intense fire fight, Captain Berry and his men rode to Bullitt County to scatter and reassemble in ten days at Merriman's farm. Thomas Berry was taken to Colonel Stower's place and Dr. John Conn, who lived Samuel's Depot, attended to his wounds. Twelve more recruits joined Captain Sam Berry's men. After disbanding, Magruder, Jerome Clarke, and Bill Wilson rode to Louisville to obtain supplies.[36]

Sam Berry hid out at Merriman's farm. While at Merriman's farm, Captain Berry equipped his men with cut off shotguns and four to six pistols in holsters and belt for each man. Captain Berry assembled fifty-six men. After the men reformed, Sam told his refreshed men: "Men, we have plenty of work for you. Forward March!"[37]

Sam Berry recruited seventy-nine men. Sam wrote to his brother Thomas to bring his company to Camp Charity. Captain Berry heard that General Morgan was at Hustonville, which was about fourteen miles from Danville. Thomas Berry had seventy-five men. Sam and Thomas met at Camp Charity. Sam and Thomas made Henry Magruder, Jerome Clarke, and George Enloe as first lieutenants. Captain Berry rode out on the road between Harrodsburg and Lawrenceburg, when they came across a company of the 9th Michigan Cavalry. Captain Berry's men charged the Federal company. Captain Berry's men were hemmed in by fences on both sides. The Federals retreated and part of them formed on the road. Captain Berry formed his men into fours across the road and charged. As the Federals rear guard rode through a gap, Captain Berry charged them. The Federals fired a volley, but the rear pushed Captain

Berry's men through and over the Federals. Captain Berry pressed to keep them from reforming and hurried through Lawrenceburg. Twenty-five of the Federal cavalry surrendered.[38]

After leaving Lawrenceburg, Captain Berry rode towards Shryock's Ferry on the Kentucky River. His men crossed the river on the ferry and reached Mortonsville, near Woodford County. The next day Captain Berry rode to Sligo, about seven miles from Lexington, where they captured some Home Guards. They took the prisoners from the 9th Michigan, along with the Home Guards, and offered them to General Morgan. General Morgan met them and assured both Sam and Thomas they would be assigned to his command. They turned over their prisoners to Confederate General Edmund Kirby Smith. According to the official records, Sam enlisted on October 6, 1862, in the 6th Kentucky Cavalry, Company G, Captain T. W. Gray's Company, Grigsby's Regiment, General Absalom Buford's Brigade, Confederate States, under Confederate General John Hunt Morgan and rose to the rank of 1st Sergeant in Lexington, Kentucky.[39]

CHAPTER FIVE

The 1862 Confederate Invasion of Kentucky

Sam received information before leaving camp that a Union stockade was located on the south side of the Salt River, on the Louisville & Nashville Railroad, which protected the bridge. The stockade was garrisoned by 150 Federal soldiers. Captain Berry relayed the information to General Morgan. Three days later, three companies were sent to attack the bridge and stockade. Major Hutchinson, of Morgan's command, and Sam Berry was given the assignment to attack the stockade. Captain Hutchinson and Sam Berry rode out and reached their destination on the second day. Captain Hutchinson placed his men around the stockade and planted two mountain howitzers aiming for the stockade. Major Hutchinson sent Captain Bowles to the stockade with a message for the Union force to surrender. Morgan's artillery fired and two shells burst above the stockade while Captain Bowles still had a flag of truce. He rode back, waving his white flag, shouting: "Don't shoot anymore; they'll be all right directly!" The garrison came out waving handkerchiefs. As soon as the artillery fired, the Confederate skirmishers moved forward, driving the Union soldiers back into the stockade. The Union prisoners were paroled.[40]

During the Confederate invasion of Kentucky, Sam and Thomas were assigned to Morgan's command and sent across the river from Cincinnati to act as scouts for General Henry Heath's front. Confederate General Edmund Kirby Smith was commander of the Department of East Tennessee and wanted to take Cincinnati, while Confederate General Braxton Bragg's Army of the Mississippi was heading towards Louisville, Kentucky. Smith sent General Henry Heath's force from Lexington, Kentucky to take Cincinnati. Heath withdrew when he discovered fifteen to twenty thousand Union troops at Cincinnati. Heath marched to Georgetown and Frankfort. General Morgan was ordered to support Confederate General Humphrey Marshall's command and ordered to cut off and capture Union General George Morgan's Union force, who was retreating through the Cumberland Gap. General Edmund Kirby Smith wanted General

John H. Morgan to blockade the roads in the Federal front and to slow Union General Morgan's retreat. Marshall remained inactive and did not chase Union General Morgan. Sam and Thomas, along with the rest of Confederate General Morgan's command, returned to General Heath's command.[41]

Morgan's command rode to the Georgetown Road and saw ten cavalry pickets. Reconnaissance revealed that a Union infantry regiment were located on the road. Morgan captured the scouts. Lieutenant Jerome Clarke, commanding the advance guard, rode into the middle of the Union pickets. One of the howitzers was unlimbered and ready to fire. Clarke pointed his pistol at the head of the Union commanding officer demanding his surrender. The Union infantry surrendered. Clarke had ridden into the Union infantry camp, captured one company, and had forced the rest of the Union soldiers back into their camps. The various Union regiments began to form, and the Union artillery was placed into position. Thomas Berry's company took eighty-nine Union prisoners, who were taken without a shot being fired. They took the prisoners to Glasgow and turned them over to General Heath.[42]

Sam and Thomas were sent to the Ohio River, since some of the Union Home Guards were formed near Carrolton, Kentucky. Sam and Thomas had orders to capture them. Sam and Thomas dispersed the Home Guards and encountered one company of Colonel Harvey Buckley's 54th Kentucky Mounted Infantry regiment. Sam and Berry drove Buckley to Covington. They headed towards Frankfort. Once they arrived, they found the Confederate army marching towards Lawrenceburg. After reaching Lawrenceburg, Morgan was sent to the front. The 9th Michigan Cavalry fired on them. The Union cavalry had set a trap for Morgan's men. The entire Confederate force moved forward, with flanking columns sent forward and the Confederate force charged and forced the Union lines back. The 9th Michigan Cavalry was the masking force for General Don Carlos Buell's Army of the Ohio, who was on the extreme right wing.[43]

On October 8, 1862, Confederate General Braxton Bragg and the Army of the Mississippi fought at the Battle of Perryville, Kentucky. The result was over seven thousand casualties. Bragg, along with Confederate General Edmund Kirby Smith's Army of Kentucky, left Kentucky never to return. After the battle General Smith's army marched to Big Hill and Cumberland Gap. Bragg's army marched to Lancaster and eventually Murfreesboro, Tennessee. General Morgan asked to stay behind the army and select his own route out of Kentucky. Morgan had three regiments and two battalions, amounting to three thousand men and six rifled cannons.[44]

CHAPTER SIX

Confederate General John Hunt Morgan Captures Gallatin, Tennessee

On October 17, Morgan headed for Gum Springs. Information reached Morgan that the 4th Ohio Cavalry was camped in Lexington. Morgan's men crossed Clay's Ferry. Morgan represented himself as Union Colonel Frank Wolford of the 1st Kentucky Cavalry. Morgan found a pro-Union man who would guide him to the Union camp. Confederate Colonels Richard Gano and William C. P. Breckinridge moved forward to attack the 4th Ohio Cavalry. The main Union cavalry force was camped at Ashland, which was at the Henry Clay mansion, about two miles away. Sam and Thomas were detailed to enter the town from the east and capture two companies of Provost Guards. Two more of Morgan's companies were sent to enter the city from the north and intercept the Union cavalry if they tried to escape before they could surround the camp. The next morning, Morgan attacked, and the Union camp surrendered after two or three volleys. Twenty-seven Federals were killed and sixty-one wounded. Morgan lost five killed and fourteen wounded. The fight with the Provost Guard at the courthouse was intense, but Morgan's artillery was brought forward, and the Provost Guard surrendered. Sam Berry was slightly wounded, and his brother Thomas was also wounded. Morgan captured eight hundred prisoners and some arms and ammunition.[45]

Morgan's men marched to Tyree Springs and with three hundred of his men set up an ambush on the east side of the road in the thick brush. Soon a small Union advance guard passed by them and two sutler's wagons came up, which were captured and sent to the woods. In a few minutes a small advance guard passed by, then came the Union infantry. Suddenly, Morgan's men heard gunfire and a second later a volley from shotguns. The Union soldiers fell back and rallied. A third volley at close range reached the Union ranks. Morgan's men could hear and see Union officers rallying their men and charged a hill. Morgan's men fired and the artillery was put into place. Union artillery was brought up and fired into Morgan's men.[46]

Morgan moved forward through the woods to reach the extreme rear of his columns. Morgan reached the road about three or four miles from Tyree Springs. Morgan captured thirty prisoners and eight commissary wagons. After reaching the Confederate line, Morgan paroled the prisoners. Morgan's men headed back to Gallatin. After Gallatin, Morgan's men headed to Lebanon, Tennessee.

On November 10, 1862, Morgan's men discovered a Union foraging party with six wagons with corn, hay, and fodder. Morgan's men set the wagons on fire. The Union soldiers were in the house having lunch from the man who they were plundering. Morgan's men opened fire and charged the Union soldiers. They divided into two squads. Thomas Berry was wounded, and Lieutenant Jerome Clarke took command. Morgan's men encountered thirty Union soldiers. The Yankees took Thomas Berry prisoner, along with Jerome Clarke. Thomas Berry rode into the Union ranks and Berry quickly leaped on his horse over a fence. Clarke also jumped the fence. The Yankees fired a volley. Thomas and Clarke rode into the woods, and they rode to safety. Suddenly a sharp volley was heard, and the Yankees were approaching. Clarke set up an ambush and the Union soldiers walked into the trap. Two volleys were fired at the Union detachment. The battle was over.[47]

Morgan decided to attack the Federal garrison at Gallatin. He received orders to destroy the railroad between Nashville and Louisville. Morgan and

Confederate General John Hunt Morgan's men raiding a town. (Harper's Weekly)

his men rode through Hartsville. As Morgan's men entered Gallatin a small party was sent to capture Colonel William Boone, commander of the 28th Kentucky Volunteer Union Infantry. Captain Joe Desha, of Morgan's command, reached the house where Boone was sleeping. Three of Morgan's men entered the house and woke Boone. Boone reached for his pistols on a table nearby, but the three men told Boone not to cause any trouble and that he was their prisoner.[48]

After Boone was captured, Captain Desha took him to Morgan. Morgan told Boone to write a letter to the officer at Gallatin and urged him to surrender. Boone wrote the letter, and he was sent to the officer under a flag of truce. The entire garrison surrendered. Morgan paroled Boone and his command. Morgan captured 450 Union soldiers, five hundred Springfield rifles, and a train of wagons, and one hundred horses. The next day a train loaded with forage for the cavalry was captured.[49]

While at Gallatin, Morgan destroyed the tunnel by running train cars into the tunnel and set them on fire. The tunnel was located six miles from Gallatin. When Morgan left Gallatin, three hundred Union soldiers returned to the town and arrested every man and boy and sent them to Nashville. One of Morgan's men had been captured and the Union troops kicked and cuffed to death one of their prisoners and shot him. Morgan's men found the dead soldier and his men were determined to find the culprit who murdered Morgan's soldier. Morgan's men overtook the Union soldiers at Bald Knob. The Union soldiers released the men and boys they were taking to Nashville. Some of the prisoners were shot and beaten over the head.[50]

The Union soldiers fled and hid in culverts and under bridges, in heaps in shocks of fodder. About one hundred Union soldiers decided to make a stand and began firing at Morgan's men. Morgan's men charged the Union soldiers. Few of the Union soldiers were left after the charge. Morgan scolded his men for taking no quarter. Morgan's men demanded to attack the Union stockade. Morgan's men attacked the first stockade. The gates were opened, and the Union soldiers surrendered the stockade with no problem. The other stockades were taken, but Morgan lost several men, including several officers and men before they were captured. Morgan lost twenty-two men and seventeen killed. Union losses were three hundred men and thirty-five prisoners. Morgan's men brought the male citizens back to Gallatin.[51]

CHAPTER SEVEN

The Battle of Castalian Springs and Hartsville, Tennessee

On August 21, 1862, while camped at Gallatin, Morgan received news that a large Federal force was in Castalian Springs, ten miles from Gallatin. The Union force was approaching Gallatin and were in line with artillery. Colonel Gano of Morgan's command gave the order to attack. Morgan's men had two battalions dismounted on the right of the line and three on the left, with his artillery in the center. Gano's battalion was in the rear of the column. Gano ordered his force to charge, and the Union force fell back, but reformed and charged. Morgan's held their fire until the Union soldiers were thirty yards away and then opened fire. Two-thirds of the Union cavalry force were unsaddled. Morgan's men rose up and poured a volley into the Union route.[52]

Gano reformed his men on the right and ordered three companies under Sam and Thomas, along with Captain Ralph Sheldon to charge. The Union cavalry under General Richard Johnson retreated for a mile and reformed on a hill. Gano readjusted his lines and charged. The Union cavalry retreated. General Johnson retreated for three miles, and sent a flag of truce, asking for an armistice so that he could bury his dead. Morgan demanded unconditional surrender. General Johnson refused. Morgan charged Johnson's men and Johnson finally surrendered. Johnson lost sixty-nine killed and 107 wounded. General Johnson had twenty-four companies and specific orders to either destroy or capture Morgan.[53]

After the battle of Perryville, Morgan refused to follow Confederate General Braxton Bragg's line of retreat, which was through the mountains of southern Kentucky and Tennessee. Morgan rode along the rear of the Federal columns as they passed south through toward Nashville and Middle Tennessee. Morgan reached Gallatin on the Louisville & Nashville railroad. Morgan's task was to interrupt the railroad. After the Battle of Perryville, General Don Carlos Buell was relieved of command of the Army of the Ohio and replaced with Union General William Rosecrans. The Army of the Ohio was changed to the Army of the Cumberland. Morgan planned to ambush two hundred Union soldiers belonging to Union General Thomas Crittenden's corps at Tyree Springs, about twenty-five miles from Nashville. After a fight with the head of the column, Morgan made a wide detour. Morgan sent out small detachments to capture Union stragglers. The Union army learned of Morgan's plan and sent Colonel William B. Stokes' 5th Regiment of Tennessee Cavalry from Tyree Springs to stop Morgan. Stokes' attacked Morgan's small squad at a sharp turn in the road. Morgan and his men wore Confederate uniforms, but Morgan was determined to fool the Yankees into thinking he was a Union officer. He was questioned by Stokes men and Morgan told him he was a Colonel of a Michigan cavalry regiment and that the prisoners were his men, who he arrested for straggling. Colonel Stokes men found Morgan's story hard to believe and insisted that Morgan ride with them to Colonel Stokes. Morgan told the Union soldiers he did not like being questioned and would not ride with them. Morgan told his men to follow him. Morgan wheeled his horse and galloped away before anyone could stop him. Morgan leaped a fence at full speed and with his men rode into a thicket and escaped.[54]

On December 1, 1862, the cavalry under the command of Confederate General Basil Duke, of Morgan's command, which consisted of Colonels Richard Gano, Bennett Young, and Clark and Chenault, and Stearn's battalions joined two infantry regiments from the Kentucky brigade, under General John C. Breckinridge, to attack Hartsville, Tennessee. He also chose Cobb's battery. The Second Kentucky Infantry, under the command of Thomas Hunt, and the 9th Kentucky Infantry, were the two regiments sent to attack Hartsville, Tennessee. Morgan requested that Hunt command the infantry. Seven hundred infantry joined Morgan's cavalry, which amounted to 2,200 men. Morgan's force would attack Hartsville. The Union command at Hartsville was Colonel Joseph Scott's brigade. The 2nd Indiana Cavalry was also ordered to Colonel Scott's cavalry. Colonel John Harlan's brigade was the commander at Hartsville but ordered to Castalian. Scott placed a section of the 13th Indiana Battery under Lieutenant Ezekiel Green near the Lebanon Pike Ford. Outposts were established on the right bank of the Cumberland River. The road leading from Hartsville to Gallatin was left unguarded. One Union company was assigned duty in Hartsville. On December 2, Scott received orders to rejoin 19th Illinois, which was his regiment. Colonel Absalom Moore, the ranking officer in the brigade, took command of the Hartsville garrison.[55]

On December 6, Colonel Moore sent the brigade's provision train to Gallatin to bring supplies to the garrison. To protect the wagon train, Moore sent two hundred men, which consisted of three companies of infantry, one company of cavalry, and thirty mounted men. On December 7, Morgan left Hager's Shop. Morgan's men approached the Federal outpost. After firing one volley, the Union pickets fled, but the alarm was sent, and the Union troops formed into line and were ready for Morgan's attack. Morgan order Duke to form his command opposite to and partially outflanking the Union right. Duke was ordered to break the Union right flank and drive them back to the center. Morgan ordered Colonel Hunt to bring his infantry forward and deploy his men on the cavalry's right. Only the 8th and 11th Kentucky cavalry were deployed on the field. Duke only had 450 men. Colonel Roy Cluke's 8th Kentucky was on the left and Colonel David Chenault on Cluke's left. Duke ordered his men to dismount. Hunt had deployed his infantry and artillery. Duke ordered an attack. The Union infantry fired by rank. Cluke's men moved against the 106th Ohio's front, and Chenault's men passed beyond the right flank of the 108th Ohio, threatening to capture the Union camp. The Union soldiers fell back and reformed their lines. Hunt deployed the 2nd Kentucky Infantry and Robert Cobb's battery of four guns unlimbered. Green's 10 pd. Parrot rifles fired at the Confederates. Hunt was to attack the Union center and left. Captain James T. Morehead of the 9th Kentucky Infantry attacked. The 2nd Kentucky and 9th Kentucky began to fire by volley. The Confederate infantry charged with bayonets. Cobb moved his guns to a new position. Cobb fired on the Union left.[56]

Colonel Moore was informed of Morgan's attack and formed his men. The Union pickets on the Lebanon pike fell back into Hartsville. Moore called for his chief of cavalry. Scott ordered the 2nd Indiana Cavalry and Company E, 11th Kentucky Cavalry to mount and move out. The men were dismounted and deployed on the Lebanon Road. Lieutenant Colonel Gustavus Tafel, of the 106th Ohio held the Union left flank and formed his regiment on the left of 104th Illinois, under Lieutenant Colonel Douglas Hapeman. Captain Carlo Piepho, commander of the 108th Ohio, waited for orders. His five companies covered the camp of the 108th Ohio.[57]

An artillery duel broke out between Cobb's battery and Green's battery. The Union cavalrymen on the right of Moore's line was attacked by Chenault's turning movement and quickly broke, falling back in disorder and fleeing back to camp. The right flank of the 108th Ohio was exposed, and they fell back one hundred yards. Chenault rode around the 108th Ohio and the Union right flank. Cluke's regiment headed for the 106th Ohio and approached to within eighty yards, when the Ohio troops broke and ran. Moore tried to form a new line and ordered the 104th Illinois to hold their ground. Green's battery continued their artillery duel with Cobb. Hunt moved to attack the battery. The 2nd Kentucky got to within fifty paces with 104th Illinois. The 2nd Kentucky, along with the 9th Kentucky Infantry, charged. The Confederates killed the horses in Green's battery. The 104th Illinois fell back. Hunt pushed forward. The retreated turned into a rout. The 7th Kentucky Cavalry with one hundred men arrived and Duke ordered his men to dismount and support Cluke and Chenault. Duke attacked. The Confederate soldiers reached the wagon park of the 108th Ohio. The remnants of the 106th Ohio under Tafel had rallied in the wagon park. Tafel halted Duke's assault but observed Hunt's infantry occupied the camps of the 104th Illinois and the 108th Ohio on his left. Tafel fell back. Tafel learned that Moore had surrendered the battery and part of the brigade. The Confederates closed in on the 104th Illinois and Moore surrendered. Tafel refused to surrender, until the 9th Kentucky surrounded him. Tafel surrendered. The 106th Ohio also surrendered. The Confederates moved into Hartsville and captured another 450 Union soldiers.[58]

The battle lasted ninety minutes and Morgan captured 1,840 Union prisoners, killed fifty-eight men, and wounded two hundred and four men. Morgan captured Green's battery, sixteen wagons, quartermaster stores, quantity of ammunition, clothing, and 1,800 weapons. Morgan lost 139 officers and men, twenty-one killed, 104 wounded, and fourteen missing. Some of the men drowned while crossing the river and three froze to death. Morgan had twenty thousand Union soldiers coming for his force. Morgan was made a brigadier general for his actions at Hartsville.

CHAPTER EIGHT

Confederate General John Hunt Morgan's Christmas Raid in Kentucky

Confederate General Braxton Bragg, commander of the Army of Tennessee, ordered Morgan to destroy the Louisville & Nashville Railroad bridges and telegraph lines in the rear of Union General William Rosecrans' Army of the Cumberland. On December 22, Morgan left Alexandria, Tennessee. On December 23, Morgan's men reached Kentucky and entered Tompkinsville, Kentucky. The following morning, on December 24, Morgan reached Glasgow, where they skirmished with Union cavalry. Morgan captured a large Union sutler's wagon filled with Christmas goods. The sutler was heading for Glasgow. The wagon was pulled by twenty horses. On Christmas Day, Morgan's force moved towards the garrison at Munfordville, which guarded a vital bridge along the Louisville & Nashville Railroad. Rather than attack the bridge, Morgan sent a force to hold the attention of the garrison, while the main force was moving toward his main target which was Elizabethtown.[59]

According to an account in *The Louisville Courier-Journal* in 1882, Dr. Evans, who was a staunch Confederate sympathizer who lived near Bardstown, Kentucky, had two sons who were fighting in the Confederate army. Federal authorities kept watch on Dr. Evans home, who thought his home was being used as a headquarters for the Confederates. The Union officers took possession of Dr. Evans's home and on Christmas Day 1862, the Union soldiers had ordered their dinner. They had taken their seats at the table, with their guns thrown across their knees and their pistols beside their plates. Their horses were hitched to the fence in their yard about ten feet away from the house, while on the west side of the house about two hundred yards away ten thousand Union soldiers were camped. Sam Berry, Bill Marion, and two others rode up to the house at full gallop and drawing their pistols proceeded to shoot the Federal horses. They killed all the horses except a white charger, which Berry chose for himself, as he quickly dismounted and shot his own horse and jumped on the white horse. Before leaving they fired a volley into the windows at the Union officers and rode off. A detachment of Union soldiers from the Union camp had seen them and chased after Berry and his men. There was two inches of slushy snow on the ground. Berry and his men were well acquainted with the area and easily made their escape.[60]

While the Union soldiers chased Berry and his men, a man in the road that Berry knew and checking his horse he pointed to a Federal army on his horse's flank and Berry said with a laugh: "See what a fine Christmas gift I have caught" and rode on. Berry rode the white horse until he was captured in 1866.

On December 26, 1862, Morgan's force reached Bear Wallow and was informed by his scouts that seven or eight Union companies were stationed at Elizabethtown, Kentucky. Elizabethtown was eight miles north of Nolin and he decided to capture the garrison. There were seven companies of the 91st Illinois stationed along the railroad track north of Elizabethtown. The companies were given the task of guarding the Louisville and Nashville trestles in the Muldraugh's Hill area. The regiments other three companies were garrisoned at the stockades at Bacon Creek and Nolin. Informed of Morgan's approach, Lieutenant Colonel Harry Smith, the 91st Illinois commander, concentrated his force at Elizabethtown. Smith posted his men in several brick buildings in Elizabethtown located south of the town. Colonel Smith sent a messenger with a letter informing Morgan to surrender. Morgan returned a reply stating that Smith should surrender. Smith stated he would not surrender. On December 27, Morgan formed his division. He ordered Duke's brigade to take position on the right and Colonel William Campbell Preston Breckinridge's brigade on the left. The railroad tracks would serve as the boundary between the two brigades. The two brigades had the task of cutting off the Union line of retreat and inform Morgan if the Union soldiers at Elizabethtown would be reinforced. The remainder of the division would be held in reserve. Corbett's artillery placed his 10 pd. Parrot rifle on the Nolin pike. Corbett fired his gun into Elizabethtown. Captain Baylor Palmer's situated his four artillery pieces on the left of the Nolin pike about six hundred yards south of Elizabethtown and opened fire. Morgan directed Palmer's artillery to fire.[61]

Confederate Colonels Roy Cluke and Robert Stoner, of Morgan's command, ordered their men to charge. The Confederates reached the houses and Stoner's men began to beat down the doors with their rifle butts. Stoner's men entered the houses and forced the Union soldiers to surrender. To the east of the railroad, Cluke's men of the 8th Kentucky encountered no opposition as they entered into Elizabethtown. While on the edge of town, Union soldiers opened fire on them. The Union soldiers were posted in several buildings near the center of the town. Palmer loaded up his two 6 lb. cannons and placed the guns where one of the roads entered town. Palmer focused his fire on a large building where a Union flag had been hoisted on the building, which was Colonel Smith's headquarters. Duke sent for one of his mountain howitzers. Corbett placed the piece on the railroad embankment and fired at the Union headquarters. After each round from the artillery, the Union soldiers would run out into the streets. The Union soldiers would fire at the artillery. A member of Morgan's staff rode up and ordered Company A, of the 9th Kentucky Cavalry to charge. The men fell back. When the Union soldiers in the headquarters saw Company A retreating, they ran out into the street and fired down the street at the howitzer. The gun was abandoned. Lieutenant Corbett refused to leave. The Union soldiers fell back into the building. Corbett rallied his men. The gun began to fire again. Soon a white flag appeared from one of the buildings. The division quartermaster Major D. H. Llewellyn had a white handkerchief. Colonel Smith's men came out of the building and threw down their arms. The entire garrison of 652 officers and men were captured and paroled. Morgan captured six hundred converted flintlock to percussion muskets.[62]

Morgan's men spent the night at Elizabethtown. Morgan sent out men to burn three railroad bridges and destroyed several miles of track on either side of Elizabethtown. On the morning of December 28, Morgan left camp at Bear Wallow and destroyed the railroad as they advanced. Four miles north of Elizabethtown, Morgan halted and broke his force into two forces. Colonel W. C. P. Breckinridge's brigade was to capture the Sulphur Fork trestle and Morgan along with Duke's force would attack the upper trestle. Union Lieutenant Colonel Courtland Matson with five hundred men of the 71st Indiana and Companies B and C of the 78th Illinois were at the Sulphur Fork trestle. Two hundred Union soldiers were positioned at the upper trestle. Morgan surrounded the Union force. Morgan sent a flag of truce to Colonel Matson. The Union force refused to surrender. When Morgan and Breckinridge gave the word, the Confederate artillery opened fire. Corbett's battery fired on the Sulphur Ford trestle, while Palmer's artillery fired on the upper trestle. The shelling lasted an hour, and the Union force raised the white flag. Morgan captured seven hundred Union prisoners, including twenty-seven officers. Morgan's men burned the trestles. By nightfall, Morgan camped on the south bank of the Rolling Fork River. Morgan dispatched patrols in all directions.

Morgan's men burned the Cave Run Bridge and two bridges on the Lebanon branch of the L & N.[63]

On December 29, Morgan's men rode onto the Rolling Fork Bridge, near Boston, which had a strong Union force protecting the bridge of two hundred and fifty Union soldiers in two stockades. Morgan met with stubborn resistance. Morgan fired his artillery into the two stockades and the bridges the Union force surrendered. Morgan charged the bridge and cleared the bridge. Morgan captured twelve Union pickets. Colonel John Harlan's force of 2,300 men caught up with Morgan. Harlan launched an attack against Confederate General Basil Duke's force of eight hundred men. Duke sent a portion of his force to capture a Union battery on the Confederate right giving his men time to ford a river. Duke was injured by an artillery shell. The Confederates rode south to Bardstown.[64]

On December 30, Morgan rode out of Bardstown. He was aware of a force in Lebanon. Morgan wanted to confuse the Union force as to where his force was heading, so he sent a detachment to Springfield and another detachment to Lebanon. On December 31, Morgan learned that Joseph Reynold's five-thousand-man division was heading toward Lebanon. Morgan rode around Lebanon and rode into Campbellsville. Morgan found out that Haskin left his brigade wagon in Lebanon. Morgan left the city and rode to the Green River Bridge, where Morgan burned the bridge and Union stockade. When the Union force caught up with Morgan, the Confederate cavalry was several hours ahead of them. On January 1, 1863, Morgan made his way back to Smithville, Tennessee ending the raid. Morgan managed to destroy one million dollars in damages to the Union and captured two thousand Union soldiers and crippled Rosecrans supply lines. Morgan only lost twenty-six men.[65]

CHAPTER NINE

Confederate General John Hunt Morgan's Great Raid

S am Berry was promoted orderly sergeant of Company D, of Colonel Grigsby's regiment. Morgan was camped at Liberty, Tennessee and occupied the right wing of the army. Morgan's men fought daily, engaging in two battles at Alexandria, two at Snow Hill, one at Smithville and one at Black's Shops. Union General William Rosecrans army fought General Braxton Bragg's army at the Battle of Stone's River, also known as Murfreesboro on December 31, 1862, to January 2, 1863. The battle was a stalemate and Bragg retreated.

Morgan sent his men to destroy the bridges and trestles between Murfreesboro and Tullahoma. Morgan had 1,200 men under Colonel Hutchinson and Lieutenant Colonel Martin, of Confederate General Adam Rankin Johnson's regiment. Morgan's men destroyed a number of bridges and were in the process of returning to camp when a strong Federal force confronted the Confederate force and planned to capture them. Colonel Jim Bowles joined Hutchinson and Martin's force, bringing the force to 1,400 men. The Union force was 3,600 men. Colonel Hutchinson placed himself at the head of the force and gave the order to charge. There were charges and counter charges and hand to hand combat. Artillery opened up on the Union soldiers. Hutchinson list (in, killed, captured, and wounded) 1,907 men. The battle was fought near Woodbury, Tennessee. Half of Hutchinson's men received wounds.[66]

On January 24, 1863, the 2nd Kentucky was at Big Springs, six miles from Woodbury. During the night Union soldiers had surrounded their camp. The first volley wounded several men. With shotguns, Hutchinson charged the Union force. Severe fighting broke out as Hutchinson's men tried to make his escape. Colonel Hutchinson was severely wounded and died on the field.[67]

On March 19, Morgan's men were garrisoned at Liberty and attacked by a large Union force under Union Colonel Albert S. Hall with the 105th Ohio Infantry, 80th and 123rd Illinois, and the 101st Indiana. W.C.P. Breckinridge, commanding the garrison, fell back along the Murfreesboro pike, fighting a delaying action hoping that the 8th Texas Cavalry, Terry's Texas Rangers, would arrive to support him. Morgan rode up. He was in Auburn, ten miles away. Morgan attacked, but his men ran out of ammunition and had to fall back. Morgan took heavy losses.[68]

On April 5, Morgan left his division at Liberty and rode back to McMinnville to visit his new wife Martha Ready. He stayed there for fifteen days. On April 20, a Union force under the command of Colonel Robert Minty's Michigan cavalry rode into town. Major McCann of Morgan's brigade delayed the pursuit of Morgan by yelling he was Morgan and was severely wounded by a Union sabre and captured. Lieutenant Colonel R.M. Martin was struck down at Morgan's side, but Morgan escaped. Minty captured Morgan's wife, but he released her.[69]

In May, Morgan's force was concentrated at Liberty and Alexandria, Tennessee. His force comprised of 2,800 men. Duke commanded the First Brigade and Adam Rankin Johnson commanded the Second Brigade. New uniforms and equipment, including rifles were issued to Morgan's men.[70]

On June 10, Morgan rejoined his division at Alexandria and immediately told his men he planned to ride into Ohio in spite of Confederate General Braxton Bragg's orders not to cross the Ohio River. In front of Morgan was 12,000 Union troops and five thousand Union cavalry under General Henry Judah and Union General Edward Hobson. The next day on June 11, Morgan moved his division across the Cumberland to attack the Federal garrison at Carthage. One of Bragg's staff arrived and ordered Morgan to march toward Knoxville to meet a threat toward East Tennessee. Morgan returned to McMinnville, Tennessee. Bragg ordered Morgan into Kentucky. On July 2, Morgan moved north out of Burkesville, Kentucky. General Judah's brigade was only eight miles away at Marrowbone. Judah moved up to attack Morgan, but Morgan had already crossed the Cumberland River. Morgan attacked Judah and forced the Federal force to retreat. Morgan took five companies of Gano's regiment and charged, driving Judah back to Marrowbone, where they encountered his artillery and four regiments of infantry. Morgan's men crossed the river unmolested. Gano lost two killed, and Captains Tom Quirk and Mitchell.[71]

On July 3, Morgan's division rode towards Columbia, Kentucky. Towards evening, Union infantry, comprised of 150 men, located near Columbia attacked Morgan. Morgan sent four companies to charge the Union force. Morgan's artillery fired grape and canister into the Union ranks just before Morgan's men charged. The Union force broke. Morgan captured the force and paroled them. The Union cavalry fell back into town and fought Morgan's men from the houses. Morgan lost seven wounded and four killed, including Captain Cassell who was severely wounded. Captain Tom Franks took command. That night Morgan camped ten miles from Columbia.[72]

The next morning on July 4th, Morgan rode toward the Green River Bridge at Tebb's Bend and found the bridge heavily fortified by Colonel Orlando Moore and his two hundred men of the 25th Michigan Cavalry. Morgan's scouts reported that during the night they heard trees falling and the sound of axes. Moore sent a flag of truce and demanded Morgan's surrender and Morgan replied that the 4th of July was a bad day to surrender. The breastworks were a hundred yards long. Moore built ditches, abattis, and earth works. Moore's men fashioned sharp ends on the limbs of the trees that were cut. Moore built three forts besides the earth and abattis works across the road. Rifle pits were built, and the stockade poured fire into Morgan's men.[73]

Colonel Basil Duke led his men on the left and Colonel Chenault led his men on the right. Chenault was killed, ten feet from the stockade. Chenault's men retreated and reformed. Another charge was made with no success. Morgan called off the attack and decided to ride towards Lebanon, Kentucky. Morgan lost thirty-six killed, and fifty-four wounded. Among the killed was Major Brent, Captain Treble, Captain Cowan, Lieutenants Halloway and Ferguson.

A scene depicting panic as Morgan's forces neared Louisville in his Great Raid of 1863. (Smithsonian Magazine)

He also lost Magenis, Assistant Adjutant of the Division, who was shot and killed by Captain Murphy, also of the division, who was under arrest for having stolen a watch from a civilian prisoner.[74]

On July 5th, Morgan approached Lebanon. The town was protected by Colonel Charles Hanson, of the 20th Kentucky, supported by two Michigan regiments. Morgan sent scouts to confuse the Union army as to where Morgan was headed. Scouts were sent to Jimtown, Harrodsburg, and Springfield. Morgan ordered Hanson to surrender, but he refused. Cluke's and Chenault's regiments formed on the left, and Colonel Grigsby and Ward's regiments formed on the right. Hanson held the railroad depot, and the Michigan regiments came to his assistance. Morgan ordered an assault on the depot. The assault was made from four different directions. Hanson's men fell back from the houses and streets into the depot. Morgan's artillery fired on the depot. A breach was made in the walls from the artillery. The artillery stopped fire to allow for an assaulting force. Morgan's made for the breach in the wall and towards two ends of the depot. When Morgan's men entered the depot, Hanson's men surrendered. Morgan captured a large quantity of stores and fixed ammunition, including Sharpe and Springfield rifles. Morgan lost twelve killed and thirty-six wounded. Captain Tom Franks led a party to set fire to the depot doors, carrying dry bundles of wood and hay, placing the fire, under a hail of bullets. He was seriously wounded. Among the prisoners was Colonel Sanders Bruce, the brother of Rebecca Morgan. In the very moment the white flag of surrender was hoisted, Lieutenant Thomas Morgan, of the 2nd Kentucky, who was only nineteen, fell dead in his brother Calvin's arms, shot through the heart. Morgan and Colonel Hanson who were childhood friends told Hanson that when he returned home, he should tell mother that he killed Tom.[75]

Morgan took Colonel Hanson and his men to Springfield and paroled them. During the night, Morgan rode towards Springfield. On July 6th Morgan rode into Bardstown. Morgan's men rested in Bardstown for six hours. Morgan learned through his telegraph operator George A. "Lightening" Ellsworth, that the Federals expected Morgan

The Springfield .69 caliber rifle that was sawed off to use a carbine, which was found in the attic of Pauline Clarke, which was the home of Jerome Clarke aka Sue Mundy. (Special Thanks to Octagon Hall Museum, Franklin County, Kentucky)

to attack Louisville. Morgan sent a diversionary force around Louisville while his main force headed for Brandenburg.[76]

The next day on July 7th, Captain Taylor and Merriwether of the 10th Kentucky were sent ahead to the Ohio River to capture boats for the crossing into Indiana and Adam Johnson headed for the river to try and capture a regular packet. Two companies were ordered to head for the shore and drive off any Indiana militia facing Brandenburg, Kentucky. The main column made camp at Garnettsville.[77]

On July 8th, Morgan's men rode to Brandenburg and rode down to the wharf on the Ohio River. Leaning against the dock, Morgan met Captain Thomas Hines. Hines managed to capture a packet called the *McComb*. Firing came from the Indiana shore and some of Morgan's men were hit. The Indiana militia were hidden in haystacks and farmhouses. Morgan's single battery of Parrott rifles opened fire, driving the militia back to a ridge. The 2nd Kentucky crossed the river in the *McComb* supported by the 9th Tennessee. They made a bridgehead five hundred yards deep. While loading the horses onto the packet, a Union tin clad came into view and fired on the Indiana shore and then the Kentucky shore. Morgan ordered his two 10 pd. Parrott rifles on a high hill above Brandenburg to silence the tin clad and to command the river and town below. One of the solid shots hit the cabin of the tinclad gunboat and knocked the hurricane post into the river. The gunboat turned around and headed back for Louisville. Soon the *Alice Dean*, which was "the pride of all Cincinnati River and finest boat now running the Memphis trade" came around the bend of the river. Morgan set a trap for the boat. The *McComb* sent a distress signal and as soon as *Alice Dean* came alongside the *McComb*, Morgan's boarded her and captured the ship. Now Morgan had two boats to transport his men to the Indiana shores. Adam Johnson's men were the last to arrive on the Indiana shore. Morgan burned the *Alice Dean* but let the *McComb* resume her journey. The fire from the *Alice Dean* was visible to the Union troops two miles away.[78]

After resting for thirty-six hours, Morgan headed for Corydon, Indiana. The Indiana militia under Colonel Lewis Jordan prepared for Morgan's approach into town and defended the town with four hundred men. The militia fired small arms. Morgan began to shell the town. After a short skirmish, Morgan captured about two hundred Home Guards and charged over some rifle pits. The fight lasted about forty-five minutes. Morgan lost eight killed and thirty-three wounded. Morgan had dinner at the Kintner hotel in town. Morgan's men plundered the town with the men taking money from the citizens, robbing the stores, stealing food, and even taking birdcages and dresses. Morgan told the residents that he would burn the flourmill if he was not paid a ransom of $2,100. During the night two of Morgan's wounded died. Morgan left his wounded in town.[79]

On July 10, Morgan headed for Salem, Indiana and captured the town and about five hundred Indiana militia. Morgan moved onto Vienna, Indiana. Morgan rested while Ellsworth tapped into the telegraph lines and learned the whereabouts of the Union cavalry, including General Hobson's troops, who was catching up with Morgan. Thirty thousand Union soldiers were after Morgan. Morgan's men were under constant fire. As they approached towns and villages, the locals would flee, leaving their homes unoccupied with food on the table and hot coffee on the stove.[80]

On July 11, Morgan's division was just outside of Vernon, Indiana, where he met a force of two thousand Union soldiers under General George Love. Love asked Morgan to surrender twice. Morgan refused and rode around the city and headed for Dupont, Indiana and captured the town. Morgan destroyed the railroad bridges in the area, cut the telegraph lines, stolen clothes, food, and other items. The next day, Morgan rode toward Ohio. General Hobson arrived in Dupont six hours later. On July 13, Morgan was heading towards Ohio and burned the White River Bridge, which delayed Hobson for several hours. The next day, on July 14, Morgan rode to Glendale, Ohio and after leaving the town, he divided his command. Morgan rode to Camp Denson, while Duke rode to Montgomery. Morgan found six hundred entrenched Union soldiers at Camp Denson. Morgan avoided Camp Denson and rode onto Little Miami River Bridge where he found a small force of Union soldiers. Morgan fought the Federal force for about an hour and Morgan was not able to cross the bridge, so he crossed two miles upstream. Duke reunited with Morgan and moved towards Williamsburg, Ohio. When Morgan reached the town, his men rested. Morgan had ridden ninety miles in thirty-five hours. Morgan's force had been reduced to 1,200 men. Hobson had three thousand men. Morgan was hoping to reach Buffington Island, where he hoped to cross the sand bar in the Ohio River and cross his men into West Virginia.

By July 18, Morgan reached Rutland, Ohio and after resting he rode towards Buffington Island, but Morgan found a small fort at Middleport with ninety Union soldiers. Morgan surrounded the fort and the men surrendered. Morgan reached the shores of Buffington Island. Approaching Morgan's force was General

Hobson, along with other Union forces. Naval gunboats patrolled the Ohio River and Union troops were waiting for Morgan in West Virginia. The next day, on July 19, General Hobson's force attacked Morgan's 1,800 men. Many of Morgan's men were low on ammunition. The battle of Buffington Island lasted four hours. Morgan retreated with only a few hundred men, while the rest of his force was captured. Only a few of Morgan's men were able to cross into West Virginia, including Adam Johnson. Union forces caught up with Morgan at West Point, Ohio and on July 26, Morgan surrendered. Morgan rode one thousand miles in three and a half weeks, destroyed hundreds of thousands of dollars in not only Union supplies, but civilian property. On July 21, Tom Berry was taken aboard a steamboat to take him to prison of war camp at Cincinnati. Tom Berry escaped by putting on a civilian suit.[81]

Confederate General John Hunt Morgan's Great Raid in 1863. A sketch from Harper's Weekly showing Morgan's men attacking Washington, Ohio. (Harper's Weekly)

CHAPTER TEN

Union Authorities Cracks Down on Guerillas in Kentucky

While Sam Berry and the rest of Morgan's men that managed to escape Buffington Island, escaped to Kentucky, conditions were changing for the guerillas in Kentucky. By early 1864, Kentucky was overrun by guerillas. The guerrillas attacked both loyal citizens and Confederate sympathizers and the people of Kentucky demanded that the government address the problem. The Governor of Kentucky and the United States government began to implement laws and orders. In January 1864, Kentucky Governor Thomas Bramlette issued a proclamation directing the arrest of Confederate sympathizers. He requested that the various military commanders in Kentucky arrest at least five of the most prominent and active rebel sympathizers for every loyal citizen that was taken away by guerrillas. Governor Bramlette stated that the Confederate sympathizers would be held as hostages until the loyal citizens were returned by the guerillas.[82] Union General Jeremiah Boyle was replaced with Union General Stephen Gano Burbridge as commander of the military district of Kentucky.

On February 14, 1864, Major General Ulysses Grant ordered Brigadier General Burbridge to Camp Nelson, located in southern Jessamine County, Kentucky, to command the District of Kentucky until relieved by General Jacob Ammen, who was on court-martial duty. When relieved by General Ammen, Burbridge would report to Grant for an assignment. By Order Number 41, Burbridge was assigned to command the District of Kentucky.[83]

On February 25, 1864, Burbridge issued his first order as commander of Kentucky. He ordered Colonel C. J. True, commanding the 40th Kentucky Mounted Infantry, to send two companies of his command, under an experienced and discreet officer, to protect the loyal citizens of Owen County, Kentucky, and break up all the bands of guerillas in the area. He ordered Colonel True to prevent his men from committing crimes on the citizens of Kentucky, including their property, and give proper vouchers for forage and subsistence taken by his men, indorsing the loyalty or disloyalty of the citizens from whom the forage or subsistence was taken.[84]

On March 8, 1864, Governor Thomas Bramlette wrote to General Grant that General Jacob Ammen did not desire the command of Kentucky and he asked if General Burbridge be retained as commander in Kentucky. Governor Bramlette telegraphed Union General John Schofield and hoped he ordered for Burbridge to stay in Kentucky.[85]

On that same day, March 8, 1864, General Burbridge laid the groundwork on how to deal with guerrilla warfare and who he claimed were disloyal citizens. To show that he did not invent his orders against guerrillas, he published the Acts of the Kentucky Legislature. Burbridge used the acts in almost every one of his controversial orders during his military command in Kentucky. What Kentucky citizens failed to realize was that he only carried out Kentucky's acts passed by the Legislature. Burbridge carried out the Kentucky acts to the letter of the law with no restraint. He stated that all acts passed by the Kentucky Legislature concerning civil law would be relied on in military cases.[86]

"Your money or your life." Guerillas plagued the turnpikes, robbing private citizens, killing Union soldiers or stagecoaches. (Library of Congress)

In Act 548 of the Kentucky Legislature, the act stated that if any person should counsel, advise, aid, assist, encourage, or induce any officer or soldier of the Confederate States, or either of them, or any guerilla, robber, bandit, or armed band, or persons or person engaged, or professing to be engaged in making or levying war upon the government of the United States or State of Kentucky, or upon any citizen or resident of Kentucky, to destroy or injure any property of Kentucky, or shall counsel, encourage, aid, advise, or assist any such person or persons to injure, arrest, kidnap, or otherwise maltreat any citizen or resident of Kentucky, or shall harbor or conceal or shall voluntarily receive or aid any such persons, knowing them to be such, shall be guilty of a high misdemeanor, and upon conviction shall be fined not less than $100.00 and not more than $10,000 dollars, or confined in the county jail not less than six months and not any more than twelve months, and may be both fined and jailed at the discretion of the jury.[87]

If any person spoke or wrote against the government of the United States or of Kentucky, or in favor of the Confederate States shall willfully endeavor to excite the people of Kentucky or any of them to insurrection or rebellion against the authority or laws of Kentucky or of the United States, or who shall willfully attempt to terrify or prevent by threats or otherwise the people of Kentucky or any of them from supporting and maintaining the legal and constitutional authority of the Federal Government or of Kentucky, or endeavor to prevent or shall oppose the suppression of the existing rebellion against the authority of the Federal government, every such person being legally convicted would be fined $100 to $5,000 dollars, or confined in the county jail between six months to a year, or both. The act stated that the constitutional right of speaking or writing in reference to the manner of administering the government, state or national, or against the conduct of any officer of either, when done in good faith with the intent of defending and preserving either of the said governments or of exposing and correcting the maladministration of either government or the misconduct of any officer, civil or military, would not be interred with.[88]

The act also stated that any person who did not give information to the nearest military authorities or civil officer of the presence in, or raid, or approach of any guerilla or guerillas in the vicinity would be guilty of a misdemeanor and if convicted would be fined between $100 to $1,000 dollars or confined in a county jail between three months and six months, or both.[89]

In any trial, the jury would hear whether the character and reputation of the accused were loyal or disloyal to the government of the United States. The test of loyalty of the defendant or defendants would be whether they adhered to and supported the Constitution of the United States and Kentucky and complied with all their laws. Any Kentucky attorney who violated any of the provisions of the act would be debarred from practicing law.[90]

The act also stated that if any Confederate soldier or body of soldiers, or armed bands belonging to the Confederacy, or the Confederate Provisional government of Kentucky, or any armed band not acting under the authority of the U.S. or Kentucky, or any guerilla or guerillas, should injure or destroy or take or carry away any property of any person, county, city, corporate body, association, or congregation of Kentucky, or shall arrest, kidnap, imprison, or wound shall be entitled to recover damages as a jury may find and if dead, his wife or personal representative or heir of law, should be entitled to recover damages to the same extent that the person himself might for any of said injuries if death had not ensued and for the property injured, destroyed, taken or carried away, the person, city, corporation, body, association, or congregation so injured should be entitled to recover double the value of damages and the damages of any of said injuries may be recovered of any persons doing any of said wrongful acts, and of any person or persons who shall aid, advise, abet, encourage or counsel such acts, would harbor conceal, aid, or encourage such wrongdoing or would permit, when it was in his power to prevent it, any member of his family living with him under his control so to aid, abet, advise, encourage, or counsel such acts, or harbor, conceal, aid or encourage such wrongdoers may be sued jointly with or without such wrongdoers, or some or any or all may be sued until the damages sustained as above provided may have been recovered by the party or parties aggrieved. Any disloyal person who has knowledge of the presence within the county of his residence of such guerilla or guerillas or predatory band and fails to give immediate notice to either civil or military authorities would be guilty of aiding, harboring, and abetting the wrongdoer and be held jointly and severally reliable with such wrongdoers for all illegal acts done by such guerillas or predatory band.[91]

During the first week of March 1864, Burbridge dealt with his first Confederate invasion of the state. The Confederate War Department gave Confederate Major General Nathan Bedford Forrest permission to raid the state. Born in Bedford City, Tennessee, Nathan Bedford Forrest became known during the Civil War as the "Wizard in the Saddle." His father was a blacksmith, who barely made a living for his family. At the age of sixteen, Forrest took care of his family. He became a successful slave trader and planter by 1861.

He enlisted in the Confederate army in 1861 as a private, but promoted to brigadier general on July 21, 1862, and major general by December 4, 1863. Despite a lack of military training, he displayed extraordinary ability as a tactician and strategist. He once made the statement that "War means fightin and fightin means killin." He became one of the most feared cavalry leaders in the Western Theater.[92]

During the battle of Paducah, Kentucky, Forrest destroyed sixty bales of cotton, a steamer in dry dock, took fifty prisoners, and four hundred horses and mules, and a considerable number of supplies. Colonel Stephen Hicks reported fourteen killed, and forty-six wounded. Forrest reported twenty-five lost, with General Abraham Buford reporting ten killed, and forty wounded.[93]

On March 28, Burbridge received word of Forrest capturing Paducah and his command was between the Tennessee and Cumberland Rivers. He thought that Forrest was going to cut the Nashville Railroad. Burbridge reported to Union General John Schofield that he had enough men to protect the railroad. He ordered four mounted regiments in supporting distance of General Samuel Sturgis's force at Mount Sterling, Kentucky.[94]

The next day, Union Assistant Adjutant General R. M. Sawyer reported to General William T. Sherman that a small party of guerillas captured a train in Lebanon, Kentucky. Burbridge sent a force to pursue the guerrilla party. Burbridge reported to Sawyer that the Rebel squad that captured the train at Lebanon was small and thought that the force was only returned rebel soldiers organized in the state. They were being pursued by several detachments. One of Forrest's soldiers who surrendered to Burbridge at Eddyville told Burbridge that Forrest started from Demopolis on February 28, with fifteen thousand men, part went toward Memphis, part into Middle Tennessee, and the remaining four thousand went with Forrest to Paducah. Those who crossed the Cumberland were furloughed for six days, with orders to report to Mayfield. Burbridge's men were on the hunt for the Confederate soldiers at Mayfield.[95]

On April 2, 1864, Burbridge reported that Confederate General George B. Hodge's brigade passed through Pound Gap and Union Lieutenant Colonel Ferguson drove his advance to Prestonsburg, but the Confederates forced him to fall back. Citizen scouts reported that Confederate General John Hunt Morgan was at Abingdon with a large force and moved toward Kentucky.[96] Morgan had escaped from the Ohio State Penitentiary along with some of his officers on November 27, 1863, and crossed into Boone County, Kentucky. He reformed his force and began raiding.

On that same day, April 2, 1864, Sherman ordered Burbridge to concentrate all his forces at Lexington, Kentucky. General Grant wanted to move into southwest Virginia which would stop any move through Pound Gap and by the way of East Tennessee. Confederate General James Longstreet headed back into Virginia and sent a small force through the Cumberland Gap to cover his movements. Union scouts reported General Forrest at Jackson, Tennessee. Sherman had an infantry force at Purdy and stated that if General Stephen Hurlbut acted with energy, Forrest would not be able to leave the state.[97]

On April 6, Burbridge reported Confederate General Hodge's brigade at Pound Gap, General John Breckinridge at Tazwell, and General John Hunt Morgan at Abington. Burbridge rode to Paris, Kentucky to look for General Hodge's force.[98]

On April 13, Burbridge reported to Union General John Schofield that the Confederates appeared at Proctor and General John Hunt Morgan passed through Pound Gap with three thousand cavalry, supported by infantry.[99]

The next day, one thousand Rebels attacked Colonel Gallop at Paintsville. Burbridge ordered General Hobson to send the Union troops at West Liberty to Salyersville road toward Pound Gap and unite with Colonel Gallop. Burbridge also ordered the 11th Michigan to support the force moving from West Liberty. He ordered General Hobson to hold the balance of his command in preparation to move in any direction.[100]

Sherman sent General Samuel Sturgis to take command of all the cavalry and whip Forrest, and if necessary, mount enough men to seize any and all the homes of Memphis, Tennessee. Bramlette assured Sherman that all the steps taken and undertaken by his militia, and the troops under Burbridge, they could catch the wandering guerillas and keep peace in the state.[101]

CHAPTER ELEVEN

Confederate General Morgan's
Attack of Mt. Sterling

Sam Berry met his brother Tom in Richmond, Virginia. Tom was on special detached service to recruit men for the Confederate army in the state of Kentucky. Sam had also received a commission while in Richmond. Morgan had made his escape from the Ohio State Penitentiary and was making his way back to into Confederate lines to form a new army. Sam and his brother reached Abingdon, Virginia. On March 24, General Morgan left Richmond, Virginia for Abington, Virginia to command the Department of Southwestern Virginia and to reorganize his brigade for the spring offensive. Colonel Giltner's regiment was added to Morgan's force. The final concentration of his army was accomplished by late April. Colonel Adam R. Johnson reported to Morgan at Abington.[102]

On May 31, 1864, General John Hunt Morgan started on his expedition with three brigades of three thousand men. Morgan's force reached Pound Gap on June 2. Sam and Tom Berry procured horses and reported to General Morgan, showing him their commissions.[103] Confederate General Simon B. Buckner, commander in East Tennessee, gave orders for Morgan to strike a blow at the Yankees in Kentucky. While Morgan planned to move out, Union forces rode into the Kanawha Valley in the direction of the Tennessee railroad. Morgan felt he should remain with his command and cooperate with the other forces in the area to protect the public interests. Since the repulse of the Union forces, Morgan obtained permission from General William Jones to carry out the original plan to ride into Kentucky.[104]

Morgan learned that Union General Edward Hobson left Mount Sterling on May 23, 1864, with six regiments of cavalry for Louisa. At Louisa, there was another force of about 2,500 cavalry, under the 11th Michigan regiment.[105]

He learned that General Edward Hobson planned to unite with the 11th Michigan regiment and cooperate with Union Generals William Averell and George Crook in another movement upon the salt works and lead mines of southwestern Virginia. Generals Averell and Crook established themselves in Mercer County, Virginia and awaited the arrival of General Hobson for a combined movement upon the works directed by three different lines of approach. Morgan decided to move at once into Kentucky and divert the plans of the Federal forces by initiating a movement within their own lines. He had 2,200 men. Morgan planned to move through Pound Gap, detach a portion of his command to move toward the Yankees at Louisa, with instructions to join him in the interior of the state, while he moved with his main force to strike for Lexington and Frankfort. He would destroy as much of the Covington and Lexington Railroad and push toward the Louisville and Frankfort and Louisville and Nashville Railroads and damage them. Morgan would try to avoid contact with the Union force at Louisa and make his way back into the department south of the Kentucky River, and through some of the passes in the Cumberland Mountains between Pound and Cumberland Gaps. If pursued too strongly, he would change his course and turn south toward some passes between Tennessee and Kentucky and make his way back through East Tennessee. He planned to destroy the road between Knoxville and Chattanooga.[106]

On June 4, 1864, Union Colonel Mires returned with the badly needed supplies for Burbridge's entire command. In the meantime, Burbridge sent Colonel John Mason Brown, of the 45th Kentucky, to Pound Gap to watch Morgan's movements, with instructions to keep him informed of all movements. Colonel Brown reported that Morgan was in force on the Virginia side of the mountain. Morgan flanked Brown's five hundred Federals on the Stony Gap Road and forced Brown to withdraw. Colonel Brown left a small scouting party to watch Morgan's movements. Morgan rode toward Mount Sterling. Mount Sterling was an important depot for Federal supplies. On June 5, Burbridge started with his command to Pound Gap, but a courier from Colonel Brown informed him that Morgan rode through the gap. Burbridge called together for consultation with General Hobson and his brigade commanders, and they decided that General Hobson should return to prepare for Morgan's force. Burbridge sent Colonel John Brown, with his regiment and a detachment of the 39th Kentucky, with instructions to watch Morgan's men and, if possible, slow their progress until Burbridge could attack him in the rear, but with discretionary power as to when and where he should reveal himself to Morgan, thereby letting him know his movements were observed. With the rest of the command, Burbridge moved on toward Pound Gap, intending to throw General Morgan off his guard and also give him time that would allow Burbridge to overtake Morgan in a country where he could not follow his favorite course of tactics, which included breaking up his command into small squads, following secret paths and the fastness of the country.[107]

On June 5, 1864, Burbridge arrived about twenty miles from Pound Gap and learned from one of his scouts that Morgan camped on the Rockhouse fork of the Kentucky River. The next day Burbridge sent Colonel Grider, 52nd Kentucky, with a part of his regiment and a detachment of the 37th Kentucky, toward Pound Gap, with instructions to obstruct the gaps and roads so that if Morgan should attempt to return before Burbridge reached him, Colonel Grider could easily hold his position until he could come up with his command. With the remainder of the command, Burbridge marched back to the mouth of Beaver Creek, where he selected all the men and horses who could rapidly march. Burbridge left the rest of his command, along with his artillery, except the two mountain howitzers, under the command of Colonel C. J. True, 40th Kentucky, to ride to Louisa as soon as possible. Burbridge retraced his steps as far as Prestonsburg.[108]

Four days later, on June 8, 1864, Burbridge took the direct line of pursuit. When he arrived at Salyersville, he received a courier from Colonel John Brown informing him he was on the tail of Morgan's main force. Burbridge ordered Colonel Brown to continue scouting in advance, and pushed forward the command, traveling without resting.[109]

On that same day, June 8, 1864, Morgan completely surprised the Union force at Mount Sterling, who fought Morgan

Although the sketching portrays Colonel John S. Mosby's partisan rangers destroying Union supplies, the scene played out in Kentucky with Morgan's men and guerillas. (Harper's Weekly)

stubbornly for some time, but were driven from the field, with Morgan capturing all their camp equipage, transportation, etc., with supplies, and about 380 prisoners. Morgan's men also robbed the bank at Mount Sterling of $80,000. Morgan remained in Mount Sterling for one day and moved on to Lexington. Morgan left Colonel Giltner's 4th Kentucky and Lt. Colonel Robert Martin's dismounted regiments behind to complete the destruction of the Federals' stores and search for horses to remount Martin's regiment. He also sent Captain Peter Everett to Maysville with one hundred men to capture the town and return to Mount Sterling within three days. Morgan sent Captain Jenkins and a small company to wreck the bridges on the railroad between Frankfort and Louisville and Major Chenoweth to destroy the bridges on the Kentucky Central between Cincinnati and Lexington.[110]

Meanwhile, Burbridge rode to within ten miles of Mount Sterling, when Colonel Brown reported to him in person that he had followed until he found Morgan, who had already taken Mount Sterling and the small Union garrison. Morgan's cavalry and his infantry arrived and had gone into camp without any suspicion that Colonel Brown had also arrived near Mount Sterling.[111]

On June 9 at 4 a.m., Burbridge ordered Colonel John Brown, with the 45th Kentucky and the 11th Michigan Cavalry to advance and ordered them to charge and attack one camp. Colonel Ratliff, of the 12th Ohio Cavalry, with the 37th and 39th Kentucky and one battalion of the 12th Ohio Cavalry was to take the center and attack the other camp. Union Colonel Charles Hanson, of the 37th Kentucky, with the 40th Kentucky, two battalions, 12th Ohio Cavalry and the two twelve-pound howitzers was to comprise the reserve. Unfortunately, Burbridge's plans did not go as planned; one of the howitzers was sent to the front, blocking the road, cutting off a portion of the 11th Michigan from Colonel Brown's brigade, and prevented them and the entire center brigade from reaching their assigned position in time to join effectively in the charge. At that point, the horses being all killed by their sharpshooters, the howitzer was captured by Morgan's men. Burbridge called for volunteers to retake the gun, and Captain Hicks, 12th Ohio Cavalry, sprang forward with his company and charged, recapturing the gun. The attack was a "thorough surprise," and after a battle lasting two hours, the Confederates ran in every direction. From the prisoners taken during the engagement, Burbridge learned that General Morgan had left, with a considerable part of his cavalry, toward Lexington. Burbridge was apprehensive that Morgan would collect and reinforce his defeated men and attack him again before his men had any chance of rest. Burbridge decided to stay at Mount Sterling, giving his men a rest. According to Union Captain J. Bates Dickson, Assistant Adjutant General, his men buried two hundred Confederates, and Union losses amounted to twenty-five killed. Union forces captured nearly two hundred Confederates.[112]

On June 10, 1864, Morgan rode into Lexington at 2 a.m. and captured Captain Hawes' Union battery, seized a number of outposts, and took the city.[113] After Tom was injured and captured, Sam took Tom's commission and made his way to Spencer and Nelson Counties. Morgan seized two thousand U.S. horses found in the stables and about five thousand horses that had been sent to Lexington for protection. Morgan's entire command was "elegantly mounted", and the greater portion of his command were clothed and shod. After burning the Government stables, depot, etc., and securing two hundred prisoners, Morgan moved to Georgetown. Morgan sent Captain Cooper with a detachment to Frankfort to make a reconnaissance and to take Fort Clay. Union Colonel George W. Monroe, 22nd Kentucky Infantry, and his 150 men defended Fort Clay against Captain Cooper's men. During one of the assaults against Fort Clay, Captain Cooper's men managed to take Frankfort's four-pound gun, but Monroe's men managed to recapture the gun. Captain Cooper made several assaults on Fort Clay, but Colonel Monroe held his ground. Captain Cooper burned the barracks at the edge of town, but Captain Cooper never took Fort Clay.[114]

A sketching from Harper's Weekly Confederate General John Hunt Morgan raiders. (Harper's Weekly)

On June 10, 1864, Union General William T. Sherman sent Burbridge a message stating that he should not assume a defensive stance toward Morgan but should follow him and "cut him off from every direction with infantry and cavalry. Morgan would have to scatter for food, and infantry could pick up his detachments. He should never be permitted to leave Kentucky, and I will be disappointed if he succeeded to escape." Meanwhile, Burbridge marched for Lexington, taking all his prisoners captured at Mount Sterling, except the wounded. When Burbridge started his expedition, he had left his assistant adjutant general, Captain J. Bates Dickson, in charge, who upon Morgan's approach to the city, put Colonel Wickliffe Cooper, 4th Kentucky Cavalry, at home on leave, in command of the place and the troops in the vicinity. Under the direction of these two officers, all the Government property, except a few horses, were moved to Fort Clay, and Colonel Cooper, after skirmishing with Morgan's advance, with the few men at his command, withdrew to the fort, from which he presented such a formidable front that Morgan did not venture to attack him. According to Burbridge, all the damage done by Morgan at Lexington consisted of the loss of the horses, except that he robbed the bank and citizens of their money, watches, and goods of various descriptions. Union Colonel Israel Garrard, of the 1st Brigade, Union General George Stoneman's cavalry, reported to Burbridge at Lexington, and Burbridge spent the rest of the day in obtaining fresh horses, rations, and ammunition. Burbridge thought that Morgan headed for Paris and planned to attack and destroy the railroad bridge at Paris. Burbridge moved with his command on the road to Paris.[115]

CHAPTER TWELVE

Battle of Cynthiana, Kentucky

On June 10, 1864, at 2 p.m., General Morgan heard General Edward Hobson advancing and, although Morgan was almost out of ammunition, he decided to meet him in battle. General Hobson, with six hundred men and the 171st Ohio National Guard, arrived on a train at Keller's Bridge, about one mile north of Cynthiana. Union Colonel Joel F. Asper, of the 171st Ohio, got his men off the train cars and was in the process of distributing rations and extra ammunition to his men, when firing was heard in the direction of Cynthiana. A man from the town reported that a detachment from the 168th Ohio needed help. Colonel Asper sent two companies to reconnoiter from a small hill and determine how close the Rebels were to General Hobson's position. The two Union companies reached the top of the hill, when a small Confederate squad of cavalry rushed towards the train. The two Union companies fired into them, and they turned and ran. A few seconds later, a Rebel cavalry force moved to Hobson's right, as if to intercept the train, which had been ordered back with the horses. Hobson observed a line of Rebel skirmishers advancing through a field. Captain J. S. Butler, Assistant Adjutant General of Hobson's staff, mounted one of his horses and one company from the 171st Ohio National Guard and some convalescent men of the Fifty-Second Kentucky, threw out a line of skirmishers and attacked the Rebels in the field and drove them until they were reinforced and sheltered themselves in the woods. Hobson's line reinforced and skirmishing kept up for an hour, when the town was seen to be on fire and the firing ceased in Cynthiana. The shouts from the rebels led Hobson to believe that the detachment from the 168th Ohio had been captured. Hobson observed the Rebel cavalry to the right and a large, dismounted force advanced upon Hobson's front. Hobson's line of skirmishers was pushed back on the main force, and the detachment of the 47th Kentucky, about thirty men under Captain Wilson, was driven back from the protection of a fence. The 171st Ohio National Guard had never been under fire and

Hobson moved them to the rear and formed on a small hill in the woods, to prevent from being flanked by a Rebel force still moving to Hobson's right. Hobson defended the small hill for five hours.[116]

Colonel Giltner's First Brigade, of Morgan's force arrived at Keller's Bridge with 1,500 men. Morgan arrived on the field. General Hobson reported that he drove the Rebel force back, but Hobson's men had been reduced in force to only four hundred men, who were exhausted from the lack of sleep and hard fighting. Morgan's men rallied and attacked Hobson's rear and flanks. Taking command of Major Cassell's battalion in person, Morgan maneuvered his command to get in the rear of General Hobson, surrounding him. By this time, Morgan reduced Hobson's force to only three hundred men. General Morgan sent in two flags of truce and demanded Hobson surrender. Colonel Asper met the flags and reported Morgan's terms of surrender as prisoners of war. Hobson called his staff and the field officers of the 171st Ohio National Guard. Hobson realized that his force had been reduced, and knowing there was no chance of being reinforced, and the troops in town surrendering, the train being captured, and nothing more could be accomplished from fighting, and 2,500 Confederates surrounded him, General Hobson's decided to surrender his entire command. Morgan rode up to General Hobson and modified the terms of surrender allowing Hobson's officers to retain their side arms and private property, and the men to keep their haversacks, private property, and blankets. After Hobson surrendered, Morgan captured three railroad trains, with baggage and horses, and destroyed 1,500 muskets. General Hobson and his staff were sent under a flag of truce to Falmouth, Kentucky and arranged with General Samuel Heintzelman for an exchange. If an exchange could not be obtained, Hobson was to report to Morgan in Virginia. In the meantime, Confederate Major Chenoweth had destroyed the railroad between Lexington and Boyd's Station on the Kentucky Central Railroad; Captain Jenkins had destroyed the railroad between Louisville and Frankfort; Captain Cooper took the fortifications around Frankfort, and Captain Everett took Maysville.[117]

Morgan rode onto Cynthiana, where he arrived on June 11, 1864, and met a force of four hundred Union soldiers under Colonel George W. Berry. A severe engagement broke out between Morgan's men and the Union force. The Federal soldiers took shelter in the houses in town and fired on Morgan's men. Morgan's men set the houses on fire that contained the Union soldiers. Unfortunately, the fire spread from the Union soldier's refuge to the entire town. Twenty-seven buildings caught fire in Cynthiana. During the engagement Colonel G. W. Berry was killed.[118]

Burbridge received word that Morgan was in Cynthiana and had taken the town and destroyed nearly all the businesses and that General Hobson had surrendered with his command. Burbridge moved out with his command, with Colonel Garrard's brigade, with 2,400 men, in the direction of Cynthiana, sending Colonel Brown on a reconnaissance toward Cynthiana, Millersburg, and Carlisle.[119]

On June 12, Morgan's command consisted of only 1,200 men. Most of his command guarded prisoners and protected the wagon trains, but they also destroyed two lines of the railroad. On that same day at 2:30 a.m., Burbridge's advance, under Major Tyler, 52nd Kentucky approached Morgan's pickets two miles and a half from the town of Cynthiana, drove them back upon their skirmish line, and held them there until the column closed up. Burbridge formed his line of battle across the turnpike leading to Millersburg, and on either side of the road, three dismounted regiments formed the center, with a cavalry regiment on each flank, and the cavalry brigade of Colonel Garrard served as a reserve. At the word "Forward" the line advanced, driving Morgan's men back from their first line. The command "Charge" was given. The Confederates were driven in, except upon their flanks, where they took refuge behind stone walls and high rail fences. Burbridge had to send in an additional force. He ordered Colonel Garrard to send one cavalry regiment to the right and one to the left to attack the extreme Rebel flanks, leaving one cavalry regiment as a reserve. Finding Morgan's men repulsing his attack on the left, Burbridge sent the 7th Ohio Cavalry to the left to assist in the charge. Burbridge's entire cavalry force, aided by the dismounted men, succeeded in completely routing Morgan's force in the area from which the most desperate resistance occurred. Meanwhile, in the center and right the Union force took the town and pushed Morgan's men back from their positions. Morgan's men fled in the "wildest confusion." Many of Morgan's men drowned in their attempt to cross the Licking River, which was the only other avenue of escape, since Burbridge blocked the escape on the right. Only two hundred and fifty men from Morgan's command managed to escape from Cynthiana. Having learned from the citizens and prisoners that General Morgan, when he learned the tide of battle had turned against him, had fled with his best troops in the direction of Claysville, Burbridge ordered Colonel Garrard, with his brigade, to pursue Morgan. Morgan had no choice but to release General Hobson's prisoners.

According to Union Captain J. Bates Dickson, Union forces captured five hundred of Morgan's men and killed three hundred. At Flemingsburg, Morgan abandoned the greater part of his transportation, together with his sick and wounded. Colonel Garrard continued to pursue Morgan until he reached the mountains, when he turned back, determining any further pursuit useless. After several hours of rest at Cynthiana, Burbridge ordered Colonel Hanson to move with his brigade through Carlisle and Mount Sterling and to dispose of Morgan's forces and to

Confederate General John Hunt Morgan. (Library of Congress)

scatter and capture as many of Morgan's retreating men as possible. Burbridge ordered the remainder of his forces to Lexington by the way of Georgetown, determining that Morgan's men were so completely demoralized, they would not make any further stand in Kentucky. He placed his prisoners for safe conduct under Colonel John Mason Brown. On June 13, Burbridge reached his headquarters at Lexington. Burbridge lost fifty-three killed, 156 wounded, and 205 missing.[120]

On June 20, 1864, Morgan made his way back to Abington, Virginia. According to Morgan, he lost eighty killed, 125 wounded, and 150 captured. He stated that recruits who enlisted in Kentucky made up for his losses and his command would be as strong as when he entered Kentucky. He stated that during his raid, he defeated the Union plans to capture the salt works and lead mines of southwest Virginia. He also remounted nine hundred men with horses and equipment. He captured a sufficient amount of clothing and shoes to equip his command. He claimed that he destroyed two million dollars-worth of U.S. property. He claimed that he managed to break up Union black recruiting operations in Middle and Eastern Kentucky and the discovery on the part of the people of an almost "unanimous sentiment of sympathy with our cause, and which promises much support to any advance of our troops in the state."[121]

Although Morgan tried to put a successful spin on his raid, the Confederate government began to investigate the bank robbery at Mount Sterling that occurred on June 7, 1864. Confederate Colonel R.A. Alston wrote to Confederate Kentucky Governor Richard Hawes, in Abington, Virginia, asking him to investigate Morgan's raid in Kentucky. He regretted to state that plundering prevailed on the whole raid. Alston stated that property was forcibly taken from citizens for private purposes; houses were plundered of silver-plate, and even the clothing and jewelry were taken from women, and violence was threatened against them if they did not give up their jewelry. He stated that a staff officer drew his pistol on Miss Todd of Cynthiana and ordered the ladies to deliver their money and jewelry to him. Mrs. Hamilton was riding to Mount Sterling with delicacies for the Confederate wounded when she was halted, made to give up her watch and other jewelry and her horse to the Confederates. Banks were robbed. He stated that the conduct of Morgan's command of the raid "was such as to disgrace the country and cause a man to blush at the name of Confederate soldier." "The conduct of our command in Kentucky is to be deeply regretted, not only for the discredit which it brought to our arms, but I feel that in the disaster which was brought on us by converting the expedition into one of plunder and robbery we lost the greatest political opportunity which has yet been offered in Kentucky.... Men who six months ago would have offered rewards for our capture were out to greet us and say, 'God speed.'" Recruits were flocking to us every hour, and but for the reckless mismanagement of the whole expedition, which was directly the result of our unlicensed and thieving course, we would this day have been in Kentucky with an army of 20,000 men, and Sherman would have been fleeing before our army in Georgia. The State would have stood self-redeemed before the world."[122]

CHAPTER THIRTEEN

Union General Stephen Gano Burbridge's Order No. 59

According to Confederate Colonel Jack Allen, Sam Berry came to Kentucky in August of 1864 after Confederate General John H. Morgan's last raid. Two-thirds of his command were cut off and Colonel Allen was ordered to bring into Kentucky what was left of Morgan's command. Allen ordered Berry to come with him to Kentucky in order to save what was left of Morgan's command. Captain Campbell ordered Sam Berry, who was an orderly sergeant of his company, to Kentucky. Campbell had been a prisoner in the winter of 1863 and made his escape. According to Allen, the Confederate army did not tolerate guerillas. He asked Berry to collect what guerillas were in the state and bring them to the Confederate army and he would give them a commission. Allen did not consider Berry a deserter because he was reported to be sick, and Berry asked Allen to wait for him since he was not strong enough to ride.[123]

Berry returned to Bloomfield, in Nelson County, Kentucky and organized a gang of guerillas, including Marcellus Jerome Clark aka Sue Mundy, Enloe, Texas, Tom Henry, Bill Merriman, John Hudgins, Bill Morrison, John Suder, Bill Walch, and Henry Magruder.[124] Tom Berry had managed to escape after being wounded in Lexington. On July 28, Tom had reached South Fork, and the next day he crossed the Salt River. While in Spencer County, Tom met a friend Judge Jonathon Davis where Tom learned about the whereabouts of his brother Sam. Tom rode to Dr. Evans's farm near Nazareth, Kentucky and found Jim Evans and Miss Alice. Tom searched for recruits. Tom Berry rode from Henry to Meade County, from the Ohio River to Lancaster, and by September 15, Tom had recruited three companies. His brother Sam had recruited 320 men.[125]

After Morgan's raid in Mount Sterling and Cynthiana, Burbridge sought advice from General William T. Sherman on how to handle the guerilla situation in Kentucky. On June 21, 1864, General Sherman wrote to General

Burbridge a letter advising him on how to deal with guerilla warfare in Kentucky. He wrote that General Morgan's recent raid and the acts of men who called themselves Confederate partisans or guerillas called for action on his part. Even on the southern states' rights theory, Kentucky had not seceded. Sherman stated to Burbridge that the people of Kentucky by their vote and by their actions adhered to their allegiance to the National government and the South would try to coerce Kentucky out of the Union and into the Confederacy. The very dogma of coercion upon which so much stress had been laid at the outset of the war carried into rebellion into the middle and border slave states. Sherman stated that the acts of partisans and guerillas "were nothing more than murder, horse stealing, arson, and other well-defined crimes, which do not sound as well under their true names as the more agreeable ones such as warfare." Sherman knew that the Confederate campaign would cause problems and asked Governor Bramlette to organize at once in each county a small trustworthy band under the sheriff and arrest every man who was dangerous to the community, and also every man who was hanging around the towns, villages, and cross roads, who had no honest calling, which Sherman thought made the material out of which guerillas are made up, but the Governor thought that this sweeping exhibition of power was arbitrary. Sherman felt that the citizen's personal liberties were so secure that public safety was lost in the country's laws and constitutions, and the Union army was thrown back a "hundred years in civilization, law and everything else, and will go straight to anarchy and the devil if somebody don't arrest our downward progress." Sherman stated that the military must protect the citizen's rights and had the right and law on their side. He wrote to Burbridge that all governments and communities had the right to guard against real or even supposed danger. He also wrote that the people of Kentucky must not be kept in a state of suspense and real danger unless a few innocent men should be wrongfully accused.[126]

Sherman ordered Burbridge to tell all his post and district commanders that guerillas are not soldiers but "wild beasts unknown to the usages of war." He wrote to Burbridge that to be recognized as soldiers, they must be enlisted, enrolled, officered, uniformed, armed, and equipped by the Confederate government and must be of sufficient strength with written orders from an army commander, to do some military thing. Sherman stated that the Union army denied the Confederacy their right to the Union's lands, territories, rivers, coasts, and nationality. He also stated that the Union army did not admit the right for the Confederacy to rebel. He suggested that the Confederates move to some other country where laws and customs are more in accordance with their own ideas and prejudices.[127]

Sherman wrote to Burbridge that since the civil power was insufficient to protect life and property, to prevent anarchy the military should step in and was constitutionally lawfully right to do so. Under this law everybody can be made to "stay at home and mind his or her own business," and if they will not do it, they can be sent away where they will not keep their honest neighbors in fear of danger, robbery, and insult.[128]

Sherman ordered Burbridge to tell his military command, provost marshals, and other agents they could arrest all males and females who had encouraged or harbored guerillas and robbers, and have them collected in Louisville, and when he had enough citizens, around three or four hundred, Sherman would send them down the Mississippi through the guerilla gauntlet and by sailing ship send them to a land where they would take their slaves and make a colony with laws and a future of their own. If they would not live in peace in Kentucky, the Union army would send them to another better land.[129]

He advised Burbridge that the civil authorities in Kentucky should enforce the arrests, but if they were not able to, then the military would step in and perform their duties. Sherman stated that there must be an end to the civil strife and the honest, industrious people of Kentucky, and the whole world, would benefit and rejoice at the conclusion. Sherman did not object to women and men having Southern feelings, if confined to love of country and peace, honor, and security, and even family pride, but these become a crime when enlarged to mean love of murder, of war, desolation, famine, and anarchy.[130]

On June 23, 1864, Union General Henry Halleck ordered Burbridge to arrest and punish all disloyal citizens in Kentucky. The order arose from reports from Cynthiana that disloyal citizens assisted Morgan's raid and, after the battle, buried Morgan's dead with honors, while the Union dead was treated with insult.[131]

On June 25, 1864, General Halleck ordered Burbridge to declare martial law in Kentucky. He was to arrest all disloyal citizens in Kentucky that gave aid and assistance to armed rebels and sought to incite insurrection and rebellion in the state. He also stated that among the aiders and abettors of rebellion and treason were distinguished officers of state government and members of Congress. Secretary of War Stanton directed Burbridge, under the authority of the President, to arrest and send all persons inciting insurrection or aiding and abetting the enemy to Washington. The President gave Burbridge authority to use the military, and if necessary to call upon Major General Samuel Heintzelman and the commanding officer in Tennessee for assistance. Halleck instructed him to use discretion, but at the same time promptly and energetically arrest the people guilty of insurrection and aiding or abetting the enemy. He wrote to Burbridge that any attempt at rebellion in Kentucky "must be put down with a strong hand, and traitors must be punished without regard to their rank or sex."

On June 25, 1864, Thomas Sawyers, Deputy Provost Marshall for Pulaski County, wrote to General Burbridge requesting a squad of twenty-five men to Somerset, Kentucky. He stated that citizens and deserters were banding together for the purpose of murdering Union men, stealing, and resisting the enlistment of blacks and several Union men had already been killed in his sector and many more had been threatened. Burbridge acted on Halleck's orders.[132]

On July 5, President Abraham Lincoln renewed the suspension of the writ of habeas corpus in Kentucky and declared martial law. Guerilla warfare increased and word of the atrocities reached Richmond, Virginia. On July 10, six guerillas boarded the steamer Tarascon, at Lewisburg. Captain Tom Henry and the twelve guerillas claimed they only wanted a drink. They met a Federal soldier from Company B of the 44th Indiana Volunteers and demanded he have a drink with them. When they toasted to the health of Confederate President Jefferson Davis, the Union soldier declined, but was soon persuaded that if he refused, the consequences would be too costly, so he lifted his glass. Because he drank with the guerillas and to the health of President Davis, the Confederate did not harm him. When the women aboard the steamer refused to grant the guerillas a "Southern air and a Southern song," they left the boat and waved farewell.[133] On July 13, *The Richmond Daily Dispatch* reported that passengers on the Tarascon, who resided in Union County, Kentucky, told the newspaper that guerillas overran the country, and the lives and property of Union men were no longer safe in the state. Guerillas robbed Union and Southern supporters. They stated that at Caseyville and Uniontown, guerillas raised the "black flag" and killed every citizen and Union soldier. Union citizens fought back and decided to take no prisoners, which resulted in daily murders. According to the *New Albany Daily Ledger*, in New Albany, Indiana, Henderson County, Kentucky swarmed with hordes of rebel guerillas. Union Lieutenant Colonel Graham Fitch of the gunboat fleet stated that no one could conduct business safely and property could no longer be protected from the guerillas. According to Fitch the guerillas operated from the Green River to the end of Union County. Fitch demanded immediate attention from military authorities to take necessary steps to rid the country of "pestilent robbers and cutthroat highwaymen."[134]

As a result of the guerilla raids in Kentucky, on July 16, Burbridge issued Order Number 59, which stated that a rapid increase in his district of lawless bands of armed men engaged in interrupting railroad and telegraphic communications, plundering and murdering peaceful Union citizens, destroying the mails, etc., called for the adoption of stringent measures by the military for their suppression. In his order, he stated that all guerillas, armed prowlers, or by whatever name they were known, and Rebel sympathizers, were warned and that in future stern retaliatory measures would be adopted and strictly enforced, whenever the lives or property of peaceful citizens were jeopardized by the lawless acts of such men. He wrote that any Rebel sympathizers living within five miles of any scene of outrage committed by armed men, not recognized as public enemies by the rules and usages of war, would be arrested and sent beyond the limited of the United States. The property of Rebel sympathizers would be used to repay the government or loyal citizens for losses incurred by the acts of lawless men would be seized and appropriated to those who had lost property. Burbridge stated that whenever an unarmed Union citizen was murdered, four guerillas would be selected from the prisoners in the hands of the military authorities and publicly shot to death in the most convenient place near the scene of outrage.[135] The *Louisville Daily Journal* published his Order Number 59 on July 20, 1864, and added that that murder of Union men would be avenged. The paper asked that the guerillas bands lay down their arms and quietly return to the "peaceable pursuits of life." The paper also stated that the guerilla bands have "trampled all laws under their feet and erased all forms that might grant to them a show of trial." According to the paper, General Burbridge's order "falls like a stream of golden sunshine upon the dark storm clouds of an angry sky."[136]

On July 26, Burbridge issued Order Number 61, in which he stated that citizens who had been banished from Missouri and other states on account of their Rebel sympathies and other acts that weaken the authority of the United States government and those who encouraged Confederate soldiers who fought against the United States were to leave the district within twenty days and not to return to Kentucky. Burbridge ordered all military officers and provost marshals to arrest and send to his headquarters for transportation beyond the limits of the United States all persons failing to comply with his order.[137]

On July 31, 1864, Judge Advocate General Joseph Holt gave his report to Secretary of War Edwin Stanton. Holt met with Governor Thomas Bramlette, General Burbridge, and General Hugh Ewing, Colonel Fairleigh, Major Sidell, and others connected with the civil and military administration. He also had interviews with various prominent and well instructed citizens upon the public affairs in the state. He reported that Kentucky was in a deplorable state. He wrote to Stanton that a very large part of the state was completely overrun with guerillas who plundered farmhouses, and fields, and villages at will, and murdered helpless victims of their robberies. These thieves and murders moved in small bodies of from four to five to twenty men. They were mounted on the best horses and armed with weapons that they concealed in boots and under their clothes. They encountered no opposition. With the exception of a single guerilla, who was shot while trying to force his way into a store at Bardstown, Kentucky, the guerillas had met no resistance on the part of the citizens. The citizens feared a greater calamity would fall upon them if they

During the Civil War, President Abraham Lincoln declared martial law on July 5, 1864—under Proclamation 113 and Proclamation 146—in order to control guerilla warfare in the state. Martial law was not repealed until October 12, 1865. (Library of Congress)

resisted, rather than submitting to the guerillas. They preferred giving up their horses, goods, and other portable valuables than to having their houses burned over their heads, and their lives sacrificed, which would occur if they tried to defend themselves. The guerilla bands were the fruit of Lincoln's amnesty proclamation. Burbridge wrote a letter to Holt expressing his opinion that nine-tenths of the guerillas infesting Kentucky had taken the oath under the amnesty proclamation.[138]

According to Holt, the Rebels do not regard any oath administered to them by Federal authority. He stated that the guerillas mocked the oaths, which they take only because "they can make them instrumental in advancing their personal interests and treasonable enterprises."[139] The rebels used the proclamation and the oath as a means of returning to Kentucky, visiting their friends, making observations on the Union military affairs, and then arming, mounting, and equipping themselves either for the Confederate service or for the career of robbers and cut throats. General Burbridge urged for the suspension of the proclamation in Kentucky and Holt supported Burbridge's recommendation. Holt stated that the existence of a conspiracy in Kentucky and the adjoining states for an armed cooperation with the Rebels furnished an additional and powerful reason why Burbridge's proposal to end the proclamation should be requested. In Holt's opinion, the government was too weak in Kentucky to justify the state to allow the buildup of active treasonable elements, which was a result of the proclamation. He added that that recent orders from Burbridge in enforcing compensation from rebel sympathizers for the thefts and robberies of guerillas and directing the execution of guerilla prisoners in retaliation for murders committed by the guerilla bands, produced the "happiest effect in mitigating the committed atrocities."[140] According to Holt, a number of executions had already taken place and no murder by guerillas had occurred since the executions. He pointed out that the outlaws banded together in the same interests and were animated by the same spirit and sought the accomplishment of the same guilty ends. "They are a brotherhood of traitors and felons, and the public safety demands that they should be held responsible for their crimes of each and all of their members."[141] Burbridge's executions had inspired a most "wholesome terror" and Holt hoped that the stern, but necessary policy inaugurated by Burbridge would not be relaxed.[142]

On July 19th or July 29th, Henry Magruder, Jerome Clarke, Isaiah "Big Zay" Coulter, and several other guerillas came to Joe Miller's house. Isaiah Coulter aka Coalter, aka Colter, was twenty years old, six foot six inches tall, dark skin, "magnificent eyes, and hair as a raven's wing. He looked like an Indian chief."[143] According to a newspaper account, Coulter's form was proportionately faultless." He was described as handsome and graceful "and his whole physique is splendid." "His nature partakes more of beast or ferocious animal." Supposedly his father and brother were killed by the Federals or Home Guard early in the war, and that he sought revenge and vengeance. He boasted of killing nineteen men with his own hands. Most of the men Coulter killed had to do with the murder of his father and brother. According to the article, "His whole family are notoriously bad."[144] Miller was a farmer living in New Haven. Miller was a relative of Henry Magruder. The guerillas rode in front of Miller's house. He thought they were citizens because they wore yellow jackets and dusters, but when Miller's wife came to the gate, she said: "They are guerillas." Joe Miller got up and went to the front door and met the guerillas and two or three of the guerillas pushed into the house and grabbed Miller and drew their pistols and had them cocked at his right breast and demanded his buggy mare, gold watch, shotguns, and pistols and money. They also took a gold pen. After the guerillas rode to his house, they attacked a train in Nelson County. Miller's gold pen was found by a lady who lived near where the guerillas attacked the train.[145]

On the night of August 29, 1864, Berry and another man came to the home of A. L. Lewis, who was a tollkeeper in Taylorsville. Lewis was asleep, but when Berry entered his home, A. L. Lewis exclaimed: "Berry, Berry, it is possible you are on this business? Berry demanded that Lewis give Berry the money from the tollgate. His wife Caroline Lewis told Berry that her husband was sick, and they were old people and told Berry not to harm them. Caroline told her husband to give Berry the money. Berry told his companion to "take the last damned cent." According to Mrs. Lewis, Berry took ten dollars.[146]

CHAPTER FOURTEEN

September 1864: Berry Fights Union Captain Harvey Buckley and the Robbing of the Lebanon Train

During the month of September 1864, Berry, along with "Big Zay" Coulter, and Marcellus Jerome Clarke, robbed the drug store belonging to Mr. Jacob Perkins. Berry took the knives. Perkins had been to Louisville and bought goods for his store. Mr. Derr and two of the Home Guards were in the store. Perkins was standing behind the counter, loading a pistol, and was putting the percussion caps on the nipples of the pistol. Clarke stepped up to Perkins with his own pistol and said: "You Goddamn son of a bitch, what are you doing with that?" Perkins looked up and did not know what to say. He told Clarke that he was loading the pistol. Clarke said: "What the hell are you loading it for?" Perkins said: "Well, just to have it loaded." Clarke said: "Give up that pistol, you Goddamn son of a bitch or I'll blow the heart out of you!" Perkins gave up his pistol and one of the guerillas knocked Mr. Derr in the head with a pistol and he fell against one of the showcases and Mr. Sweeney, who was in the room, caught Derr. Blood was running down Derr's face and the guerillas took all they wanted, and Coulter called Perkins "Peck" and said: "Peck, I want some whiskey." Perkins said that he did not have any. He said: "You Goddamn liar, I know you have, and I want some of that good whiskey you keep for medicinal purposes." Perkins did not have any whiskey of his own but had some that belonged to another man. Coulter said he wanted some whiskey and walked with Perkins into the front room of his store in order to bring out the whiskey. Perkins put the whiskey on the counter and Clarke stated that he wanted Perkins to drink first. Perkins enjoyed whiskey but in small quantities. The guerillas drank all of the whiskey.[147]

On September 7, 1864, Tom Berry met Jim Evans and Captain Wainwright, who was a Confederate recruiting officer, in Henry County. They had recruited thirty men and were heading back to Owen County when they were attacked by a company under the command of Union Colonel Harvey Buckley. According to the *Louisville Daily Journal*, Colonel Buckley overtook Confederate

Colonel George Jesse's gang several miles north of Shelbyville, drew up in a line of battle as the Union troops approached. According to the newspaper report, Jesse's gang fled and after a long chase, the gang stopped four miles from LaGrange and prepared for a fight. Colonel Buckley charged, and the gang fled in every direction. The gang threw away their guns, knapsacks, and blankets. Colonel Buckley searched the area as the gang made their way back to Owen County.[148] According to Tom Berry, his force pushed Buckley back to Port Royal, killing a number of Union soldiers. Another *Louisville Daily Journal* report stated that Colonel Jesse Craddock's regiment, along with a squad from Buckley, started from Port Royal, when a messenger informed Craddock that Jesse's gang was camped at Smith's old pork house. Craddock countermarched and took the road to Smithfield. Jesse rode back to Port Royal. As soon as Craddock was aware that Jesse had eluded him, he also rode back to Port Royal in pursuit of Jesse. A few shots were exchanged between Jesse's men and Craddock's men, and some of the guerillas were wounded, but nightfall brought an end to the chase. The next day, Jesse's gang formed as line of battle near Campbellsburg, but when he discovered no Federals, he rode to Port Royal.[149]

Captain Wainwright, Jim Evans, Tom Berry, and the thirty recruits crossed the Kentucky River and arrived near Drennon Springs. Tom left for a week and when he returned, he found Jim Evans, his brother Sam, and eight others waiting for Captain Wainwright. The party left for Big Eagle where fourteen men were waiting to join Captain Wainwright. The men reached Little Eagle Creek and picked up more recruits. Captain Wainwright picked up eight more recruits at Stamping Ground. With over sixty men, Captain Wainwright rode to Captain John Carter, two miles away. Tom introduced his brother Sam to Captain Carter. According to Tom Berry, General Burbridge had robbed Carter of his horses, hogs, and a large drove of cattle. Sam and his brother, along with the rest of the party, camped for the night at Captain Carter's house. Early in the morning, Federal soldiers were approaching the farm. Stepping to the north window, Tom Berry saw the house was being surrounded. Tom woke up his brother, Sam, Captain Wainwright, and Evans, and told them that they were surrounded by Union soldiers. The house was a two-story log house with two bay windows. In the front of the house was a door. Carter had seven double barrel shotguns and several pistols. Captain Cook dismounted his men down in a ravine behind the tobacco barn about two hundred yards from the house. Cook sent a lieutenant to demand that the party in the house surrender. If they did not comply in five minutes, Cook would set the house on fire. Captain Carter yelled: "Come and take us!"[150]

Cook's men opened fire on the windows and sent men forwarded with bundles of tobacco and dry shingles and clapboards to set the house on fire. Evans and Tom Berry returned fire on the men who were determined to set the house on fire, killing six of them. More Union soldiers ran up and took the bundles and threw them against the house. The party in the house shot away the flaming bundles. The Union soldiers charged the house. While the Union soldiers were charging, four of the party had descended the hall. They threw open the door and made a rush at the oncoming Union force. The Union soldiers recoiled. Now Tom, Sam, Evans, and Wainwright charged, each with a double barrel shotgun with twenty-four buckshot in each barrel. After discharging their shotguns, both Berry's, along with the rest of the party, switched to pistols. The Union soldiers fell back. The party had left their horses in the middle of the tobacco barn, and they quickly mounted them. Cook returned to the fight, rallying twenty of his men, who pursued the Berry brother towards the barn to set the barn on fire. The party drove the Yankees back. Carter opened fire on the Federal force with his shotguns. Captain Cook was approaching Sam Berry. Berry fired on Cook, seriously wounding him. With Cook wounded, his men fled to the road. As they reached the road, the party followed the Federals and captured all their horses. Captain Wainwright with his men soon came to reinforce the Berry brothers, along with Evans. Wainwright charged the Union soldiers. Wainwright charged the fleeing Union soldiers for about four miles. Out of the sixty soldiers that were assigned to kill the Berry brothers and Jim Evans, fifty-three men were killed and wounded in the yard. Captain Cook begged Sam Berry to kill him and end his suffering. Captain Wainwright took up his march to Licking Hills on his way south. Sam Berry, Jim Evans, and Tom Berry rode into the upper Eagle Hills.[151]

Several days later, Tom, Sam, and Jim Evans were eating dinner in the woods, when Arch Edges approached the Berry brothers. Edges was a Confederate sympathizer and had a home on a round hill about a mile and half west of Leesburg. The house was made of logs and one story. Edges invited the Berry brothers to eat dinner at his house. While eating dinner, they were alarmed by a shot. A company of Federal soldiers were dismount and deploying towards the home. In dismounting, one of the Union soldiers caught his gun in the saddle and the pistol discharged. At the same time, an African American boy ran in the house and informed Edges that the Yankees were coming. There were five young ladies at the table trembling in fear. Tom Berry called for Evans and Sam to bring their shotguns to the front. The door was opened, and seven Union soldiers were in the doorway. Sam and Tom unloaded their shotguns, and all seven soldiers went down. Captain Barker led his men with a rush at the salient angle of the door. Captain Barker yelled: "Charge the door! Charge the door! Follow me." Sam and Tom waited for the Federal soldiers. A young lieutenant led six soldiers and the Berry brothers unloaded their shotguns. All six fell. Before charging the Union soldiers, Sam and Tom loaded their shotguns with twenty buckshot in each barrel, and their revolvers. Sam and Tom leaped over the pile of dead Union soldiers and fired on the fleeing Union soldiers. The enemy fled through the woods.[152]

Sam and Tom left the home of Edges and rode towards the Williamstown road. When they reached the road, they could see the light from the flames that was consuming the Georgetown Female College. According to Tom Berry, Union African American soldiers had burned the college. Sam and Tom fired at the soldiers who ran off. Sam and Tom were almost caught, when the Union soldiers began crossing the creek to attack. Tom and Sam rode onto Woodford County. They rode until they reached Shelby County.[153]

On September 12, 1864, John Morgan, who was no relation to General John H. Morgan, was a student and riding a train that left Louisville around 7 pm. He took a seat on the left side of the train car and was reading his book. When the train traveled about seven miles below Lebanon, where the track runs through a cut, with the sides of the cut about thirty feet high at one side and low on the other side, he heard firing, and he looked up and saw a bunch of men on the hill with guns. They were firing at the train. The train came to halt and heard a men cry out: "Lie down!" and everyone on the train headed for the floor of the passenger car. Magruder and Clarke were the first to enter the car. Magruder had four or five pistols buckled around him. He came in cursing and swearing and ordered everyone out of the car. He called out to the men: "You God Damned sons of bitches, get out of here." Some of the men hesitated. Most of the men ran up the bank of the hill. After Morgan reached the bank of the hill, a young man demanded his money. He took thirty-five dollars from Morgan. Morgan saw the engine was off the track where the ties had been pulled up under the rails. The baggage car was set on fire. The passenger and baggage cars were pushed back. The guerillas demanded money. Morgan noticed Sam Berry because he had only one arm. He came up and took Morgan's hat and another guerilla took his coat. Morgan saw one man wounded in the wrist, who was an Irish laborer. The baggage was saved from the flames, but the baggage car was burned. Magruder rode to the left, taking with him four or five prisoners. Morgan counted around thirteen guerillas. Morgan stated there were four Federal privates and one Second Lieutenant on the train that were taken as prisoners. After a half an hour they came back to the train.[154]

CHAPTER FIFTEEN

October 1864: The Robbery of Harrodsburg and Perryville, Kentucky

On October 7, 1864, William Williamson was a stagecoach driver that ran the route from Harrodsburg to Nicholasville. He knew Sam Berry for four years. One day he was on his route and five men rode up to him about five miles and a half from Harrodsburg. The first three men that rode up were Coulter, Froman, and Clarke. Coulter halted Wilkinson and demanded the mail. Wilkinson told Coulter that he could not throw the mailbag off the coach, but he might take the bag off. Wilkinson intended to keep the Louisville mail hidden, but Coulter took the three bags. There was a Union soldier on the coach, and they ordered him off the coach and made him open the letters. They took sixty cents from the soldier. Clarke ordered Wilkinson to unhitch the horse, but when he found he was not a good riding horse he refused to take the horse. About this time Sam Berry rode up and called Wilkinson by his name and laughed and began talking to Wilkinson. He said: "Billy, are you well?" Berry then turned his attention to the ladies in the coach. Wilkinson asked Coulter if he could get the mail back after Coulter searched the bags. Coulter stated he would give the mail back. Soon after Froman told Wilkinson that he must go back to Nicholasville. The gang wanted to use the road that night and Wilkinson was not to pass until after 3 o'clock a.m. They stated they would burn every coach if guards were put on them. Wilkinson left the safe open on the road. There was nothing in the safe. The gang did not rob the women, but they did rob the men and took twenty-four dollars from Wilkinson.[155]

According to Wilkinson, he originally saw Berry one hundred yards away on the road before he rode up to the coach. He was guarding about twenty prisoners. They had one soldier whose name was William Robinson. The reason why Berry took prisoners was because he did not want anyone to pass and wanted to catch the coach. After the guerillas robbed the coach and mail, they let the prisoners go, except Robinson and another young soldier who was also in the 11th Kentucky Infantry, who was with Wilkinson. The gang rode onto Harrodsburg with their two Union soldiers, who they put on the coach horses. According to Jesse Cager, who was a liquor merchant in Harrodsburg, knew Berry for about six years. He was coming home from Harrodsburg, when about four miles from town, he met Berry and others. They had prisoners and stopped Cager and several others until the stage was robbed. The guerillas told Cager they stopped them to prevent information to reach the stage.[156]

On October 7, R. W. Cecil, who was a farmer in Mercer County, left home for some business in Shakertown. As he was coming back about a half mile west of Shakertown, he saw some wagons stop there and he noticed a couple of men talking to some people standing in the road. He saw William Robinson who was with his wife. Berry and the guerillas came up to Cecil's horse and laid their hands on his shoulder and requested him to ride by the side of the road, about a hundred yards into a deep hollow of timber and brush, with the balance of the guerillas. Cecil told them that it was unnecessary to ride there. The guerillas stated they would treat him as a gentleman. Cecil refused to go with them, but the guerillas insisted. Coulter and Berry drew their pistols and told Cecil if he did not ride with the prisoner Robinson and his wife, they would blow Cecil's brains out. Cecil started off with one on each side of him and rode about twenty steps. The other guerillas demanded that Cecil give over his pocketbook. Cecil told the guerilla he had no pocketbook. The guerilla was not satisfied with his answer and began searching Cecil's pocket and took out the pocketbook. Cecil claimed he had forty to fifty dollars in the pocketbook. In today's value, the money is worth $1,949.53. Berry was nearby when Cecil was robbed. After taking the money out of his wallet, they handed the pocketbook back to him. The guerillas took Cecil into the hollow, where there were two other men and five or six horses, and another man standing back on the hill, as a sentinel, with a gun. They demanded Cecil get off his horse and stay with them. Cecil stayed with the guerillas for about two hours, until the stagecoach arrived. One of them came from the road and ordered Cecil to get on his horse and ride up the road with Robinson and his wife. When they got to the stagecoach, Cecil saw forty or fifty men and women stopped at the coach. When they heard the stage coming, the guerillas made Cecil, Robinson, and his wife, to fall back, and take a position behind a stone wall and hold the guerillas horses. As the stage approached the bridge, four of the guerillas jumped on their horses, met the stage, and robbed the passengers. One of the guerillas sat on his horse guarding Cecil, Robinson, and his wife. After the guerillas robbed the stage, they turned the stage around back toward Shakertown. The guerillas ordered the company back and told them to stay there for two hours. The guerillas started back with the men who did the robbing, but only two or three men had galloped up toward the tollgate and Cecil turned his horse and galloped off and left them. Cecil rode home as fast as he could in order to report the guerillas conduct at Harrodsburg. But before Cecil got to Harrodsburg, he met a man who told him the guerillas had been in town and attacked the bank. The guerillas put Robinson and another soldier from the 11th Kentucky Infantry on horses and put pistols in their hands. According to Cecil, Robinson knew Coulter. They were neighbors. One of the Shakers told Cecil that Berry had lived with them for several years.[157]

The next day on October 8, 1864, Berry, along with Jerome Clarke, Henry Magruder, Lieutenant Milton, Richard "Dick" Little and "Big Zay" Coulter, decided to rob the First National Bank in Harrodsburg. The bank was built in 1858 by Dennis Haley. The cashier was Captain J. W. Cardwell and William Vance was the president of the bank.[158]

Thomas Stagg was a cabinet maker from Harrodsburg and knew Sam Berry for two or three years before the war and was in Harrodsburg. He was standing at his door, looked up the street, and saw two men riding on horseback, one of them was Berry, who rode up to the bank with Jerome Clarke and fired into the bank. Due to the quick thinking of Cardwell, he hastily bolted the iron shutters and door and refused to surrender the bank. According to Jesse Cager, the guerillas began firing into the bank through the door and almost killed the cashier. The guerillas shot through the iron slats.[159]

When the firing on the bank began, Stagg shut his door and went out into the street and saw Berry speaking with a Mrs. Carter. He said to her: "Mrs. Carter, you must get your watch, my name is Berry. Stagg met Berry in the street and he said: "Tom, will you shake hands with me? The last time you met me I was a gentleman, but now I am a damn thief, murderer, robber, etc." Stagg shook Berry's hand; the guerillas gave a whoop and some of the citizens of the town fired at them. Stagg fired at Berry, and he fired at Stagg, then fired at each other again. The gang galloped their horses out the Perryville Street, followed by the Home Guard. Jesse Cager saw the Home Guard come around his house and saw them shooting at the guerillas. Robinson was still with them and as they turned around the street, a jeweler named Comstock fired at Clarke and killed his horse. Clarke turned and shot Robinson. Robinson's foot was still in the stirrup and Clarke came up and threw him off his horse and jumped on his horse. When Clarke fired at Robinson, the members of the gang also fired at Robinson, and he died immediately from six bullets entering his body. Another Union soldier of the 11th Kentucky managed to break free from the gang and rode around a sharp turn in the street and made his escape. According to Stagg's testimony, Berry fired at Robinson first. One or two of the gang members had a shotgun, and one had a Spencer rifle. Ironically the bank was never robbed. Berry said he wanted to see Captain Cardwell and would take off his arms if would let him in.[160]

During the raid on Harrodsburg, ex-Kentucky Governor Beriah Magoffin, who was from Harrodsburg, was at the courthouse and was walking out when he met Clarke. Going up to Magoffin, Clarke introduced himself and shook hands. In the meantime, the rest of the gang were robbing the stores, and riding up and down the streets. Magoffin was embarrassed by being taken by Clarke and tried to lighten the situation by suggesting to Clarke that they both walk over to a fire since the day was cold. Clarke told the ex-governor: "I'd rather you wouldn't go, Governor, the fact is the people here think I am holding you as a hostage, for my men and that if any of the boys are attacked you will be shot. So, we'd better stay here." Magoffin smiled, but Clarke told Magoffin in a serious tone: "That is just the situation, and I hope nothing will happen." When the guerillas began to leave town, Clarke saluted Magoffin and rode off leaving the ex-Governor unharmed.[161]

According to James Temlinson, who was a farmer in Harrodsburg, knew Berry for about ten or twelve years. While the gang was in Harrodsburg, Jerome Clarke drew a gun on Temlinson and ordered him out into the streets. While Temlinson was talking with Clarke, Berry rode up to him and put a pistol on his arm and they had a conversation. He asked Temlinson what he intended to do while he was in town, and he stated he did not claim to be a solider and he pretended to be a robber. In the meantime, Clarke took Sue Cardwell's watch and Temlinson asked Berry to force Clarke to give back the watch to Mrs. Cardwell which he did. He went and got the watch back from Clarke and returned the watch. He said he did not rob women. And then he rode to the bank. They fired on the bank when they first arrived in town. Berry asked Temlinson to walk up to the bank and tell Cardwell to open the bank. Temlinson told Berry he had no influence with Cardwell and Berry replied: "Goddamn you, you don't want to go." Temlinson stated that the Union soldier that escaped was another soldier from the 11th Kentucky Union infantry.[162]

According to Temlinson, the citizens of Harrodsburg began firing on Berry.

The citizens did not know that Robinson was a prisoner. When he examined Robinson's body after he was killed, he saw two pistol wounds and the others were buckshot. He also found Robinson's furlough papers in his pocket. Shots were fired from both sides. He thought that Robinson was killed by shots coming from both sides. He claimed there were about fifty or sixty citizens shooting at the guerillas, unfortunately they also fired at Robinson. He was struck in the shoulder and across the breast, but the wounds that killed him were the pistol shots. According to Temlinson, Berry told him that he wanted to rob the bank to take the arms of the Home Guards out of the bank. Berry said he only wanted the guns and did not intend to rob the bank.[163]

J. M. Smedler, a physician in Harrodsburg, saw Clarke and Berry, along with three other guerillas. They had two prisoners with them. He heard gunfire and the cry of the guerillas. He wanted out of his house and saw Berry and Clarke. Smedler spoke with Berry and said he wished he would leave the town. Berry said: "I know you Doctor Smedler, you are an abolitionist. Doctor, we have two prisoners and if you or any of the citizens shoot at us, we will kill the prisoners." Smedler left and came back after the guerillas had left town and saw Robinson lying dead. When he went out into the streets, he saw Clarke cursing and telling Berry to order the guerillas to burn the buildings and if he refused to burn the buildings, he would report him to Captain Jesse.[164] Berry told Smedler that his reason for robbing the bank, he said: "Doctor, there are arms in there, and I want to get them out." Smedler told Berry there were no arms, but only arms that belonged to private citizens. Berry insisted and he was told there were arms in the bank and he wanted to check for himself whether the arms were in the bank or not. Berry told Smedler "Doctor, I wish you would go and tell Carter to open the door." Smedler told him he would not. Berry said he wanted the door open to see if the arms were there.[165]

John Young was a stable keeper and boarding housekeeper in Harrodsburg. He saw Robinson shot. According to Young, Robinson fell after the first shot. Young was only fifty yards away. He thought Clarke shot and killed him. Young knew Berry when both were boys. He saw the citizen's fire at Clarke. The guerillas shot Robinson. Young saw Clarke shoot Robinson in the left side. He saw Clarke's horse killed.[166]

On October 26, Burbridge issued Order Number 8, in which he stated that irregular bands of armed men within his lines, disconnected from the Rebel army, who prowled through the country and subsisted by destroying the property of citizens and the government are guerrillas, and would be treated as such. Burbridge stated that they were without an idea of permanent occupancy, or with a reasonable hope of seriously injuring his communications. They formed no part of the original army of the rebellion, and when captured were not entitled to the treatment prescribed for regular soldiers, but by the laws of war, they have forfeited their lives. Frequent robberies and murders committed by these outlaws demanded that the laws of war be stringently meted out to them. Burbridge declared that from "hereafter no guerillas will be received as prisoners, and any officer who may capture such and extend to them the courtesies due prisoners of war will be held accountable for disobedience of orders.[167]

On October 30, 1864, the local citizens in Bloomfield were going to arrest three African American boys, under the names of Elijah Dugan, Alfred Harrington, and John Sutherland, and three white boys, under the names of John Violet, along with one of his brothers. Another white boy went by the name of Gist. One of the African American boys belonged to Mrs. Sutherland, another was owned by James Dugan, and went by the name of Dugan, and other went by the name of Tansley. Two of the African-American men were captured at Francis Hester's house. Three of the men escaped and two of the Violet boys made their way back home. Gist also escaped and made his way back home. Some of party watched for their return and caught them. The party were taking them to jail when Jerome Clarke came up and wanted to kill the boys in the street. Jerome and Sam Berry accused the Violets of robbing stores and blaming the robberies on the guerillas. The African Americans were accused of robbing under the disguise stating they were Sue Mundy, Magruder, and Berry. Henry Tinsley and other residents of Bloomfield interfered and prevented the killing. Sometime after, King White and Berry rode to Tinsley's house. Tinsley was a local tailor and saloon keeper. King White and Berry were angry with Tinsley for not allowing Clarke to kill the three African-American boys. They said they would kill them and leave the house. Jerome Clarke, along with Holmes, Tandall, Warford, along with several others, stopped the party of John Green, Henry Russell, Eli Snyder, William Milton, John Henry, Thomas and Milton Grier, about two and a half miles from Bloomfield to Bardstown. The escort party had the three African-American men with them near James Grier's house. The party had stopped for refreshments at Grier's house when the guerillas approached them. Jerome Clarke ordered two of the African Americans over into the road and once the two men had crossed over into the road from the fence, Clarke shot them. One of the African Americans was not completely dead, so Harvey Warford shot him dead. Russel tried to prevent Clarke from firing again by pinning Clarke's arms while pushing him back against a fence, but another guerilla drew his gun and Russell was forced to release Jerome. Mitch Russell followed the guerillas out of concern for his father, Henry, who was in command of the prisoner escort. Henry told the African Americans to jump over the fence and escape and Clarke tried to shoot Henry with his pistol. Berry ran in and grabbed Clarke. In the confusion, the third African American and the three white men escaped. Foreman handed John Violet over to Berry, who allowed him to escape.[168] After killing the African American men, Clarke and the rest of the guerillas rode back to Bloomfield.[169]

Henry Tinsley was a tailor and tavern owner in Bloomfield. Tinsley was home on October 30, 1864. He stated that there was no jail in Bloomfield and some of the citizens were taking the African Americans from the jail at Bardstown. He saw the citizens had three African Americans and three white men. Two of them were the Violets. The six prisoners were being taken to the Bardstown jail. Four or five guerillas wanted to kill them. Colonel Stone came and got them quietly and said there might be trouble in town. They then ordered dinner at Tinsley's house. When they finished dinner, Berry and Clarke came to his house. They were angry for letting the prisoners to pass. The guerillas knocked over everything and gathered up the band and started out. They came back, when the black prisoners were killed. Berry and Clarke told Tinsley that the white men had robbed stores and accused the guerillas of doing the robbing. The African Americans were trying to pass themselves off as Clarke, Magruder, and Berry. Tinsley stated that Berry and Clarke were the ones who stated that the prisoners should be killed. Tinsley never saw the blacks or whites again. Tinsley stated that the bodies were buried two and a half miles from Bloomfield.[170]

Tinsley stated that the last time he saw Berry was when Berry and King White were captured on his property. Tinsley had been downtown and heard his bell ring and started home. He saw Berry and King in front of the public room. He had heard that they had made some threats against Tinsley, and he went around the backway. Berry had threatened to wear out a pistol over Tinsley's head and to cowhide him. Berry came to his wife and said King White wanted to see Tinsley. Tinsley sent White to the public room. White came in and asked Tinsley how much he owned him. White said he owed Tinsley eleven dollars for making a suit of clothes and for eating there several time with Berry and others. Tinsley told White he understood that White owed Tinsley $150.00. White said Tinsley was an infernal scoundrel and a liar and only owed Tinsley eleven dollars. Berry rushed in and spoke about the coat and said he got the coat from Clarke. Tinsley told Berry he should pay Tinsley. As soon as Berry came in the door, Tinsley's son put his hand on his pistol. Berry instantly put a pistol to Tinsley son's breast and told him not to draw the pistol or he would blow his brains out. Berry told Tinsley's son to take off his coat.[171]

While they were arguing, Tinsley slipped out the back and got his gun. Berry was determined to kill his son. Berry turned and fired at Tinsley. Tinsley dodged and as he went out of Tinsley's house, he fired at Tinsley again. Tinsley's son began firing with his pistol and wounded Berry and his horse. Tinsley found three or four of his neighbors and brought them back. Tinsley had made Berry and his guerillas roundabouts and pantaloons. He made gray, black, and red clothes. He said Bill Marion wore black frock coats. Tinsley stated that he saw Berry with Bill Marion, Tom Henry, Clarke, and Magruder. He also saw Coulter and Warford. Clarke told Tinsley that he had killed Tom Sutherland. Tinsley stated that Warford and Parkhurst killed the African American prisoners. The guerillas stated that they wanted to kill Captain Russel because he prevented Clarke from killing the three white men.[172]

Butler Thomas was a farmer living in Bloomfield and October 30, 1864, he stated that Captain Russell and other citizens had in their custody an African American who was the property of Mrs. Sutherland and another African American who belonged to Dugan and three white prisoners. Thomas said the white men were captured by a group of citizens in his neighborhood at the home of Forster. They were with two men by the name of Violet. They were at the house of his mother. Another of the black men belonged to Harrington. His name was Alfred. The gentleman who belonged to Dugan went by the name of Elijah and the slave who belonged to Sutherland went by John. Before he got to Bloomfield, the guerillas overtook them. He remembered the names as Froman, Taylor, Parkhurst, Flowers, Mackay, and Warford.[173]

James F. Moore, who was a schoolteacher and surveyor in Bloomfield, was in Bloomfield when he saw citizens taking the African-Americans, Gist, and the two Violets to Bardstown. He was at his hotel and saw a crowd at the other end of town, which attracted his attention, and walked down and saw the crowd gathering around some people. He saw the African-Americans and the white men. Moore saw around seven or eight guerillas in town who wanted to take them out of town and shoot them and the citizens of town persuaded

A sketch depicting rebel raiders attacking a western town. This same scenario was carried out in many areas of Kentucky, including Harrodsburg, Perryville, and Bardstown by Sam Berry. (Library of Congress)

them from shooting them. The townsfolk said the prisoners were in the hands of the civil authorities and they had better leave them to take onto Bardstown. The citizens finally persuaded the guerillas to stop, and the citizens began to take the prisoners towards Bardstown. Around dinner time, Moore walked up to the hotel to have dinner, when Berry, Clarke, and Mundy rode up to the hotel and stated they heard about the African-American prisoners being taken to Bardstown. The guerillas were angry and spoke about following the citizens with the prisoners and kill the prisoners. They jumped on their horses and rode out of town.[174]

John Thomasson lived in Nelson County and was a farmer. He was also the brother of Mollie Thomasson, Jerome Clarke's girlfriend, whom he wrote from military prison a few hours before his execution. He saw Clarke kill the African Americans. He stated that Berry was not present during the killing but came after the killing. Captain Russell tried to save the black prisoners, when a guerilla by the name of Wright drew his pistol on Russell and Berry said he would kill Wright if he touched Russell. Thomasson was about ten yards away when Clarke came up and got off his horse. Berry came up in about three or four minutes after the black prisoners were killed. He was standing alongside a fence, near Captain Russel. Clarke came up and jumped off his horse with his pistol in his hand. Clarke ordered the black prisoners over the fence and then jumped over the fence himself.[175]

Berry had issues with Tinsley and his son. Berry held a pistol to Tinsley son's breast and threatened to kill him if he even moved. Tinsley heard Berry and his men say they had killed the African American boys and some of them wanted to kill Captain Russell for preventing Clarke from killing them. Tinsley stated that he had made Bill Marion a coat and pants for $400.00 but was never paid. He even made red clothes for them. Red clothes were the sign of retaliation and no quarter. Tinsley stated that he was forced to make clothes for Jim Davis, Bill Henry, Henry Magruder, Bill Marion, and others. Tinley told them he could get into trouble for making them their clothes, but the guerillas told him that if anyone harmed him for making the clothes, they would kill them.[176]

CHAPTER SIXTEEN

November 1864: Berry Gang Rampage of Murder and Robbery

On November 2, 1864, Elijah Jones, a farmer in Edmonson County, was reading a newspaper at Rocky Hill Station, when someone came in and stated that some soldiers were riding into town. Jones looked out the station window and saw that the riders were not soldiers, but guerillas under the command of Henry Magruder, Jerome Clarke, and others. He saw the riders turn to the left and came up the railroad and he heard a pistol shot and the train car was set ablaze. One of the riders rode up to a storehouse where Jones was standing with other citizens and asked what the hell they were doing there. One of the bystanders stated that he was selling goods to his customers and friends. The man on the horse asked how long before the train showed up at the station. The storekeeper told the man on the horse that the train would arrive in an hour. The men on the horse said: "Hurry up, boys." Jones tried to get away but one of the men on horseback called him back. One of the guerillas searched his pockets, but Jones did not have his wallet on him.[177]

Some men were talking to Jones, and he saw one of the guerillas extended his hand with a pistol and fired nine or ten shots. A Federal soldier named William Fox was walking away from the guerilla with his hands up until he got to the fence, when he fell from the bullets. The guerilla who shot him went up to Fox and pulled him away from the fence and rolled him over on his back and was stooping over him. After the guerilla left, Jones walked over to the soldier and saw that the bullet had entered over his eye, and he was still breathing. The soldier died an hour later.[178]

William Durham was at the Station and stated that a squad of guerillas rode into the station at 2 am and captured William Fox as they came in the station and as they left, they killed Fox. Fox was outside and Durham was inside the station. The guerillas rode in from Old Rocky Hill on the south side of the railroad and set some boarding cars on fire, standing alongside the tracks, belonging to a construction train. The guerillas came to the door, and one of the guerillas asked Durham for the time. He told the guerilla. The guerilla dismounted and came into the house and took the money out of the cash drawer. While he was in the house, three other guerillas entered into the house. While in the house, he saw Fox pass the door, walking towards the road to Brownsville. The first guerilla who entered the house walked outside and began firing. Mrs. Fox was present and yelled that the guerillas had killed her son. Durham walked outside the door and saw the man robbing the house took hold of Fox's collar. Fox had fallen. The guerilla had a pistol in his left hand. Durham did not want to see anymore and stepped back into the house, when he heard the pistol fire for a second time. After a minute, Durham walked back outside and saw the guerilla ride off. Durham quickly went to Fox's body and turned him over on his back. The guerilla shot Fox behind the ear and the ball came out the front. He lived for about two hours and half. He described the guerilla that shot Fox as a tall man with dark hair and dark eyes and very long hair. The guerilla

stated his name was May. He said he was dressed in a gray Confederate uniform. One of the guerillas had an oil blanket and one had a brown coat.[179]

On November 5, 1864, Union soldiers executed four men named M. Jackson, J. Jackson, G. Rissinger, and N. Adams for the murder of Adam Harper. Members of Jerome Clarke aka Sue Mundy's band of guerillas murdered Harper on November 1, 1864. After the execution the Union soldier buried the four men in a shallow trench near where they fell. Eventually the men were re-interred in the city cemetery.[180] On that same day,

Mass grave of M. Jackson, J. Jackson, C. Rissinger, N. Adams, who were shot and killed under Union General Stephen G. Burbridge's Order No. 59. They were buried in Midway, Kentucky. (Photo courtesy of author)

a skirmish took place near Bloomfield, Kentucky and Union Major Samuel Martin of the 37th Kentucky Infantry, reported that one of his companies surprised some guerillas at Bardstown. Out of the fifteen men who had their horses shod and pillaging the town, his men managed to capture three men. Two men managed to escape Martin's men. The men who escaped were none other than the infamous guerillas Sue Mundy and "One-Armed Berry." Martin's men took the three men captured, Tingle or Tindle, Parkhurst and Warford, to headquarters and when the party got to within five miles of Bloomfield, they tried to escape. The Union soldiers opened fire and killed all three men, although historian James Head and Stewart Cruickshank feel that the three men were executed by the Union soldiers. The citizens of Bloomfield took the remains to town for burial, although their exact location is unknown.[181]

On November 7, Berry broke into Jacob Perkins showcase in his drug store in Maxwell, Washington County, Kentucky. Several of the guerillas were on the outside of the counter leaning against the showcase and shoved the showcase out. One of the guerillas tried to open the case and was not able to open the case. He said: "Goddamn it, I can get it open," and he raised up his foot and put his foot through the door of the showcase and proceeded to take whatever he wanted from the showcase.[182]

On November 24, 1864, James Devine was on the road in his wagon going home from visiting with his neighbor David Foster. Devine knew Sam Berry when he was a schoolteacher and Devine was a schoolboy. Captain "Big Zay" Coulter rode up to Devine and demanded Devine's money. Coulter stuck a pistol in his side and robbed him of fourteen and a half dollars. He was about to take Devine's horses when Berry rode up and said: "How are you Devine?" Berry shook hands with him and asked him what he was doing there. Devine told Berry that his men were about to take his horses. Berry told his men to leave the horses alone. They went on ahead, going towards Devine's home. Devine refused to go back to his house for the fear that the guerillas might scare his family. When he was going back, they took him along as a prisoner and rode back to David Foster's house. Devine was only twenty-five yards away from Foster's house, when he heard the guerillas shoot Foster in the house. Berry was on his horse at the time of the shooting. He heard Foster's wife cry out. According to William Riley, the guerillas rode up to Foster's home and told Riley and Foster to come out with their pocketbooks. Riley took his out and the guerillas searched the pocketbook and found there was no money. They threw the pocketbook on the ground. Foster walked Riley's dog around the house and when he came back a man met him at the porch and said something to him. Riley was standing about five or six steps away. He could not hear the conversation and then the guerilla shot Foster dead. Riley saw him fall. After the guerillas killed Foster, they rode to Devine's home. According to Devine, Berry and his men had another prisoner by the name of Enoch Warren.[183]

After they released Devine, he headed back to the Foster's and helped wash him after he was killed. According to Devine, the reason why Berry and his men killed Foster was because Foster was a Union soldier. According to Riley, one of the guerillas asked him was Foster was dead. He said yes. The guerilla asked if Foster was a soldier. Riley said that Foster was a discharged soldier. He looked at Riley and said: "They beat us that way; we have to do the same."[184] After they released Devine, they rode onto another neighbor's house about six hundred yards away and then rode into the next town.

On November 25, Berry, Dick Mitchell, Isaiah Coulter, along with the other twenty-five guerillas rode into Washington County traveling on the turnpike from Bloomfield to Springfield. When they came across a laboring Irishman, beat him on the head with a pistol and took seventeen dollars. They robbed the tollgate keeper of fifty dollars. From the tollgate the guerillas moved toward Maxville. Along the way, they came across a gentleman by the name of Beverly and robbed him of his buggy mare. They robbed one citizen of twenty dollars and two mares, a Mrs. Brown, they robbed her of a horse, and Mitchell Thompson's of a horse and small amount of money. They also robbed the citizens of Thompsonville.[185]

When the guerillas arrived at Maxville, they met Charles F. Bosley. Bosley was the sheriff and farmer in Washington County, Kentucky. He was sitting in the backroom of a drug store. The first guerilla he saw was Berry. He came in and ordered Bosley out into the front room with others. He thought Berry was a Federal soldier because he had on a Federal soldier's hat and Federal overcoat and cape. When Bosley heard a pistol shot, he asked what the shot was, and the townsfolk said the shots came from a group of drunken Federal soldiers and when he ordered Bosley into the front room, he thought he was a drunken soldier. Berry ordered Bosley a second time and he saw the man was Berry. Berry asked Bosley's name. Bosley got up and went to the front room and when he came in, he walked behind the counter and met Coulter. Coulter asked Bosley name. Bosley told Coulter his name and Coulter took Bosley's pocketbook and his money. Bosley turned around and saw Berry with his saddle bags. Bosley had two pistols in his saddlebags and all of his sheriff's papers and books and papers and told Coulter not to destroy them. Coulter told Bosley he would not destroy them, but he would take his pistols. Bosley saw Coulter put one of the pistols in one of his breech pockets and one in the other and carried his saddlebags out into the streets and put them on his horse. Coulter told Bosley about a report stating that Coulter was killed and that he was Sam Berry. Bosley noticed that the man had only one arm and knew that the man was Berry.[186]

Jacob Perkins lived in Maxwell in Washington County. About twenty guerillas came riding to his house. He was in the backroom. He had built a small addition to his house. Charles Bosley and Perkins were sitting in the backroom, along with Squire Mitchell when he heard gunshots. Squire Mitchell jumped up and said: "What does that mean?" and he walked into the front room and as he walked the guerillas passed his house. Perkins told Bosley that there were some drunken soldiers and told him to sit there and he would go outside and "settle them." Bosley said: "Never mind, I will settle them and make them behave themselves." Mr. Walker, Perkins clerk, was in the front room and said they were guerillas. Mr. Bosley said: "I reckon not, and Walker said: "Yes they are, I know them." The guerillas jumped down from their horses came in the back door and ordered Mr. Bosley and Perkins to come out. He remembers the guerillas saying "Goddamn sons of bitches! Come out of there, Goddamn you." Perkins was waiting for Bosley to go out and he was waiting for Perkins. Perkins kept waiting for Bosley to go out and he said he was waiting for Perkins. Finally, one of them came up and he said: "You Goddamn sons of bitches come out of there; do you two men intend to come out? You Goddamn fools, do you think you can resent 25 soldiers? Perkins came out of the backroom to the front room and his money was demanded, where he gave them. Another guerilla searched him. Perkins had a pistol in his right-hand side pocket, which did not belong to Perkins, but a friend of his, but they did not find the gun. Perkins also had a roll of tickets in one pocket and a pocketbook in the other. They took money from Mr. Walker and Mr. Bosley. Bosley said that the guerillas robbed him of one hundred dollars. After they stole the money, the guerillas went behind the counter and took everything they could pack away and pulled open drawers and examined Perkins papers. One of the guerillas cursed Perkins and told him that he had written a pamphlet against the guerillas. Perkins told the guerilla he knew nothing of the pamphlet. The guerillas scattered his papers all around the room and went into his backroom and examined the bed where his clerk slept and found a pistol. When the guerillas were dealing with Bosley, Perkins slipped his pistol out of his pocket and threw the pistol under the bed. One of the guerillas cocked his pistol and walked to the front part of the house and presented the pistol and cocked the weapon at Bosley. Perkins stepped to the door and begged for Bosley's life. The guerilla stopped and turned around on Perkins and put the pistol against his right side and pushed him across the room and said: "You Goddamn son of a bitch, I intend to kill you anyhow." Perkins thought that Henry Magruder had the pistol in his side. Perkins begged Coulter, who was behind the counter, to interfere, and he turned and said: "You Goddamn son of a bitch, put up that pistol, Goddamn you, and let that man alone." Magruder put his pistol in his pocket and walked to the front part of the house. Several of them were behind the counter and several were on the stairs and took some jewelry and silver that was in a trunk, and they took the pistol and some goods. The value of the items the guerillas took amounted to eight hundred dollars.[187]

On November 25, 1864, James Wilson, who was a mechanic in Mercer County, heard a knock at his door. He asked who was there. The answer was "Friend." He got up out of bed and his wife went ahead of him and opened the door and the man standing at the door was Berry. Wilson had known Sam Berry for about ten years. Wilson asked Berry why he had come to his house. He said he had come there to "play hell." Berry was going to burn Mr. Hall's store and several other things. He was also going to kill some three or four men in the area. He wanted to hang Demaree and kill Jacob Hall and Captain Burns. Berry was standing just inside Wilson's door. There were two or three guerillas that was with Berry and asked Berry: "What must be done with Demaree? Berry said: "Go and hang him." Wilson pleaded on the behalf of Demaree and asked him not to hang Demaree. In less than a minute, he countermanded the order and directed the guerillas to go and whip him. Demaree was whipped. Berry demanded a light while he was in Wilson's house and picked up a candle and candlestick and started out with a finger full of matches. Wilson asked Berry not to take the light out. Berry said: "I can take a candle and you can't help yourself." Berry went out and Wilson heard Hall's door crashing and Hall's house was searched. Berry told Wilson and his family to stay in the house.[188]

On November 26, 1864, in Washington County, Kentucky, Sam Berry and his gang of about twenty-three men, including "Big Zay" Coulter, rode in the direction of Cornishville, in Mercer County and shot down Private

Sam Green of Colonel Frank Wolford's 1st Kentucky Cavalry, who had been visiting home while on leave home for only an hour. Green tried to hide under his bed, when Berry and his men approached his house, but they discovered him and put their pistol against his head and shot him dead. The guerillas killed John Foster, who was a discharged soldier also from the 1st Kentucky Cavalry, was at home. Sam Berry and his men rode to a house of a local and found Private Isaac Butner, who was in Colonel Speed S. Fry's old regiment. He was also on furlough, when Sam Berry and his men shot him and robbed him of his money and watch.[189] After killing the soldiers, Sam Berry and his men rode up to Mrs. Martha Hall and her husband Lieutenant Colonel Thomas Hall's farm. Her husband was colonel of the local Home Guard. As soon as the guerillas approached the home, her husband told his wife and children to go upstairs. He had a gun and two pistols. He fired seventeen times at Sam Berry and managed to wound several of his men. He fired at the guerillas and after he fired his last round, he headed upstairs to join his family. He told his wife to head downstairs and pleaded for her husband's life. The guerillas, who were all armed with pistols, stated they would kill him. She went downstairs and pleaded for her husband's life, but the guerillas ordered her to get out of the way or they would blow her brains out. Her husband heard the guerillas abusing his wife, so he came to the door where the guerillas were waiting outside and told them he would give himself up and not to shoot him. One of the guerillas shot the husband in the left side. He slapped his hand on his wound and leaned over and exclaimed: "Lord have mercy," and the guerilla shot him again. The second bullet entered the husband's forehead and killed him instantly. He dropped at his wife's feet and then the guerillas shot him four more times. According to the wife, Sam Berry stood in the doorway facing her after her husband was shot. After they killed her husband, they threw his body out the door on his face. Berry stood in the doorway when her husband was shot. Berry asked the wife's husband's name three times, but she refused to answer. He went off, and finally her little son told Berry the name.[190] After killing her husband, the guerillas took all the weapons in the house and burned the children's clothing, blankets, and several other items.[191]

Doctor McCluskey lived in Nelson County and knew Berry. He attended to Berry when he was shot in the side in November 1864. He was confined to his bed until Christmas. In January 1865 Berry was wounded in his left shoulder and was confined to his bed. McCluskey did not see Berry for about six weeks because of his wounds. He remembered the affair with Colonel

Finley, of a Missouri regiment. Berry told the other guerillas not to harm the colonel, since he was a gentleman. Berry promised he would protect the colonel. McCluskey saw the colonel the day after in Bloomfield and he told McCluskey that Berry saved his life. McCluskey remembered Colonel Allen arriving with Berry in August of 1864.[192]

CHAPTER SEVENTEEN

December 1864:
The Killing of African Americans

On December 12, 1864, Samuel Snyder, who was a blacksmith and jailer in Taylorsville, Spencer County, Kentucky, had brought breakfast to four of his black prisoners in his jail. The prisoners were jailed for stealing and attempting to burn property. One of the prisoners asked him if he could purchase him some cigars. Snyder walked across the street, purchased the cigars, and had just started to go back to the jail, when a couple of men rode up with pistols drawn, and told him they wanted him to unlock the door and they pushed Snyder into the jail. The guerillas followed Snyder up the stairs into the cell and the guerillas took the four black prisoners out of the cell. Two of the guerillas were Henry Magruder and Jim Davis. Snyder was in the cell and when he walked down and looked, the guerillas were gone. He asked where they went and was told they rode across the bridge to Bloomfield. The blacks were owned by Eli Cooper, one of them belonged to widow Holms, another belonged to Colonel Grigsby, and the remaining prisoner belonged to Tickner.[193]

Joseph Watson was a farmer in Taylorsville saw the four guerillas take the four black prisoners from the jail. He claimed he saw Magruder, Jim Davis, Bill Merriman, and Sam Berry. After the guerillas took the prisoners out of the jail, they rode towards the Salt River Bridge. The bodies of two of the prisoners were found a half mile up the river in a pond that belonged to Watson's brother. According to Watson, two of the prisoners were buried by Watson and his brother-in-law. After the blacks were killed, Grigsby, who owned one the two slaves, came to Watson father's home and asked if Watson and his brother-in-law would go to the place where the blacks were killed and help get them out of the river. Watson went with them, and he helped pull them out of the river. One of the slaves was shot in the right side of his jaw and the girl, who belonged to Cooper, was shot in the chin and once in the forehead. There was also a wound in her side.[194]

According to Watson, the citizens asked for Sam Berry to meet with them, hoping that they could persuade him from taking the four black prisoners. Berry rode up to the citizens of the town and said: "Gentleman, I have done all that I can for those negroes without endangering my own life, and I will not do that for the sake of a negro. I can do nothing more than make them take these negroes from town as far as I can, but my life is in danger, and I have been threatened." Berry said he would take the four prisoners as far from the town as possible. The citizens thought the guerillas were going to kill the blacks in their jail cell and thought that Berry could not stop the rest of the guerillas, but he would take them as far as town as possible, if they would kill them.[195]

Benjamin Watson, who was a farmer and sawyer, in Spencer County, saw a black man and black woman taken out of the river. He saw some men going up the river with a black man and girl. He saw five guerillas, including Jim Davis and Berry. The woman was behind Berry. They were going in the direction of the place afterwards they found the bodies. He saw Davis shoot the black man. Davis was one hundred yards from Berry during the shooting. Berry was sitting on his horse when Davis came back, and the woman was behind him and mounted on Davis's horse. He then galloped off on the same road. Watson heard shooting and when Berry rode up to the hill near the river, he did not see the black woman behind him.[196]

John Russel was one of the black prisoners in the jail cell. The other prisoners were Cooper's Bell, Mrs. Humee's Frank, and Charles Grigsby's George. Russel stated that Abe Froman and George Jesse had put Russel and the three other prisoners in jail, because a house was burned, and Miss Hume's black woman stole the best items from the house. The black woman gave testimony against Russel. The townsfolk told the black woman if she did not tell where the items were, they would hang her. She said she gave the clothes to Russel.[197]

Russel stated that Berry came into the jail and said: "I hear there are some Goddamn niggers put in this jail for burning down barns." He wanted the jail cell opened. Russel, along with the other prisoners, were taken down the stairs from their cells by four of the guerillas and headed out with them. The guerillas took the prisoners to the bridge. The guerillas made the four prisoners ride ahead of them and when they reached the bridge each one of them took one of the prisoners up behind them. After the prisoners got up the creek, another guerilla came out and met them. As Berry led Russel up the river, he said: "Uncle, I believe they are going to kill the last damn one of you."

Russel told Berry to let him go. Berry said he could not let him go and that the Captain would punish him, and he might even kill him. Berry moved on. Russel managed to escape and jumped over a fence and Berry shot him in the left hip. Russel fell with his head down the hill. Berry shot four times at Russel. Russel raised his head and Berry had left. According to Russel, Berry was wearing a red hood on. Dick Mitchell had a black hat with a half silver moon. All of the guerillas had black overcoats.[198]

John Rusk was another one of the prisoners in the jail. The reason he was in jail was because a house had been burned and he was accused of being involved in the burning. According to Rusk, Berry shot him before he got to the creek. He asked Berry to let him go and Berry said he would be killed himself if he did let him go and the captain would kill him. Rusk dismounted the horse and ran along the field. Berry fired at him and shot him near the hip. Berry fired another three or four times but missed Rusk. Rusk rolled down the hill and saw no more of Berry. Each of the guerillas took one of the prisoners behind him on a horse.[199]

On December 30, 1864, twelve gang members, including Jerome "Sue Monday" Clarke, Sam Berry, Jim Davis, and Dick Mitchell, started on a raid of robbery and murder. The gang first visited Springfield, Kentucky, robbed the stores and private individuals of about two thousand dollars in money and property. The gang members shot and killed T. W. Lee, a wagon maker, and a gentleman named Wetherton, a shoemaker. According to G. S. Robinson, he saw Davis and Sue Mundy shoot Lee. After he saw Lee shot and killed, he examined the wound in the back of the temple of Lee's head. Robinson was in the public square and started to go home and a man came up to Robinson and demanded his pocketbook. Robinson gave the pocketbook to the guerilla and then the guerilla told Robinson if he did not go back, he would kill him. Robinson went back and after a while started back up again and he saw Davis and Mundy sitting on their horses shooting at Lee. Robinson saw Lee dead in a closet in the home of Mr. Clement. Berry was seen on a horse talking with Mrs. Knott and her daughter. Lee had a pistol in his hand and got down behind a horse and one of the guerillas rode around and came out with a gun and pistol and said: "he had sent him up." Robinson did not see Lee's dead body until after the guerillas left the town. Henry Turner, one of the guerillas, insisted that Robinson go in Mr. Clements house. He said there was a killed man in there. Robinson went in the house and saw Lee dead. Dick Mitchell was also with Turner.[200] Henry Turner was twenty years old in 1864. He had been in the Confederate army serving in the 8th Kentucky Cavalry, Company G, Cluke's Cavalry.

Another witness to the robbery and murder of Lee and Wetherton was C. B. Butler who was a lawyer in Springfield. Butler knew Berry. They both taught school in 1862 and met in the same church. Butler was sitting in his office when he heard horses coming through the streets at a high rate of speed. He looked out his window and saw the horsemen pass his office. The horsemen turned around and stopped almost at his office, fired their pistols, and yelled for everyone to come out into the streets. He saw Berry leave the horsemen and walk away. He saw the horsemen shooting. Butler said he saw one of the guerillas carry a black flag. The guerillas called for matches to burn the barn, but luckily the men did not burn the barn. Butler remained in his office. He recognized Berry and Dick Mitchell. He saw two shots fired into the meeting-house. Butler stated he saw one man robbed of his watch. Another guerilla rode up to the man and demanded money. The man said: "I have been delivered of my money," and then took his watch. He saw one of the guerillas rob Mr. Marattay. Marattay stated to the guerilla that they had robbed him of all his money. The guerilla said: "Give me fifty cents, then, I haven't got any money today." There were several women running around searching for the doctor, and they said: "Goddam you, we expected to send you after the doctor before we got there." One of the women was looking for a priest.[201]

After a short time, Butler walked to Mr. Wetherton. Wetherton told Butler he was a dead man. Butler noticed that the ball that entered Wetherton entered just above his left hip and passed through the skin near the right nipple. Butler could feel the ball. Wetherton died an hour and a half later.

Robert Symes (Simms) was a grocer and lived in Springfield. When the shooting was going on, Berry was speaking with Symes at his door. Symes was robbed and he told he was robbed of a ring, watch, chain, and money and asked for Berry to retrieve them. Berry told Symes that he would use his influence. If Symes showed Berry who robbed him, he would get them back. Berry protected Symes from having his saddle stolen.[202]

On December 3, 1864, A. C. McElroy was a merchant in Springfield. Twelve guerillas came riding into town and McElroy was informed that they were coming. He looked out his door and saw the guerillas riding into town. He went back into the store and just as he was walking into the store a man rushed up to him and said if they were fired on, they would burn the town. Two ladies were in the store. The guerilla told the ladies they could go home if they would not tell anyone that the guerillas were in the town. He threw down his pistol and demanded that McElroy hand over his money. He gave the guerilla twenty dollars. He also handed the guerilla his pocketbook, but the guerilla refused the pocketbook. There was ten dollars in the pocketbook and the guerilla took five dollars out of the pocketbook. McElroy recognized Dick Mitchell. He saw a watch taken from his brother and fifteen dollars stolen from his brother James Hughes. He stated that Captain Magruder took their money. He also saw boots and some other goods from James Hughes store. The guerilla rushed into another room and demanded money from McElroy's brother and drew a pistol on him. Shortly after the pistol was drawn, the distinct sound of a pistol went off. The guerillas were firing into a grocery store.[203] McElroy stated that he found out that Magruder was in the room when the guerillas called his name. He knew one of the guerillas who rode with Nathan Bedford Forrest as one and identified him as Dick Mitchell.[204]

James R. Hughes was a physician and merchant in Springfield and was robbed by the guerillas. His partner estimated that they were robbed of $356 dollars, which is the equivalent to $6,896.13. He saw the guerillas shooting through windows. He saw both Wetherton and Thornton Lee dead. Hughes also saw Lee dead in a closet. He saw two guerillas ride up to Mrs. Lee, who was standing on the porch with two ladies. The women began to scream. Two of the guerillas rode back to Berry and he cursed them for going and telling what they did. He told the two guerillas they should have not murdered Lee and he reprimanded them for their "hard-heartedness." The guerillas left. Hughes picked up the certificates of stock and administration papers that was scattered through the streets by the guerillas. Hughes also found Lee dead in the closet. Hughes said he recognized Berry when he came to his store on horseback and Hughes noticed that Berry had a missing arm. Berry asked Hughes' name. He told Berry his name was Hughes. He asked who the store belonged to, and Hughes told Berry that the store belonged to McElroy. Hughes brother-in-law was Hugh McElroy. McElroy was the cashier at the bank. McElroy was in the counting room at the bank and heard firing in the streets. He saw everybody run in every direction. He heard the guerillas yell at the citizens to stop running or they would shoot them. The guerillas made the citizens gather in the streets and made them stand. Another part of the guerillas were riding all over town. The guerillas asked the citizens who had the keys to the banks. The guerillas approached McElroy in the bank. McElroy stated that his cousin Charles McElroy had the keys, and he didn't know where he was. The guerillas left but came back and said that Hugh McElroy was the President of the bank and demanded he open the safe. McElroy went into the counting room and told the guerillas he did not have the keys and the vault was locked. The guerillas threatened to break open the door. One of the guerillas took a bench and smashed the bench against the vault door. McElroy told the guerillas that the drawer on the counter probably held the keys. McElroy told the guerillas to hit the drawer and the drawer should open the door. The guerilla hit the drawer and three pocketbooks fell out, full of papers, some money, and the keys. One of the pocketbooks had $150.00 in Federal money and $600.00 in Confederate money, which he received from General Braxton Bragg when he took his cattle. McElroy took the keys and opened the safe door for the guerillas. One of the guerillas saw a vault box open and took the silverware in the box. There was about $40 to 50 dollars in silver and about the same amount in money belonging to Mrs. Cunningham amounting to $50.00 in silver and sixty dollars in cash. The guerillas found an urn and two cups that belonged to the church. The guerilla took the cups but left the urn. Two of the silver cups belonged to the Fair Ground and the other two silver cups belonged to the church. The elder of the church persuaded one of the guerillas him to give back at least two of the silver cups. Two more guerillas came into the bank. Magruder was one of the men that walked into the bank. After the guerillas searched the drawers, Magruder walked up to McElroy put his pistol across his forehead and said: "Now, God Damn you tell me where the balance of that money is or I will blow your brains out." McElroy told him "that the man that was in the vault that he knew all of the money in the house that I had knowledge of." Magruder threatened to blow his brains out again. McElroy told Magruder to go ahead and blow his brains out because the man in the vault had all the money in the house. Magruder lowered his pistol and all of the guerillas walked out the bank. The incident took only fifteen minutes. He learned that Lee was killed. Lee grabbed a gun and came running towards the guerillas and the guerillas shot him dead. He confirmed that Lee ran into a house and hid in the closet after they shot him and laid down in the closet and the guerillas came into the house and shot him again.[205] Hughes saw Berry ride over to the grocery store. Berry called for items to be brought out of the store, such as cigars. According to Hughes, Berry paid for everything that was taken from the store.[206] He also recognized Henry Turner. He also heard the names of Captain Henry, Captain Mitchell, Captain Turner, Captain Davis, and Captain Mack.

J.J. Marity was a druggist in Springfield and saw four guerillas in front of his store and began shooting Mr. Bosley's home. Mr. Bosley ran into his home and shut the door. One of the guerillas followed him to the door and yelled at him to open the door. Mr. Bosely refused to open the door and the guerilla began shooting. The guerilla shot all around the house. The guerillas broke open the door and went into the home. One of the guerillas told Marity to come out of his store and demanded he give over his money. Marity gave the guerilla his money and he ordered him out into the streets among the other residents of Springfield. He saw one of the guerillas rob a man by the name of Robinson of a ring and a man by the name of Simons. He stayed there for about five minutes. One of the guerillas rode up and spoke to Marity. The guerilla agreed to allow him to return his store. Marity knew Dick Mitchell and Henry Turner.[207] Marity said that Thornton Lee's wife came to her door and screamed that her husband was killed and for someone to come to her assistance. One of the guerillas by the name of Turner was standing in front of his door. Marity asked Turner if he could go over to John Weatherton. Turner agreed. Turner said he knew Weatherton and would walk with him. Marity went to the house and saw him lying in a bed. He could barely speak and wanted a priest. Marity went out of the house to look for a priest.

G.J. Bosley was a grocer in Springfield and heard the alarm that the guerillas were coming into town. He ran to the door and saw them riding into town. He went back to his desk and grabbed some papers. Jim Davis came up to his door and shot into his house two or three times. He ran out the back door and ran into another house about thirty yards away. He saw across the street at some howling and heard one of the guerillas shout: "There goes a damn Yankee" with a gun in his hand. He saw Lee with a pistol in his hand. Bosley saw one of the guerillas ride around the blacksmith shop, yelling "Shoot the damn rascal." Lee jumped into a garden and laid his gun on the side of the stable and shot at the guerilla and then dropped his gun and ran toward the house and as he ran through the garden, he saw Jim Davis shoot Thornton Lee.[208] Bosley saw Lee's dead body about ten or fifteen yards away. The guerillas went into the house and killed Lee.[209]

R.J. Simms stated that he knew Sam Berry, Dick Mitchell, and Turner. The guerillas robbed him of his silver watch, a gold ring, and about thirty dollars in cash. He also saw the guerillas rob George Robinson. They also robbed his father of a watch, but later gave the watch back to him. Simms stated that all the guerillas were called captains.

After robbing Springfield, the gang rode to Texas and Pottsville and robbed the towns of only a small amount of money. Just after dark, the town of Perryville was informed that about one hundred guerillas were headed in their direction by the way of Mackville Road. The news threw the town into panic. The citizens of Perryville kept watch over the town during the night. The townsfolk were not armed and came to the conclusion that if the force was too large the town would not be able to offer any resistance.[210]

At 2 p.m., the next day Sue Mundy, along with Berry, and the other twelve gang members stormed into town. At the time, about two to three hundred people in Perryville were in the streets of Perryville going about their daily business, when the gang came riding in from the west and yelling loudly: "Fall in line or be shot down." A large number of Perryville residents jumped into the bushes. Dick Guthrie was standing in the blacksmith shop. He had a lot of money in his pockets and fearing that the gang would take his money hid under the forge. Harvey Walker hid in the cave on the Karrick-Parks house. About one hundred of the residents lined up directly opposite the Enterprise Hotel and were robbed at gun point. Everyone was relieved of their purses. Most of the gang never dismounted and rode up to the store doors and made the merchants bring them the contents of their cash drawers. One of the gang members, who was a large six-foot gentleman, dismounted and rifled the pockets of the line of men, all of whom had their hands in the air. Money was the sole object of the raid. The gang members also took several horses and saddles. Dashing across the bridge, Berry rode his horse into Wallace Green's drugstore, and took all the money from the cash drawer and rode out. When the raiders entered the next store, which was a grocery store, and the clerk was W. H. Parks. They thought they were about to be attacked by a young Federal soldier by the name of John Lawson. He was shot and mortally wounded while in the act of handing over his wallet. The gang member who shot the Federal soldier stated that he shot the soldier by mistake. Richard Lester, who was in the rear of the store, jumped out the back window, and into the Chaplin River. He swam across the river and hid in the tall woods on the Wingate farm east of town, where he remained for three days without food before returning to town. The gang members were going to kill Lester because he had been discourteous to the gang members on a previous raid. The gang next entered the store of Peg Leg Jones, a local merchant. Jones had just opened his store, having moved from Harrodsburg just a few days before the raid. Henry McGraw, who lived in Perryville, was an uncle of Sam Berry and his appearance on the scene prevented a further attack on the town.[211] The gang stayed in the town for only twenty minutes. From Perryville, the gang rode onto Nevada and Cornishville. They were headed towards Bloomfield. About an hour after the raid, Federal Captains Fiddler and Wharton, from Lebanon, in command of a detachment of thirty-five soldiers and armed citizens, arrived and were in hot pursuit of the gang members.[212] While looking for the gang members, they ransacked homes and businesses and taking horses. Some of the citizens were repaid for their horses.

During Christmas dinner, on December 25, 1864, Dr. Evans, Miss Rhoda and Miss Alice invited Captain Berry and his men to feast with them. While at the table someone proposed capturing Bardstown. Nearly all of them had drank too much wine and whiskey. Dr. Evans tried to dissuade the men, knowing that Captain Taylor had sixty-five men in the Bardstown courthouse. Tom tried to convince his brother not to attack Bardstown. The courthouse was in the center of the square in town with four streets that cross and center into the square. Captain Berry would not listen to his brother. On January 16, 1865, Captain Berry, along with Clarke, Magruder, Henry Turner, Pat Ball, James Pratt, Bill Merriman, Billy Hughes, Sam Jones, and others attacked with fifty-five men with disastrous results. Captain Robert Young had a detachment of the 54th Kentucky Mounted Infantry in the courthouse. The old frame depot on the edge of town was burned by Captain Berry and Captain Berry charged as far as Market Street, where Captain Berry's men were brought to a stand. Captain Berry called on the "damned" Yankees to come on and Young mounted part of his men and charged Captain Berry's force and routed him. Magruder described the scene: *A citizen told us there were twenty-five of them; so they outnumbered us. But it was not long before they gave us abundant opportunity to tell the number of their guns. Thirty of them came out of the Courthouse-A fair challenge to battle. We declined and fell back up the turnpike, hoping to gain some advantage of position. The Federals followed us-we mounted, they on foot. The firing was lively and rapid on both sides. Thus we fell back half a mile, the Federals, one hundred and fifty yards behind us, advancing slowly. Just here I described two horsemen coming out of town, whom I at first took to be citizens coming to witness the fight. In the meantime the enemy came to a halt, and I, supposing that I had only infantry to fight, dismounted my men and placed them on the roadside. While things were in this position, twenty-five cavalrymen, who had approached the turnpike by a bridle path, appeared as suddenly as if they had fallen from the clouds, and came thundering on the charge.*

I had no time to lay low and fire when the Yankees came abreast of them, Sam Berry and I rode slowly up the road, hoping that they would follow us and come near enough for my boys to empty their saddles. In this I was disappointed. They saw the trap and started back. I wheeled, and the boys, anticipating the move, were all in their saddle, so that when Berry and I reached them they joined us, and we charged the cavalry, now retreating in turn. The Federal infantry had been moved forward and in perfect fully we rushed into the very fate we had prepared for the Yankees. I and Berry were in advance of my squad some fifty yards. The boys in the rear saw the game in time to escape, but Berry and I got the full discharge of twenty-five "Brindleback" muskets. My horse fell dead under me, pierced by a dozen balls. Berry was severely wounded in the left shoulder, and his horse mortally wounded. The noble animal, of the best blood of Kentucky, had strength enough to bear us both away. When my horse fell, I saw Berry reel in his saddle, and in an instant I sprang to his crupper, and, holding the wounded rider, guided the bleeding, panting horse back to where my men stood covering my retreat. We then retreated, bearing our wounded man along, until we reached Mr. John Mackey's, some five miles from Bardstown. Here the mettled horse fell under his wounded master and died in the road. I at once "pressed" a horse and buggy for Berry and a horse for myself and continued the flight to Bloomfield.[213] During the "brisk" fight, according to the *Louisville Daily Journal*, Captain James Pratt and Lieutenant J. P. Ball of Sam Berry's force were killed. Several of Berry's men were chased by Young's men and left their horses and ran into the brush. Darkness ended the chase. According to the newspaper, Sue Mundy, aka Jerome Clarke, was shot in the hand. Captain Berry lost four men killed and thirteen wounded including Captain Berry.[214] The doors on the west side of the courthouse were reached and battered down, killing nine men inside and nineteen wounded. Tom Berry was also wounded. The attack was repulsed.

Tom Berry has a slightly different story of the retreat from Bardstown. According to Tom Berry, he saw his brother Sam shot, falling from his horse. Tom rode to his brother amid a shower of bullets, dismounted, lifted his brother on his saddle. Six men of Berry's command came to Tom Berry, keeping Young's force at bay. Retreating slowly with his brother, they came across Captain Lancaster in his buggy. Tom placed his brother inside the buggy, he formed the men and charged the advancing Union troops, driving them back a mile and a half. The pursuit ended. Tom took his brother to Dr. Evans, who tended to Sam's wound.[215]

After recovering from their wounds, Tom Berry, along with Jerome Clarke, and Henry Magruder, King White, rode to Boston, Nelson County, and to the Rolling Fork Bridge, which they burned after a sharp battle. The Union force was located inside a stockade and a hand-to-hand combat took place and the Union force surrendered. Leaving Boston, Tom Berry rode to Meade, Hardin, and Hancock Counties. Captain Berry captured the steamboat *General Lytle*, which docked at Hawesville. When they boarded the ship, the Union soldiers fired on Captain Berry's men. King White stole $2,300 from the captain. Jerome Clarke and Henry Magruder were seriously wounded and had to be left behind. Captain Berry made his way back to Nelson County, where he found his brother Captain Berry ready to take command. Captain Tom Berry and his brother Sam thought that his force should scatter. Captain Berry needed more ammunition, so they sent Rude and Texas to ride to Louisville and secure the ammunition. They dressed as women and seven days later returned with the much-needed ammunition.[216]

While Texas and Rude rode to Louisville, Sam Berry stayed at Dr. McCloskey's farm near Bloomfield. Later one evening Sam and his brother Tom were riding towards Fairfield. Reaching the top of a hill, they heard a horse cough and looking ahead saw Captain Taylor at the head of forty Union soldiers. He had also reached the top of hill on the same road. Captain Taylor was marching towards Bardstown. Both Captain Taylor and Sam and Tom drew their pistols. Captain Taylor saw Sam and Tom's pistols drawn and continued to ride by not willing to risk being shot. Sam and Tom rode off.[217]

Sam and Tom rode to the Salt River and camped. While they were eating dinner, Captain James Bridgewater's troopers surrounded them. They drove Sam and Tom through an open field when the brothers jumped a fence. There was a gate in front of a lot with two corn cribs, near the bank of the river. There were high fences on three sides. The Union soldiers followed the brothers into the lot. The Union soldiers came from two sides and cut the brothers off. Sam and Tom took shelter behind the corn cribs. The brothers had six pistols each and cut off double barrel shotguns. They had thirty-eight shots apiece. They held off the Union troops for twenty-five minutes. Tom had a Sharps repeating rifle. The two brothers managed to kill eight horses, killed eleven men, and seriously wounded Captain Bridgewater. Eighteen men and horses went down when the Union troops tried to rush their position behind the cribs. Tom turned to his brother and said: "Brother, let's leave this place now." The brothers mounted their horses and leaped into the river and crossed to the other side. The brothers rode to Bullitt County and met with Captain Phillips in Jefferson County. The next night the brothers rode to Louisville and asked for a friend to buy them one hundred pistols and ammunition. The weapons were brought to them in market baskets. They were also given medicines. The brothers left Louisville and traveled to Paroquet Springs. During the evening, the brothers rode to Keesby's Ford and to Spencer County. Once they arrived in Spencer County, the brothers visited Judge Jonathan Davis's place. They were met with comrades. The brothers distributed the pistols. Fifty-six recruits were waiting for them. After nightfall, Sam and Tom Berry along with the fifty-six men rode to Dr. McCloskey. All the men had on blue overcoats. The gang rode to Bloomfield, crossed Muldraugh Hill, passed Columbia. After resting, the gang rode to Burkesville, near the Cumberland River, crossing Stagalls Ford. They camped at Blacks Shop. The gang rode deep into the South with their destination being Johnsontown on the Tennessee River, hoping to reach General Nathan Bedford Forrest's lines. Forrest received the new recruits. Two days later Forrest would fight a battle at Johnsontown.[218]

On December 29, 1864, Henry Magruder, along with Merriman, James and Thomas Pratt, Jim Davis, Dick Mitchell, Bill Marion. Magruder, Marion, and Davis were wearing red suits, meaning no quarter would be given. In all there were about fifteen guerillas, who rode about ten miles from Bardstown and surrounded Union Lieutenant Charles Spalding, who was a Union officer, who was recently discharged from the army from the 10th Kentucky Union Infantry. Magruder and his gang murdered Lieutenant Spalding. Magruder and his gang rode into Bardstown.[219]

On December 29, 1864, Mrs. William R. Grigsby, who lived in Bardstown, had her home visited by two Union officers: Dr. John L. Shirk, surgeon of the 7th Pennsylvania Cavalry and Captain Robert McCormick, Company G, 7th Pennsylvania Cavalry and brigade inspector of Colonel Robert H. G. Minty's brigade. His family extended a warm greeting to the officers. Mrs. Grigsby was a supporter of the Union cause and Union soldiers paid her visits and she always greeted them with warm hospitality. Grigsby and the two Union officers were not aware that Henry Magruder and his gang saw the Union officers approach Grigsby's house and Magruder along with his gang, rode across a narrow valley, surrounded the building, and cut off any means of escape.[220] Captain McCormick had a brother, who was Colonel Charles McCormack of the 7th Pennsylvania Cavalry, who stayed at the Grigsby's the year before when he was sick. Charles McCormick told Robert to pay his respects to the Grigsby family. There was a party that night and there lots of ladies and gentlemen in the parlor. Alphonso Kirk was attending the party at the house and witnessed the incident. After a short conversation while sitting in the parlor, the young daughter of Mrs. Grigsby began to play the piano for the officers. Twenty minutes later, the black servant came in and said that the house was surrounded by guerillas. Henry Magruder stated that while he was going through Mr. Grigsby's farm "I discovered two finely caparisoned horse tied to the fence. I knew that my time had come. I surrounded the house, and, going to the door, discovered two officers, I afterward learned them to be Major Shuck (Shirk) and Captain McCormick. As soon as we saw them, we began firing.""[221] Magruder stated he had twenty men. Cousin Billy Grigsby's sister said she had seen the guerillas coming over the fence when she was looking from the window, but she thought they were Federal soldiers. Shirk recognized some of the guerillas as Pratt's men. Shirk wanted to surrender. McCormack would not surrender. The guerillas bolted into the house and began to fire. The guerillas shot and killed Shirk immediately after they entered the house. Captain McCormack came into the family room and the guerillas were shooting at him. McCormack came out into the hall and said to Mrs. Grigsby: "They have shot me all to pieces" and fell down at her feet. Mrs. Grigsby asked for the guerillas not to shoot anymore. Kirk recognized Magruder and Merriman. Both McCormack and Shirk were dead.[222]

According to a newspaper article published after the Civil War, Magruder saw McCormack roll under the bed, and he coolly got down on his knees and crawled after McCormack and put his pistol close to McCormack and fired. Some of the blood splashed out onto his pistol barrel and as he rose to his knees, he placed the weapon to his lips and kissed the blood off the polished barrel. Mrs. Grigsby was paralyzed with terror in the room, when Magruder approached her, tipped his hat, and with a polite bow, apologized for being compelled to kill the men in her house. He said: "We could have taken them to the woods but for the soldiers that are camped close by, who might make it warm for us." He then rode off and escaped.[223]

CHAPTER EIGHTEEN

January 1865:
The Simpsonville Massacre

In January 1865, James Techener was a farmer and lived three miles and a half east of Taylorsville. Tom Henry and Berry came to his house and wanted an iron gray horse from Techener. Berry took the horse. Techener stated that Berry was armed with three or four pistols that were pointed at him. Berry left Techener a mare. Berry also gave him twenty dollars. If Berry did not come for the mare, Techener could keep the horse. Within a few weeks, Berry and Bill Marion sent a note by a black messenger stating he wanted the mare back. The man who had Techener's horse lived in Bloomington, Indiana. Techener was not able to recover his horse. Techener gave Berry his mare back. Techener stated that the value of his horse was $150.00. Later after the incident, he learned that Berry and Marion were waiting for his mare at Techener's neighbor.

On January 6, 1865, Anne Engle, who was a resident of Lebanon Junction, was at the station at Lebanon Junction and came with her brother James Engle to board a train for Louisville. While they were waiting for the train at Lebanon Junction, Jerome Clarke, Henry Magruder, Bill Merriman, and Henry Metcalf, rode into Lebanon Junction. Her brother James Engle and Charles Barnett were both Union soldiers in the 15th Kentucky Volunteer Infantry. Both Engle and Barnett were trying to get away from the guerillas and ran across an open field. Magruder and another guerilla, saw the two soldiers run across the field. The guerillas caught up with the soldiers, and James Engle and Charles Barnett surrendered. According to Anne Engle, after her brother surrendered, Bill Merriman shot him. Anne witnessed her brother being shot in front of her. One of the bullets hit his heart, and the other bullet hit his back. He was shot four times. Barnett was shot at the same time. One of the bullets entered the back of his head and lodged in his forehead. Anne described one of the guerillas wearing a red jacket and the rest were wearing blue uniforms and had blue overcoats. She said there were four guerillas on horseback.[224]

W. H. Mayfield was also a witness to the murder to Engle and Barnett. He was one hundred yards away when the shooting took place. He said he saw four men come up and fire on the engine just as the train was moving out of the station. Some of the men yelled: "They are guerillas. Mayfield ran as soon as the firing began. After the guerillas left, he saw the bodies of Engle and Barnett. He also saw the body of Jake Winstead, who was shot at the same time Engle and Barnett were killed.[225]

James D. Hill, the brother of William Hill, who was a farmer living in Lebanon Junction, was also a witness to the killing of Engle and Barnett. He stated that he saw all four of the guerillas shooting. He was also present when Winstead was killed. Hill stated he saw two Union soldiers running across an open field, and Magruder along with another man, went after the soldiers and captured them and brought them back and shot them within one hundred yards of Lebanon Junction. Bill Merriman was a cousin of Hill. Hill was within thirty yards when he witnessed the murders. Hill stated that Magruder shot Engle. Hill stated that Jerome Clarke was dressed in a red suit and the rest were dressed in blue overcoats. He also stated that each of the guerillas were armed with four revolvers apiece. He stated that four men were murdered: James Engle, Joe Barnett, Doc. Barnett, and Jake Winstead. Hill stated that he also shook hands with Bill Merriman. He also shook hands with Jerome Clarke. He stated that Merriman called Clarke by Sue Mundy. According to Hill, he stated that Barnett was killed in the field, not at the station.[226]

William Hill was a soldier in the 15th Kentucky Union Infantry and was discharged on January 14, 1865, also witnessed the murder of Barnett and Engle. He was at Lebanon Junction to board a train for Louisville to receive his discharge papers. He was standing and saw a man coming up dressed in civilian clothing, except for his Federal overcoat and the guerillas began to shoot at the engine. He was within a few feet of the guerillas when they began firing. He went back into the store. The two soldiers asked Hill what their next move was. He told them he had no answer, except the men should turn and fight. He told them not to run for if they were caught by the guerillas, they would be killed. Engle and Barnett started across the field and two of the guerillas went after them and fired at them hollering for them to Halt! And cursed at them and called them Yankee son of bitches. They overtook Engle and Barnett at the fence and brought them halfway back before the guerillas shot both Engle and Barnett. Hill went upstairs in the room above the dining room at the Mayfield Tavern to keep out of sight since he was unarmed. Hill stated he knew Merriman since he was a small boy. He also knew Henry Magruder.[227]

Harvey Wells was the hotel keeper at Lebanon Junction and had just sat down to dinner and a young man named Hunter came running into the dining room and stated that the guerillas were coming. He sat at the table and did not get up from his seat, eating his dinner, and within a few seconds he heard pistol fire towards his back and then two or three pistols firing. He threw his head over his shoulder and looked through the window and saw some men on horses. Jerome Clarke came into his house, kicked the barroom door open, and kicked the back door open leading from the barroom to the dining room. He came in with a pistol in each hand and demanded to know where the telegraph operator was located and threatened to kill Wells if he did not tell him. He had his pistols in Wells' face. Wells stated he did not know. Clarke demanded money and Wells pulled out his pocketbook and handed the pocketbook to Clarke. Clarke said: "I only want your money; I don't want any of your private property." He took the money out, and he also took Hunter's money. Clarke was joined by Magruder. Wells asked Magruder not to kick down any of the doors and that Wells would open the doors for them. Clarke stated that he would no longer kick down any doors. The stove was kicked over in the Telegraph Office and the coals were about to set the house on fire, and Wells asked if he could put out the flames. Clarke agreed and let Wells put out the flames. Wells stated that two rail cars sitting on a track in the northwest corner of his house were set on fire. He also saw two Union soldiers coming towards the station. Clarke was chopping down a telegraph pole and saw Engle and Barnett running across the field. Wells was standing on the northeast corner of the platform at the end of his house. Magruder and another guerilla, yelled at the two men and Wells turned around the corner and stood there, and heard four guns fire. Wells came around the platform and saw the two guerillas coming back after the shooting. Wells stated that two of the men were killed in the east corner of his house and the other two were killed in the northwest corner. He stated he saw Winstead lying dead on the left side of the railroad. According to Wells, he said no one was in command of the guerilla party and each man did as he pleased.[228]

James Bird was also a witness at the killing of Barnett and Engle at Lebanon Junction. He knew Magruder since he was a boy and was raised in his county. The guerillas robbed him. He stated that he saw James Engle, Dick Barnett,

Joe Barnett, and Jake Winstead. When the guerillas fired at the engine, he stepped back into his house. He confirmed that he saw the train car burning, he saw Clarke wearing a red suit, and saw Clarke, Medcalfe (Medkiff), and Magruder enter the hotel. He also confirmed that Magruder entered the bar after the shooting. Magruder spoke to Bird who was in the hotel. He stated that two of the men killed were on one side of the train cars and two on the other side of the town.[229]

Anthony Botto stated that Bill Merriman told him to retrieve coals from the engine and set the two train cars on fire. Merriman told Botto to get matches from the Mayfield home. He also told to get turpentine and chop down some telegraph poles and took the pieces to start the fire. There was a carload of hay which was also set on fire. Botto stated that Clarke and Magruder shot two of the Union soldiers. One of the soldiers was lying on the ground groaning and Clarke went back and shot the soldier. Magruder told Clarke not to kill the soldier, but Clarke ignored him. Botto said the guerillas followed Clarke's orders.

Frank Brenner stated that he knew Magruder. He knew that Magruder joined Morgan's command in September of 1861 and saw Magruder riding with Morgan, when the trestle was burned near Elizabethtown during Morgan's Christmas Raid. One of the guerillas rode up and told Brenner to burn Mayfield's house, which was the Mayfield Hotel. He went to assist Magruder. Brenner told Magruder that he was ordered the burn the house. Brenner told Magruder that Mayfield was a friend of his. He asked who ordered the burning of the house. Brenner pointed out the man, and Magruder told Brenner "Don't obey any such orders."[230]

On January 13th or 14th, at Bloomfield, F. H. McCay, who was Deputy United States Collector, stated that Magruder and Dick Mitchell arrested him a short distance from town. McKay was on his way to a mill and asked if him if he was a United States Collector. He told them he was. They asked him if he had been collecting. He told them he had been collecting about two days ago. The guerillas stated they wanted to see his papers. They went to his house and McKay opened his drawer and handed them sheets of paper eighteen to twenty inches square showing accounts made out for Nelson and Spencer counties. Dick Mitchell asked McKay what his commission was on and what he collected. Both Mitchell and Magruder were sitting near his fireplace Mitchell asked him why he did not have money on the premises. McKay told Mitchell that the law required him to make deposits after he collected the money and that Mr. Blakely, who was the District Collector, gave him a check every month for his commission. He told the guerillas that as soon as he collected the money, he sent the money to Louisville. McKay did not tell the guerillas that he had eight hundred dollars in the house. The guerillas rode off from his house with his papers and burned them.

On January 19th or 20th, 1865, D. R. Pogniard, a resident of Spencer County, and a land proprietor, noticed three men on foot that were crossing a field three or four hundred yards from his house and as they approached the house, one of them turned back and went to the stables. Two of the men came to the house. One of the men came to the back door and knocked and was let into the house by a servant. He demanded that Pogniard give him his three horses. He also wanted three saddles. Pogniard told his servant to get the horses and saddles. The men also wanted three bridles. The men also had a prisoner with them. Four or five more men rode into his yard and demanded some whiskey. Although Berry did not steal the horses personally, he was with the men who rode off with his horses. He eventually recovered his horses but in an injured condition. He recovered one of his saddles and bridles which was worth about five dollars.[231]

Confederate Captain William Quantrill rode from Missouri to Kentucky. Quantrill was one of the more infamous guerillas. He was born in Hagerstown, Maryland, on July 20, 1836. His father died when Quantrill was young, and he lived with widow mother. When he was sixteen, he went to live at Cleveland, Ohio. He had an older brother that lived in Kansas City, who encouraged his brother to leave Ohio and come live with him. In 1856, Quantrill and his brother visited California. While they were traveling to California, a group known as Lane's Jay-hawkers, who acted as abolitionists, desired freedom for Kansas came across the brothers as they camped on the Cottonwood River. Thirty Jay-hawkers fired their pistols, and the oldest brother was shot and killed. Charles William Quantrill was shot and left for dead. The Jay-hawkers robbed the brothers Golightly Spieback came across Quantrill and saved him from death. Years later, Quantrill surrounded himself with Todd, Scott, "Bloody" Bill Anderson, Blant, Yager, Hulse, and Greg, the Younger brothers, and Frank and Jesse James. Quantrill led the guerillas in Missouri. Quantrill and his band led the massacre of Lawrence, Kansas. By December 1864, Quantrill took no part in Confederate General Sterling Price's invasion of Missouri. He had a bitterness towards Price and had contempt for General Joseph Shelby. He asked for the generals for aid to take against the rising popularity of Todd.

William Quantrill's Raid in Lawrence, Kansas occurred on August 23, 1863. The Raid would be known as the Lawrence Massacre. Quantrill and his men killed approximately 150 unarmed boys and men. Lawrence was a pro-Union town. Later in the war, Quantrill would leave Kansas, and in 1865, he and his men would enter Kentucky. Quantrill would work with Jerome Clarke, Sam Berry, Henry Magruder, and others from Clarke's force. (Originally printed in Frank Leslie's Illustrated newspaper, September 12, 1863, p. 389.)

Quantrill was forced out of the guerilla band. His attempt at advancement was ignored by the Confederate command in Richmond and by General Price. With thirty-five men who supported him, Quantrill decided to take his men into Kentucky. By January 22, 1865, Quantrill and forty-five of his men, wearing Federal uniforms, arrived in Hartford, Ohio County, in the Green River, Kentucky. He represented himself as Captain Clark, commander of the Fourth Missouri Cavalry, in order to fool Union soldiers. Quantrill claimed to be riding toward the Ohio River over the Hawesville Road, pretending to need a guide. Private Andrew Martin Barnett, of the 26th Kentucky Infantry was recruiting, and Isaac H. Axton was also recruiting in the Hartford area. Barnett agreed to ride with Quantrill. Walter B. Lawton, a soldier in the 3rd Kentucky Cavalry, who was at Hartford on furlough to see his family and for safe conduct, also agreed to ride with Quantrill and Barnett. Just after leaving town, Axton became suspicious and told Quantrill he would meet him later up the road after he got his best pistol and money. As Axton left, Quantrill sent three men to follow Axton. Axton went to Joe Barnett's, Andrew's father, and told him that Joe and Lawton were in danger. Barnett sent his hired hand, James Wisley Townsley, who was formerly in the 3rd Kentucky Cavalry to bring Andrew back. Townsley was stopped by Quantrill's men. Quantrill's men took his reins, cut them, strangled the horse, then three miles down the road in some woods, the men hung Townsley. Nine miles further down the road, Quantrill's men shot Lawton. Sixteen miles from Hartford, Quantrill's men shot Barnett.[232]

On January 23, 1865, Berry, Bill Marion, and Turner, rode into Taylorsville, Spencer County, Kentucky and told Samuel Snyder, who was the jailer for Taylorsville, they were going to burn the courthouse. Snyder asked Berry if he could take the chairs, benches, and tables out of the building. Berry told Snyder he could take anything out of the building. They proceeded to burn the courthouse. The guerillas forced the black citizens of town to set the building on fire. The guerillas also burned the jail.

On January 25, 1865, Company E, of the 5th United States Colored Cavalry, numbering eighty men were assigned to drive a herd of cattle from Camp Nelson to Louisville to supply the city with beef. The men were spread out over a large area, driving the head of cattle. According to Tom Berry, two hundred cattle were in the herd. Captain Sam Berry recruited eighteen men whose families had been brutally treated by Union soldiers, especially Captain Edwin Terrill, who was raiding in Spencer, Washington, Shelby, and Jefferson County, killing citizens, arresting citizens, and stealing cattle and horses. He also had men from Morgan's old command who had been cut off during Morgan's Mount Sterling Raid. Captain Berry and his brother, Tom Berry, had eighteen men, and rode towards Shelby County. Near Shelbyville, Sam and his brother received word from their Uncle Louis Berry and John McGraw that the Union force had stolen a hundred head from Uncle Louis and forty cattle from McGraw. Sam and Tom Berry with his force waited for the 5th U.S.C.C, Company E, to approach. Near Simpsonville, near the county line of Shelby and Jefferson County, Captain Sam Berry and his men prepared themselves with ten long tin horns which could be heard a mile away. The men with the long horns were placed a half mile apart and on either side of the road with five men on each side. They were instructed to blow their horns at intervals of twenty minutes and each pair on either side was directed to answer each other's calls along the line of march, but all the men were instructed to stay out of sight and reach the Union column and when within one mile and a half from Simpsonville, to hurry forward ahead of the Union column. The Union force was divided into small groups, herding a group of cattle. The Union soldiers were puzzled by the horns. They were told they were dinner horns. Captain Sam Berry prepared his men for attack. The advance passed the village which was at the crossroads. The captain commanding the cattle drive stopped at a spring. The cattle were grazing. The captain was drinking in a saloon with some of his men. Captain Sam Berry charged the Union soldiers. They tried to rally and fired two volleys, then broke and

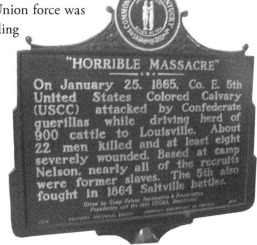

Kentucky Historical Society marker indicating the massacre of African-Americans in the 5th U.S. Colored Calvary in Simpsonville, Kentucky, which was carried out by Sam "One-Armed" Berry. (Photo courtesy of author)

fled. Berry and his men fired into the Union soldiers. The cattle stampeded. The battle lasted only forty minutes. Tom Berry reported that they lost one man killed and seventeen wounded. According to Tom Berry, the Union force amounted to sixty white soldiers and 180 black soldiers. Captain Berry and his men killed seventy-nine and wounded 114 soldiers. Captain Berry and his men collected the cattle and drove them to the hills. According to Tom Berry, the captain did not fight but slipped out the side door of the bar and hid under the platform.[233]

According to Henry Magruder, he reached Simpsonville at 10 am and rode straight into town and saw six or eight cavalry horses hitched. The local citizens told the guerillas that a "train" of cattle had just passed. "I sent Dick Mitchell toward Louisville to see what was coming in that direction. By this time the negroes fired on him. He came back, and the negroes, thinking him alone came on. I formed and charged them with a yell. As we came in view, thundering down on them, they fired a few shots, and, throwing away their arms, ran in among the cattle. At the first fire they killed my horse. I was mounted again in a moment and went for them with a yell. They had no officers, or at least they did not show themselves. Well, to make a long story short, we just went in among the cattle and killed the negroes wherever we could find them. I don't know how many I killed, but I plenty of wool." I got ahold of a Government agent and took three hundred dollars from him. Magruder claimed he had fifteen men with him. According to Magruder, the gang was made up of Whitesides, Merryfield, Froman, Johnson, Hughes, Jimmy Jones, Bill Marion, Dick Mitchell, Berry, Merriman, Clarke, Coulter.[234]

The *Louisville Journal* has a different take on the massacre. On January 26, 1865, the paper reported that the Union officers stopped to warm themselves at various houses along the road, and their men were allowed to straggle along by themselves. Half of the command marched in front of the cattle, while the other half kept in the rear of the cattle drive. The cattle and soldiers were not even out of sight of Simpsonville, when fifteen guerillas, under Coulter, dashed into town. Three of the white officers were in a tavern but made their escape. The guerillas robbed the citizens of $1,200 dollars. After robbing the citizens, the guerillas headed for the African American soldiers guarding the cattle. The guerillas overtook the soldiers and firing began. In about a half hour, the guerillas returned to town, loaded with goods and stated they had killed twenty-five of the black soldiers. The guerillas rode off in the direction of Shelbyville. A gentleman who was detained at Simpsonville by the guerillas resumed his journey after the guerillas had left town and headed towards Louisville. About a half mile up the road, he saw a horrible scene. "The ground was stained with blood, and the dead bodies of negro soldiers were stretched out along the road. It was evident that the guerillas had dashed upon the part guarding the rear of the cattle and taken them completely by surprise. They could have not offered any serious resistance, as none of the outlaws were wounded. It is presumed that the negroes surrendered and were shot down in cold blood, as but two of the entire number escaped-one of them by secreting behind a wagon, the other by running, as he was met several miles from the scene of tragedy wounded and nearly exhausted."[235] Thirty-five African-American soldiers lined the road. The paper reported that the scene was "horrible butchery." The paper correctly reported that Sam Berry, Coulter, and Jerome Clarke were the leaders. The newspaper also reported that one of the gang members was an African American, who boasted when the guerillas returned to Simpsonville, that he killed three African American soldiers himself. The African American belonged to Tom Berry. The African American boy's name was Tom and he belonged to his family. He was sent into the ranks of the 5th U.S.C.C on a work mule with blind bridle, trace chains, back band, collar and harness. He was instructed to fall in casually with the soldiers and learn the number of soldiers, cattle, and gain all the information he could and report his findings to Tom Berry.

After the Simpsonville Massacre, Captain Clarke, Captain Sam Berry, Tom Berry rode to Spencer County and onto Nelson County. While at Bloomfield, Tom Berry's servant, Tom, was killed by Bill Marion. After the massacre, Captain Clarke, Mundy, and the rest of the guerillas were riding along, and Tom happened to be riding by the side of Bill Marion. Lightly touching his leg with his hand, he said: "The fight was a hot one, wasn't it, Marse Bill?" At this moment, Bill Marion turned on him and started to yell at Tom and told him he was going to kill him, but first he was going to order his coffin. Tom apologized to Marion, but he would not accept the apology. He rode to Bloomfield, ordered a coffin, paid for the coffin, came back to camp, and early in the morning, Sam Berry and the other guerillas learned that Marion had killed Tom and left the camp. Tom Berry did not learn about the killing until after Marion left. He never saw Bill Marion again because the day after he rode out of camp, he was killed by Union Colonel James Bridgewater's men near Chaplintown, Kentucky. According to Tom Berry, he never knew his real name, but Bill Marion told the guerillas about his life. He said that his mother and two sisters had been stripped and whipped with hickory switches until blood ran down their legs and were left to untie themselves. All three were found unconscious and his mother died soon after the beating. His father was killed, and his sisters lingered between life and death for months. Tom Berry stated that Marion took no prisoners and killed everyone he met. He had no friends in the world except his pistols.[236]

After a few day's rest, Captain Berry and Tom Berry began recruiting. Captain Berry recruited 180 men. Tom Berry took charge of the recruits and started south with the new recruits. Tom Berry found Morgan at Alexandria, Tennessee. His advance outposts were a few miles from Lebanon. Morgan had skirmishes and battles at Sparta, Smithville, Snows Hill, Dry Creek, and Alexander Blacks Shop. Tom Berry reported to Morgan and turned over the new recruits. After resting for two days, Tom Berry returned to Kentucky. Captain Sam Berry had sent 130 men south and had three skirmishes with Union soldiers and had a received a serious wound. Tom Berry found his brother under the care of Dr. John Cook.

On January 28, 1865, Quantrill was three miles east of Chaplintown. The next day, his men were at Danville, where he stood the townsfolk into line while he plundered a store, robbed some citizens, and destroyed the telegraph office. Quantrill pretended to be with the 4th Missouri Cavalry. His men left the town and headed for the Perryville road. Captain James Bridgewater pursued Quantrill from Danville and caught up with Quantrill about five miles west of Harrodsburg in the evening. At least two of Quantrill's men stopped at Stanford and one of the men began to drink and they began to talk, which led Union Captain James Bridgewater and his scouts, who were recruited from Stanford and Hall's Gap area, to discover the identity of the men. The scout's official designation was Company A, Hall's Battalion, Kentucky State Guard. Bridgewater's men had been alerted at Stanford and followed Quantrill's men as they rode out of Stanford. Quantrill's men broke up into three squads and stopped at three houses along the road for dinner. The last squad was near the Oakland Church and was under the command of Sergeant John Barker. Bridgewater's men surrounded the house and took positions behind any cover they could find. Bridgewater's men opened fire into the windows and the doors. Sergeant Barker and his men were only equipped with revolvers and the three were killed, including Barker. The survivors tried to make a run for safety, but they did not make their escape. The remainder of the men were either captured or wounded, including Jim Younger. Allen Parmer and Frank James rushed from the next house up the road but determined they could not escape. Quantrill's Second Lieutenant Chatham "Chad" Renick, who was in charge of the next squad, was killed. Parmer, James, and the rest of the men made their way back to Quantrill and retreated to Nelson County. People in the neighborhood buried the four men in the Oakland cemetery. The prisoners were taken to Lexington, Kentucky. Five of the guerillas, including Jim Younger, escaped from the Federal prison in Louisville and made their way back to Nelson County.[237]

On that same day on January 28, Dick Taylor, along with some of the members of the gang, visited the home of his father Grayson Taylor on Hammond's Creek in Anderson County, where they spent the night. After his son and the other members of the guerilla gang left, Grayson rode to Lawrenceburg and reported that the guerillas had spent the night on his farm. Captain Lorenzo Brown's Company D, 54th Kentucky Mounted Infantry were sent out to capture Dick Taylor and the members of the gang. Taylor and his fellow guerillas had taken shelter from the weather under a pile of fence rails. Brown's men discovered Taylor and the guerillas and attacked. Taylor and a man named Smith were captured, but the rest of the gang escaped. As Captain Brown and his men pursued the other guerillas, Lieutenant W.T. Moore and Private Shouse were placed in charge of the prisoners, putting each on their horses behind them. After riding for some distance, a signal between Taylor and Smith initiated a grab for the guns carried by Moore and Shouse. During the scuffle, Shouse's horse became frightened and ran ahead several yards. The soldier managed to gain control of his gun and shot and killed Smith. During the scuffle on the ground between Taylor and Moore, Moore received several cuts to his face from a bowie knife that Taylor had in his possession. During the hand-to-hand combat, Taylor was shot dead.[238]

The bodies of Smith and Taylor were taken to Lawrenceburg and were carried to the home of W. R. Taylor, who was a brother of Dick Taylor, and Dick Taylor and Smith were buried in the family cemetery on the Taylor farm.

On June 4, 1904, during Decoration Day, flowers were placed on the Confederate graves in Mercer County. Among the strains of patriotic music and wagons carrying loads of flowers, the graves of the soldiers in Spring Hill Cemetery, in Harrodsburg, Kentucky were decorated. Several speeches were made including a speech given

Spring Hill Cemetery in Harrodsburg, Kentucky

by Colonel R. C. Breckinridge, from Danville, Kentucky. The memorable part of the ceremony was the reinternment of the remains of several Confederates who were buried in various parts of Mercer County during the Civil War. Among them was Sergeant John Wright of

Marker of Chad Renick, John Barker, Foster Key, James, Henry and William Noland of Quantrill's command.

the 41st Georgia Infantry, who was wounded at the Battle of Perryville and died of his wounds, Lieutenant Chat Renick, Sergeant John Barker, Private Foster Key, Privates James and Henry Noland, of Quantrill's command, who were buried in Oakland Cemetery, two miles west of Harrodsburg. Their remains were interred in the Confederate lot at Spring Hill. Frank James was invited to take part in the reinternment ceremony. He wrote a letter dated May 30, 1904. He wrote: Bridgewater killed and captured twelve guerillas including Major Edwards, without a single loss. Chat Renick and the Noland brothers were among the killed and the guerillas fled from Bridgewater.[239]

On January 28, 1865, in Spencer County, Jerome Clarke, Henry Magruder, and three other guerillas were surprised and attacked by Captain Ed Terrell's force. As the guerillas began to return fire and flee, Coulter and ten men rode to their rescue. Cheering, the five guerillas joined forces with Coulter's men attacking Terrell. Retreating from one defensive position to the farm of Squire Heady, Terrell's force took a defensive position in Heady's barn. Attempting to improve his aim, Coulter charged the barn on horseback while the bullets around him "rang like bees." Terrell shot Coulter through the chest. Coulter removed his silk bandanna and with his ramrod pushed the cloth through the wound and out of his back. He had a man tie off the bandanna in the rear and tying a knot in front, he rode off. Supposedly he rode to his aunt's home to obtain medical care and safety. He developed pneumonia and died on February 6, 1865. He was only twenty-two years old when he died.[240]

CHAPTER NINETEEN

February 1865: Berry Encounters Captain Edwin Terrell and Captain James Bridgewater, Union Guerilla Hunters

On February 2, the guerillas burned the depot at Midway, Kentucky. For several days the guerillas were pursued by Colonel James Bridgewater, who pushed the guerillas from Bradfordsville, Campbellsville, and other towns. Captain Ed Terrell with forty-five men charged Captain Sam Berry and Captain Berry's men countercharged at Chaplintown, near the line of Nelson County. Hand to hand combat took place between the two forces and Terrell was driven back. He reformed and Berry chased him for several miles. Captain Berry was wounded in the foot and had to be taken to Dr. McCloskey. They hid in a cave. While Captain Berry was recovering from his wounds, some of his men decided to make a raid through Spencer, Shelby, Oldham, Owen, Scott, Woodford, and Anderson counties. Fifty-eight men rode out and fought at Taylorsville, Smithville, Worthville, Liberty, Georgetown, and Shryock's Ferry on the Kentucky River. The guerillas lost ten killed and five wounded.[241]

Kentucky Historical Society marker indicating Jerome Clarke's and William Quantrill's raids in Midway, Kentucky.

Who was Edwin Terrell? He was born in Kentucky in 1845 and was raised by his uncle, Thomas Baker, who lived at Manton, Kentucky, which was a small village between Marion and Washington, Kentucky, five miles from the Lebanon Depot, on the Lebanon branch of the Louisville & Nashville Railroad. His uncle sent Edwin to the local school in Manton. His uncle, who was a highly respected member of Marion County, was killed by two of his slaves before the Civil War. When the Civil War broke out, he joined the Dixie Guards, 1st Kentucky Confederate Infantry Regiment in Davies County, Kentucky and later joined the 2nd Kentucky Cavalry, under the command of Confederate General John Hunt Morgan. According to a newspaper account, Bragg's army was camped at Tullahoma, Tennessee after the Battle of Stone's River, Tennessee. Terrell was attached to army headquarters as a teamster for an ambulance driver. Terrell had difficulty with a staff officer, so the officer transferred Terrell to the 9th Kentucky Infantry, under Colonel Thomas Hunt, Confederate General Ben Hardin Helm's command, which was advancing towards Manchester, Tennessee. Colonel Thomas Hunt placed Terrell in Captain Crouch's company. In April 1863, a detail was made from the brigade to proceed to McMinnville

for the purpose of guarding the commissary stores. Terrell was among those detailed to protect the stores. On April 19, 1863, a group of Federal cavalry charged into the commissary stores and Terrell along with seven others were captured. According to Terrell he was looking for a "square meal" when he was captured. Terrell under the order of General Braxton Bragg, commander of the Army of the Tennessee, was to be shot the next day. General Morgan was there, but not to witness the execution, but just happened to be in town with his escort and assisted in holding the Union cavalry in check while

Edwin Terrill (From the Barton collection. www. Bartonpara.com)

the wagon train was moved to a place of safety. Terrell escaped and joined the Union army. According to Union General John Palmer, Terrell killed an officer of his regiment and fled to join the Union army.[242]

Terrell joined the 37th Kentucky Mounted Infantry, under Colonel Charles Hanson. On December 29, 1864, Terrell was mustered out of the Union army. According to varying reports General John Palmer or General Jeremiah Boyle gave Terrell authority to raise a company of Federal scouts, raised from Spencer and Shelby County, called the Shelby County Home Guards. Terrell was made captain. General Palmer gave orders to Terrell to drive out all the guerillas from the state of Kentucky.

On February 7, 1865, Secretary of War Stanton wrote to Major General John Palmer that President Lincoln had assigned him to command the Department of the Ohio, including the state of Kentucky. The President desired General Palmer to focus his attention on Kentucky. The reason was that the Kentucky state troops were disorganized and undisciplined which rendered them almost completely useless against rebel military forces. General Palmer was to place his troops, both white and black, in a state of discipline and organization. Major General Burbridge was to be relieved of command and ordered to report to Major General George Thomas for duty in the field.[243]

There are several stories on when Quantrill met Magruder, Clarke, and Sam Berry. According to Tom Berry, on February 28, 1865, Captain Quantrill met with Captain Sam Berry. There were greetings and introductions were given all around. Captain Berry and Captain Quantrill inspected their combined forces. Captain Berry had twenty-eight men. Quantrill had thirty-nine men.[244] According to Henry Magruder, he heard of Quantrill's arrival and went to see him. *"He told me that he was going on a long and perilous raid, and asked me to take my men and go with him. I finally consented to do so, when he laid his plan before me. Some of his men had been captured by Bridgewater immediately after his arrival, and he was apprehensive that they would be executed as guerillas. He had learned that Colonel Weatherford and Major Bristow were in the country in the neighborhood of Danville, and he hoped to capture them, and so force an exchange of the Federals or else hand them in retaliation for his own men. I entered heartily into his project and getting all together, we started from Mr. Hinkle's at 1 p.m. and having Springfield and Lebanon to the left, we traveled all night and camped the next day at 12 o'clock. There were about forty of us, Clark (or Quantrell) first in command and I second."*[245] At sunset Quantrill and Clarke, Magruder, and Sam Berry road to New Market, and learned that two government wagons were there, guarded by some Union soldiers. On February 8, Quantrill, and Berry's gang charged them, captured and killed three guards and four were captured. The guerillas burned the wagons and killed the mules. The men robbed the stores, when they started for Harrodsburg. While riding off the Lebanon road, Fidler, with fifty men, came charging down on Quantrill and Berry's men. Quantrill along with Magruder, Berry, and Clarke fired a volley and wheeled, and ran around Fidler and cleared a path. Quantrill along with Berry, Clarke, and Magruder made a charge for Major Bristow, but he had fled. Next, they rode towards Colonel Weatherford. Quantrill, Berry, Magruder, and Clarke stopped and rested in a farmhouse. Captain Bridgewater with a squad of men rode up on the guerilla camp on the Little South Fork, west of Houstonville. He killed four guerillas and captured thirty-five horses. He surrounded the guerillas, but Quantrill and Magruder with about twenty men, cut their way out and escaped. Some of Quantrill and Berry, Magruder, and Berry's men were killed and some captured and the balance of the men scattered in every direction.[246] Quantrill gave Magruder the command and told him to lead what was left of the gang out. Magruder ran the men between Harrodsburg and Lebanon and reached a point three miles from Springfield, when Magruder heard that Union soldiers were in force in Springfield. Magruder rode around the town to the Bloomfield pike, going to Bloomfield and stopped on a hill to rest. While they were there, they saw one hundred men pass on the pike, going to Bloomfield to cut Quantrill, Berry, Magruder, and Clarke off. The guerillas turned off to the right and over on the Chaplin River, and camped, then rode three miles from Bloomfield. The guerillas rode to Mr. Muir's and had their horses shod. The guerillas rode into Pitt's Point and robbed the stores. Magruder heard that Caldwell was at home and took a squad of four men and went over to Caldwell's house. Magruder called him out and made him surrender his arms. Magruder took him to the stable and while one of the Caldwell's was in the saddle trying to catch a horse, some of Caldwells yelled out: "Look out! look out! There were four shots fired at Caldwell. Magruder was on horseback in the stable. One of the Caldwell's exclaimed: "You have killed my brother." Magruder learned that the reason of the cry to "look out" was because there was a steep bluff near the stable, and the warning was with reference to bluff. Caldwell was with the 15th Kentucky Union Infantry. After killing Caldwell, the gang went back and camped in the Old Houses at Furnace (Belmont).[247] The gang rode to Lebanon Junction and found four cars and an engine. The cars were burned. They destroyed the telegraph office, robbed the stores, and killed two soldiers and wounded one, who later died. The gang rode to Wilson's Creek, then Samuel's Depot and camped for three days. The gang rode to Beach Fork and went over to the railroad and found two black soldiers, one of them a sergeant, both were well armed, the sergeant had three pistols. The black soldiers fired on the oncoming guerillas. The guerillas surrounded them and after a hard fight, the guerillas killed both of the black soldiers. After the killing of the black soldiers, the gang rode to Meade County, crossed the Louisville turnpike and went to Garnettsville and Big Spring.[248]

On February 9, 1865, Henry Diehl, who was a farmer and gardener, living in Jefferson County, Kentucky, was going to the market with his wagon near the junction between Bardstown and Taylorsville turnpike. He met about twenty wagons who were not allowed to enter the town. A man dressed in United States soldiers clothing rode up and Diehl asked if he could go into town. He told him not for a while. He asked Diehl if he had any money. He told the Union soldier no. Diehl thought the soldier was a private and told him he would only give his money to an officer. Berry rode up and asked Diehl to hand him his money. They took his watch and $109 dollars (worth $3,545.00 today). Diehl stated that there were nine men with Berry. He also noticed Dick Mitchell. Berry told Diehl he was collecting the Southern tax. He asked Berry to let him go. He said no. Another gentleman rode up in a rockaway. Berry and his men robbed him of $260.00 (worth $4,851 today). One of the guerillas told Diehl "Go on Dutchman, you've got to follow us for a while." The guerillas rode to Mr. Connolly's home and robbed him of nine dollars. Some of the guerillas had whiskey bottles and they made Diehl drink. He drank three times. Diehl told Berry that it was hard to rob a poor man. Berry replied he was a Southern officer. Diehl had a small bay mare and Berry said: "how does that mare suit you?" Mrs. Connolly told Berry that Diehl would be ruined if they took the mare. Once Berry and his men had their fun, they rode on. Diehl stated that Berry and his men carried pistols and bowie knives. One guerilla had a shotgun. All were dressed in cavalry clothes. Some of them had on Union cavalry uniforms and the rest were dressed in civilian clothes, except Mitchell, who had on a black hat with a half silver moon. Diehl saw the red headed Jim Henry.[249]

In a battle on the Salt River near Nelson Creek, Captain Berry had been driving back Captain Ed Terrell with fifty-two men and Captain Berry had twenty-three men. Captain Berry came across Captain James Bridgewater's company of forty-one men, reinforcing Terrell. Captain Berry now faced ninety-three men against his twenty-three men. Captain Berry held back the Union guerilla hunters. Lieutenant Jerome Clarke, aka Sue Mundy, Henry Magruder, Jim Evans, Brothers, Texas, Halee, Henry, King White charged against the oncoming Union force. Every man was wounded and King White's horse went down. White called for help. Captain Berry stood behind the dead horse, rescuing White under a hail of bullets. Hand to hand combat broke out. Ammunition ran out on both sides. Captain Berry withdrew from the field. Captain Berry lost six killed and seventeen wounded. According to Tom Berry, the Union force lost twenty-five killed and twenty-eight wounded. The fight ended.[250]

Both Captain Berry and Tom Berry received severe wounds and fell back to their camp in the woods. Dr. John McCloskey came to care for Captain Berry and the rest of the wounded. According to Tom Berry, fourteen days had passed and Tom Berry rode to check on Willie Spencer who was also wounded. Before he left, he told his brother that he would be back in about an hour and a half. Tom left Captain Berry with a servant. Just as Tom Berry left his brother, Captain Ed Terrell rode up to McCloskey's home to have the doctor attend to some of his men who had been wounded. He discovered Captain Berry and before Captain Berry could hobble for cover, Terrell captured him and took him away to hang him. Tom had hardly left his brother, when the servant stated that his brother had been captured by Captain Terrell. Willie Spencer, Tom Berry, and Jim Evans mounted their horses and met nine more of their men. Tom sent for three more men. Jesse James and Hulse joined Tom's men. Fourteen guerillas rode out in search of Captain Berry. They followed Captain Terrell's trail. Tom met five more of Berry's men. Terrell was riding towards Chaplintown. Tom Berry reached the creek, crossed the creek, and headed to the main road. Tom placed his men on either side of the road, behind trees, with double barrel shotguns loaded with twelve buck shot in each barrel. Twenty-two men were posted behind the tress waiting for Terrell. Tom Berry had a Sharps rifle with fifteen rounds and six pistols. Twenty-five minutes went by when Terrell came into sight with Captain Berry. Captain Berry's legs were tied under his horse and he was riding between Terrell and two other Union horsemen.[251]

Reaching the stream, the thirty-five Union soldiers stopped to drink. The Union soldiers were only fifteen yards away when Tom Berry ordered his men to fire. Sixteen Union soldiers fell from their saddles. Tom Berry ordered a charge and Captain Terrell who was seriously wounded escaped through the woods. When the firing began, Captain Sam Berry lowered his horse's head down stream into deep water, swam his horse around the bend of the creek, and hid behind a bluff to escape the gunfire. After the firing was over, Captain Sam Berry rode out from his cover. Tom Berry cut his rope and released his legs. They rode back to McCloskey's farm.[252]

After thirty days, Captain Berry assembled fifty-two men. Captain Berry rode out with his force and headed towards Fairfield and met the Union force and routed

Trapping Rebel guerillas in the West. Union authorities gave men like James Bridgewater and William Terrell free reign to kill guerillas onsite. (Library of Congress)

them in a charge. Captain Berry rode to Bloomfield, Taylorsville, Fisherville, and Chaplintown. Captain Terrell rode through Bloomfield to Smileytown after Captain Berry scattered his forces. The next day, Captain Berry heard that Terrell was at Taylorsville, stopping to have his horse shod. John Ennis, who had just finished shoeing his horse, dropped to the floor and asked Terrell: "How is that?" Terrell drew his pistol and shot him dead, mounted his horse and rode away. Two days later, Terrell rode into a field near Louisville where Kirk Walker was plowing and shot him dead.[253]

Also in February 1865, R. H. Sissol had been away from his home in Harrodsburg and on his way back home he saw a couple of men in front of him on the road. Berry was one of the men. They rode up to Sissol and put their hands on his shoulders and told him to ride to the other side of the road. He refused and the men stated they would treat him as a gentleman and they immediately drew their pistols at Sissol's head and stated they would blow his brain out if he did not ride with them. The guerillas rode on either side of Sissol and Coulter searched his pockets and took his pocketbook from him. Berry was standing near the guerillas, but did not rob Sissol. The guerillas along with Sissol traveled down the road until they heard the stagecoach coming, four of them jumped on their horses, rode up to the stage, and began robbing the passengers. After they robbed the stage, the guerillas turned the stagecoach around and made the driver turn back. When the four guerillas rode towards the stage, one of them stayed behind to guard Sissol and one or two more prisoners.[254]

Colonel Buckley reported that Berry, Jerome Clarke, and Quantrill passed Owen County, and pursued them from Spencer County through Shelby County. On February 1, Captain Searcy reported chasing the guerillas three miles from the road into Chaplintown. The guerillas formed on either side of the road across on John's Creek on Chaplin Hill. Ten men were posted in the road in front and nine men under Quantrill planned to charge the Union troops. The Federals rode in by two's and when they came to within fifty yards John Bushnell leaped into the road and fired a double barrel shotgun, followed by a quick volley by the rest of Quantrill's men. The Federals retreated. According to Tom Berry, thirteen Federals were killed and eleven wounded. Quantrill and his men charged over the creek. The guerillas fired from behind trees. Frank James, Allen Palmer, Joe Young led the charge. Wiggington and Hockersmith of Quantrill's men fought in the battle. The battle lasted an hour and a half. Bridgewater, with fifty-nine Federals, lost thirty-six men killed and wounded. Bridgewater withdrew.[255]

During the battle, Captain Sam Berry, Tom Berry, Lee McMurty, Williams, Basham, Bud Pence, Denny Pence, Tom Harris, White, Hall, David Hilton, Robert Hall, Jim Evans, Ike Berry, Jesse James, and Frank James participated in the fierce battle. Quantrill and Berry lost four killed and nine wounded.[256]

CHAPTER TWENTY

Henry Magruder and Marcellus Jerome Clarke aka Sue Mundy is Captured

On March 12, 1865, Union Major Cyrus Wilson, of the 26th Kentucky Infantry, along with fifty of his men surrounded the tobacco barn at the Cox residence where Marcellus Jerome Clarke, Henry Magruder, and Medkiff were hiding. Wilson was captain of the local Home Guard and originally in the 33rd Kentucky Union Volunteer Infantry. At the age of fifty-two he enlisted at Munfordville, Kentucky on September 13, 1862 and was appointed captain of Company D of the 33rd Kentucky Volunteer Infantry. In January 1864, Wilson was on detached duty on the Lebanon branch of the Louisville & Nashville Railroad guarding the bridges. On February 17, 1864, Wilson was mustered out as captain and promoted to Lieutenant Colonel of the 33rd Kentucky Infantry by the governor of Kentucky. He was mustered out of the 33rd Kentucky Infantry on March 31, 1864, and mustered into the 26th Kentucky Infantry when the 33rd and the 26th Kentucky were consolidated on April 1, 1864. When the regiments were combined, Wilson was appointed as major of the 26th Kentucky Union Infantry. On May 1, 1864, Wilson resigned from the 26th Kentucky Infantry. He stated that his family needed a protector, and his family were "living in a part of the country where guerilas are constantly robbing and plundering."[257]

On May 14, 1864, his resignation was accepted. Although his official records do not indicate when he was brought back into service into the 26th Kentucky, by 1865, he was brought out of retirement to specifically capture Jerome Clarke. Magruder had been shot through the lung during a skirmish in Hancock County and taken to the Cox family home in Breckinridge County to recuperate from his wounds. The men surrendered to Wilson and were to be taken to Louisville to be tried as guerilas.

At 11 am, a detachment of troops under the command of Wilson appeared at the Louisville wharf. The men marched ashore from a steamboat from Brandenburg forming a square and placed in the center of the square were

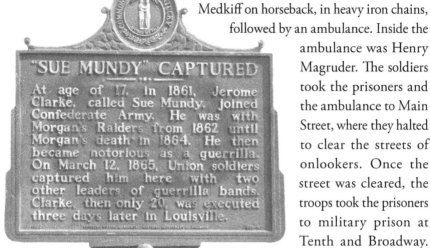

"SUE MUNDY" CAPTURED

At age of 17, in 1861, Jerome Clarke, called Sue Mundy, joined Confederate Army. He was with Morgan's Raiders from 1862 until Morgan's death in 1864. He then became notorious as a guerrilla. On March 12, 1865, Union soldiers captured him here with two other leaders of guerrilla bands. Clarke, then only 20, was executed three days later in Louisville.

Kentucky Historical Marker located in Simpson County notes the burial location of Marcellus Jerome Clarke, who was also known as "Sue Mundy". (Photo courtesy of author)

two prisoners, Jerome Clarke and Henry Medkiff on horseback, in heavy iron chains, followed by an ambulance. Inside the ambulance was Henry Magruder. The soldiers took the prisoners and the ambulance to Main Street, where they halted to clear the streets of onlookers. Once the street was cleared, the troops took the prisoners to military prison at Tenth and Broadway. Jerome Clarke was taken under heavy guard to Coyl's headquarters, located on Chestnut Street to be questioned. Mundy was led into the drawing room of the old Huffman home. Before the home was Coyl's headquarters, the building served as the paymaster's department. Mundy was informed of the charges against him and when he protested that he was a regular Confederate soldier and said that the principal crimes charged against him had been committed by Bill Marion. Mundy was told that his court-martial would not hear any of the evidence presented by Clarke. An immense crowd of people stood in the street outside waiting for a glimpse of Clarke. There was no trial. The next morning Reverend Dr. Talbot, rector of St. John's Episcopal Church, visited Clarke in prison and asked him if he knew the result of the court-martial. Clarke told Talbot: "I suppose I shall be shot since the court-martial would not hear any witnesses for my side." Reverend Talbot asked Clarke if he knew when he would be executed. Clarke said he thought in a couple weeks. The reverend asked if he would be of service to Clarke. Clarke answered that he would be happy if the reverend visited him. The reverend told Clarke to prepare in a couple hours. He told Clarke that he would be executed at 4 pm. He also told Clarke that he would be hung, not shot. Mundy protested telling the reverend that he was a Confederate soldier commissioned by Colonel Jack Allen and that he could prove that Marion killed the men that he was charged with killing.[258]

After learning the news he would be shot, Clarke asked the reverend to pray, then he dictated letters to his aunt, his sister, his cousin, and his girlfriend. He called in the guard and had several curls of hair removed from his head and enclosed a lock of his hair in each letter. Clarke wrote to his girlfriend: "I have to inform you of the sad fate which awaits your true friend. I am to suffer death this afternoon at 4 o'clock. I send you from my chains a message of true love and as I stand on the brink of the grave I tell you I do truly, fondly and forever love you." At 3 pm, Clarke was baptized.[259]

On March 15, 1865, Jerome Clarke was taken to the junction between 18th and Broadway in Louisville where a scaffold had been built with a noose. A large crowd assembled around the scaffold and since the crowd did not know when or who would be executed and sat down and waited for information. About a half mile away, a large crowd assembled around the prison. At the appointed hour, Clarke was escorted by four companies of Union soldiers with the Post band with twenty brass instruments playing the Death March. Clarke was accompanied by Reverend Talbot. Clarke was taken into a carriage with shackles around his feet, but none on his hands. In his hand, Clarke had a white handkerchief and put the handkerchief to his eyes. The carriage took Clarke to the scaffold. An express wagon passed by going in the direction of the scaffold with a rough pine coffin. Once the carriage arrived the foot of the scaffold, the carriage was halted and the commanding officer ordered his troops to push back the crowd to a respectful distance. Clarke put up the handkerchief, raised his face. His lips were constantly moving as if in prayer. He rose, walked up the steps of the scaffold, and took his place on the trap door, while the guards tied his limbs and arms. One of the crowd thought Clarke said: "Lord, have mercy upon my poor soul." Clarke was dressed in a dark blue cavalry jacket, down the front was a single row of brass buttons, bearing Kentucky coat of arms, dark cassimere trousers, and a pair of boots cut down to fit like shoes. He was wearing a black velvet cap, which was removed. The post commander read the charges and the order of death and asked if Clarke had anything to say. Clarke said a few words in a low time to Dr. Talbot and Talbot repeated them aloud to the crowd. The statement was the same he had made in prison that he was a regular soldier and not guilty of the murders charged to him. He added that he hated no one, but loved everybody and hoped to go to Heaven. He said: "I believe in and die for the Confederate cause." At this moment, a white hood was put over Clarke's head. One, two, three was counted and the trap door opened. Unfortunately the execution was botched. The rope did not break his neck and he struggled furiously while he was being strangled. The guards feared that the rope might break. After Clarke died, his body was cut down and the crowd was able to approach his body. The crowd surged forward to cut the buttons off his coat, bits of the rope or pieces of the garment. Rumored circulated in the crowd that Clarke had money sewn into his jacket, and the clothing was cut into hoping to find money, but there was no money. Three men fought to get Clarke's cap, which was stamped with "Green & Green" which was a well know hatter in Louisville. The men fought so hard over his hat, they were arrested and taken to prison. The next morning the men were fined and the hat was given to the Provost Marshall. Clarke told Dr. Talbot that he wanted his body taken to his relatives in Franklin, Kentucky. Between ten and twelve thousand people witnessed his execution. As the crowd surged forward toward the prison at Tenth and Broadway, a bull appeared in the middle of Broadway, and the animal scared the band, the crowd, and the crowd. As the bull prepared to charge, the crowd in the front pushed the crowd behind, and fearing danger, pistols were drawn and fired at the bull. The pistol shots only wounded the bull in the breast and only made the bull angrier. The pistols shots made everyone in the crowd who had a pistol draw their weapons. The crowd towards the back could not see what was happening. The crowd in the front fired another volley, and the bull fell dead. The crowd towards the back thought there was a riot, and everyone panicked for safety. Soldiers in the prison, who were kept in reserve, came running to the site of the dead bull, fixed bayonets and prepared to quell the riot. Luckily the death of the bull stopped further firing, and the crowd dispersed before the soldiers became engaged.[260]

His body was taken to Simpson County, his home, and buried in a small cemetery, but on August 11, 1914, a delegation from the Confederate Veterans in Simpson County, and relatives and friends of Jerome Clarke went to the country graveyard and reinterred him in the Greenlawn Cemetery in Franklin County, Kentucky.

Interestingly Bill Marion wrote to the *Louisville Courier-Journal*. The newspaper stated that the education Bill Marion received in his younger days "was sadly neglected. . . .He is as bad a soldier as he is a poor scholar." On March 13, from Meade County, Kentucky, Marion wrote to General Palmer that he had *"captured two of my men Clark or Sue Mondy you style him as Megruder as also Heut Medcalf. Gentlemen J. W. W. Marion, Capt. Commanding Confederate forces in Kentucky do Solemnly declare if you do treat them as guirillas that*

I will Shoot or hang fifty of your men you may think get them first but you will find that I will get them I am A Confederate soldier an my men are all regular Soldiers but you drive us to desperation, desperation let it be if you Murder those Brave men. I haunt the City of Louisville until I have revenge them look how you treated one of my men when wounded an Captured in Anderson County at Bacon Bush, you Brutally shot him while lying on the ground But you failed to kill him or keep him So far as I am Concerned I ask no quarters of you an if you don't treat those Boys as prisoners of ware I will Show none to you So if you think there is no hell for you, you pitch out."[61]

Henry Magruder was allowed to recover from his wound. On September 13, 1865, Magruder was charged with being a guerilla, murder, wounding by shooting with intent to kill and rape. He was tried and found guilty of being a guerilla was to be executed. On October 20, 1865 at 2 p.m., Magruder's mother, sister, two cousins, and aunt, visited him in prison and embraced him for the last time. During the day, Magruder was visited by his counsel General Whitaker and Father Brady, who was his adviser. He told Whitaker: "Tis hard, but I reckon it is fair." Just before the fateful hour, he stated that he held no malice toward any one and expressed serenity of mind and feature. Around two or three hundred people gathered on the rooftops of the buildings within and around the prison, where they could have a full view of execution. About one hundred spectators, belonging to executives who worked in the prison, were admitted into the courtyard of the prison. At 3:15 pm the field band of the 125th Colored Infantry played the Death March. Under direction of Captain J. P. Neal, Provost Marshall, the regiment formed a square around the scaffold, which stood in the middle of the prison yard, facing west. Around 3:40 p.m., Magruder emerged from his cell, supported by Whitaker and Father Brady. Magruder had a cigar in his mouth and passed from his cell door through an aisle lined with guards and he walked up the gallows. The group gathered on the scaffold was Captain Neal, Father Brady, General Whitaker, Magruder, and Mr. Harris. The stand was surrounded by reporters and a few Union officers. Captain Neal read to Magruder the findings and sentence of the court-martial. The reading took ten minutes and when Captain Neal finished Magruder and Father Brady prayed. Captain Neal asked if Magruder had anything to say. Magruder replied: "Not a word." Mr. Harris placed Magruder on the trap door, adjusted the rope around his neck, drew the white hood over Magruder's head, and at 4:10 pm, Magruder was hung. His body quivered for five or six minutes before he finally died. After twenty minutes, Magruder's body was cut down and transferred to his family. Magruder wore a military jacket, gray mixed pants, with a white linen handkerchief loosely tied around his neck. He was only twenty-two. He was also on the same scaffold that Clarke was hung.[262] After the death of Jerome Clarke and Henry Magruder, Sam Berry formed a new gang.

In March of 1865, J. D. Edwards, a farmer who lived two and a half miles east of Simpsonville, Kentucky, was riding with a Mr. Byers, and a Mr. Howell on their way to Simpsonville when Berry, Tom Henry, Texas, and two others were just at the head of the town. Berry asked Edwards if he had any greenbacks. He said he was collecting revenue for the government. He asked Edwards if he had any postage currency. He asked a couple more questions then demanded Edwards' pocket book. Edwards handed Berry his pocket book. Berry took what money was in the pocketbook and handed the pocketbook back to Edwards. Edwards only had a half dollar. He then asked Edwards if he knew anything about the stagecoach. When Edwards replied he did not know anything, Berry and his men rode down the turnpike about a half mile and fifteen minutes later he stopped the stagecoach. Berry rode into Simpsonville after he robbed the stagecoach. Riding with Berry was a man wearing a coon skin cap by the name of "Texas." Texas took a pistol from Mr. Howell.[263]

On March 23, 1865, Joseph G. Byers was a farmer. While riding on a highway with a group of his neighbors, Berry and six of his men halted Byers and his neighbors and drew their pistols and demanded they give over their money. Texas took a gun from one of his neighbors. Byers described Berry wearing a Confederate cavalry jacket with gold lace. The other guerilla with Berry wore gray pants and the other guerilla wore a coon skin cap.

On March 27, 1865, the mail stage was captured near Shelbyville and the passengers robbed of their money and valuables. The mailbags were opened and every letter or package were searched for valuables. H. H. Webb, a cabinet maker from Simpsonville, witnessed the robbery of the stagecoach. He was only fifty yards from the stagecoach, when four or five guerillas halted the coach and began to tear open the mail bags and were putting letters in their pockets. They told the passengers to get off the coach and proceeded to rob them. They broke open a trunk. Berry took music sheets out of the trunk and strapped them to his saddle. Webb told Berry that the music sheets might get spoiled if he left them on the saddle. Berry told Webb: "What in the hell is that to you?" Berry opened a box that was on the top of the stagecoach. There was nothing but cakes and candles inside the box. Berry stated that if he was hungry he would "pitch into them." One of the passengers on the stagecoach was a man by the name of Rogers, who lived in Simpsonville. Berry looked at Rogers and said: "You're a nice looking gentleman; you must have some money." Berry then said: "That's a very nice coat; I would like it." Rogers began to take his coat off when Berry said: "Keep your coat, I don't want it." After Berry and his men realized there was nothing else to rob, they rode on.[264]

W. H. Biddle was the stagecoach driver who lived in Louisville. The driver said that Berry, Bill Marion, and Zay Coulter were present. He stated that eight passengers were robbed on the coach. They robbed seven hundred dollars.[265]

The guerillas under Bill Marion took Willis Finley, a citizen, and took him with the guerillas as they rode off. A few of Captain Terrell's men were in town, and immediately rode in pursuit of Marion and overtook Marion's men at Bullskin Bridge, on the Taylorsville road, where a skirmish broke out and one of Terrell's men, Warren Hackett, was captured. In the meantime, Captain Black of the 185th Ohio, stationed in Shelbyville, heard of the guerilla attack and mounted his twenty men and were sent to reinforce Captain Terrell's men. After Black arrived, the guerillas left, and were followed as far as Taylorsville, where another skirmish took place with no casualties. Night came on and the pursuit was called off. The guerillas handled Finley roughly and released him. Hackett was hung near James C. Duncan's place, about three miles from Bloomfield. Before he was hung, Hackett was allowed to write to his friends and able to request that his uncle to defray the cost of his funeral. Hackett was from the 6th Kentucky Infantry.[266]

CHAPTER TWENTY-ONE

April 1865: The Civil War Comes to an End

On April 8, 1865, a free African American woman by the name of Laura, was living at Ben Adam's home as a servant in Spencer County, Kentucky. Two white women were also present in the house. Her husband was a soldier in the Union army. She lived in the upstairs of the home. Three men entered the home. She knew one of the men: Sam Berry. Berry had a pistol in his left hand. He told her to come downstairs and lay down. He pulled up her clothes and proceeded to rape her. She begged him not to rape her. He cursed at her the entire time of the rape. The rest of the guerillas came upstairs. After Berry raped her, he gave Laura a quarter. After he raped her, Berry made her unlock a trunk. He took the money out of the trunk. Berry and his gang robbed Benjamin Adams of seventy dollars.[267].

Also in April, in Simpsonville, Biddle was a driver for a stagecoach, when Berry and his gang rode up to Biddle and stopped his coach and drew their pistols on the passengers. They robbed a lady and gentleman of three to four dollars and robbed the mail. Biddle stated that Berry, Texas, Tom Henry were the only guerillas that he recognized. After they robbed the coach, the guerillas moved onto town.[268]

On April 9, 1865, Confederate General Robert E. Lee, commander of the Army of Northern Virginia, surrendered his army to Union General Ulysses S. Grant's at Appomattox Court House, Virginia. On April 12, 1865, in North Carolina, Confederate General Joseph Johnston and his army received the news of Lee's surrender. The next day, Union General William T. Sherman's Union cavalry captured Raleigh, forcing Johnston's men west. Under the pressure of Sherman's massive army, Johnston asked Sherman if he would discuss peace terms. On April 26, Sherman and Johnston signed a new surrender agreement. Johnston surrendered ninety thousand soldiers to Sherman. On May 4, Lt. General Richard Taylor surrendered ten thousand Confederate soldiers and several days later Confederate General Nathan Bedford Forrest disbanded his cavalry corps at Gainesville, Alabama. On May 26, Confederate General Edmund Kirby Smith surrendered his army at Galveston, Texas. The war had essentially come to an end. On April 6, 1866, President Andrew Johnston issued a proclamation stating the insurrection was over.

On April 12, 1865, Bill Marion threatened to hang Dr. Montgomery Miller, a Federal surgeon, who the guerillas took as a prisoner, if Medkiff or Magruder were executed or punished. Marion sent a request to Union General John Palmer that he should answer his threats through the newspapers. General Palmer ordered that if Medkiff and Magruder were to stand trial and if found guilty were to be punished accordingly. In the meantime, Captain Marion was informed that should he execute or injure Dr. Miller, Medkiff and Magruder would be instantly hung.[269]

On April 13, Major Cyrus Wilson, Captain George W. Penn, and Captain Ed Terrell attacked a band of guerillas under Quantrill, along with Bill Marion, near Bloomfield, Kentucky. The Union guerilla hunters killed two and wounded three. Marion was shot and killed by Captain Terrell's men at a still house, near Manton.[270]

Several days later, on April 15, 1865, President Lincoln was assassinated by John Wilkes Booth at Ford's Theater in Washington, D. C. Lincoln died the next morning on April 15. Quantrill was at the home of Jonathan Davis, judge of Spencer County, Kentucky. Word reached Quantrill of Lincoln's assassination and all of his men were drunk. He apologized to the ladies in the home and said: "Excuse us, ladies. We are a little in our cups today. The grand-daddy of all greenbacks, Abraham Lincoln, was shot in a theater in Washington last night." He called for

Bill Marion's grave marker. Photo courtesy of Gerald Fischer. The grave is located in Cave Hill Cemetery, Louisville, Kentucky.

glasses to be raised, and Sam Berry gave a toast stating: "Here's to the death of Abraham Lincoln, hoping that his bones may serve in hell as gridiron to fry Yankees on."[271]

On May 10, 1865, Quantrill and Captain Sam Berry did a roll call at John Bedford Russell's farm on Ashes Creek, in Spencer County at the Spencer-Nelson County line and the remnants of the two guerilla units called out their names. Nineteen men were present including Captain Sam Berry, Tom Berry, Jim Evans, John Enloe, Billy Merriman, Jim Drake, Howard West, Jake Singleton, H. Upton, Alex Grisby, John Ross, Bill Hulse, James Hockersmith, Halle, Glasscock, Bud Pence, Allen Palmer, Dave Hutton, McMurty, and Dave Hilton. "Big Zay" Coulter was also present in the group. The men moved out of the woods to the road leading to Taylorsville, in order to escape the chilling rain. The men rode to a woodland pasture and came across the farm of Captain Wakefield of Smileytown. The men took shelter in his barn. They hitched their horses and did not place any pickets. One of the guerillas saw through the pouring rain Captain Terrell and his 120 men riding up to the barn.[272]

Quantrill and Captain Berry were ambushed. Captain Terrell and his men tracked down William Quantrill. Terrell's scouts were on the pike just over the hill from the Wakefield farm, across the pasture from a blacksmith shop, when he received word that a group of horsemen were nearby. Terrell's men charged down the lane straight for the barn with pistols and carbines firing at Quantrill's men. Both Quantrill and Berry shouted: "Cut Through; cut through!" Clark Hockersmith mounted his horse and determined to save Quantrill, since he was not able to mount his horse and ran across the pasture trying to catch up with his fleeing men. Hockersmith dismounted and helped Quantrill into the saddle and sprang up behind him. As they were riding away, a Union volley killed Hockersmith and his horse. Both Hockersmith and Quantrill hit the ground. Richard Glasscock returned to assist Quantrill. The third Union volley mortally wounded Glasscock and Quantrill. Quantrill was shot in the left shoulder with the ball exiting his right groin. The second shot took off Quantrill's trigger finger. Supposedly the second shot came from Captain Terrell. The battle lasted for forty minutes.[273]

Quantrill was paralyzed from the arms down. He was taken to the Wakefield home. Terrell came to Quantrill and asked him if there was anything that he could do for him? Quantrill asked Terrell to bury Hockersmith as a soldier. Quantrill also asked Terrell if he could stay at the home. Terrell promised to leave Quantrill to die at the house but changed his mind. Hockersmith was buried. Terrell took Quantrill on a wagon to a military prison hospital in Louisville. On May 13, 1865, Quantrill arrived at the military hospital. On June 6, 1865, Quantrill died from his wounds.[274]

On May 24, Tom Berry reached Sam Berry's camp. Sam told Tom about the death of Jerome Clark and the capture of Henry Magruder. Jim Evans was sent to Louisville to learn about the fate of Magruder. Sam and Tom made plans to rescue their comrade in prison. Captain Sam and Tom Berry recruited volunteers from Nelson, Spencer, Bullitt, Washington, and Jefferson County to ride with Captain Berry and rescue the captives. The meeting place was Coger's farm, four miles from Louisville. Forty-five men were armed. All took the oath to rescue Magruder and Mundy. Unfortunately for Captain Berry, both Magruder and Clarke had been executed.[275]

Interestingly, a newspaper account from July 31, 1865, the newspaper stated that two weeks earlier, two men entered Meadeville and after drinking at a "low grocery," Bill Magruder, who was Henry Magruder's brother, asked for James Newton, and the men were directed to Newton's house. Bill Magruder and the other unidentified accomplice, found Newton with his wife and his children. Bill Magruder asked Newton if he had ever been a Federal soldier. Newton stated that he had been a Union soldier. Magruder drew a revolver and immediately shot Newton dead. Magruder quickly left the house, mounted his horse, and rode into town, and was fired upon by a man named Jackson as Magruder was leaving town. Magruder dismounted and ran into the woods.[276]

According to Tom Berry, Captain Sam Berry, along with his men, were riding to meet Major Cyrus Wilson to surrender. They rode towards Bloomfield. When they reached the Bloomfield and Chaplintown roads Union Captain Baker and forty-five soldiers were riding into the Chaplintown road. Captain Baker fired on Captain Berry and his men. Captain Berry and Captain Terrell both halted their men and both drew their pistols. When they reached thirty yards, they opened fire. The two commands stood by and watched the personal duel between Terrell and Berry. Both fired five shots a piece. Three of Berry's shots hit Terrell, including his horse that fell dead. Captain Terrell's collar bone and shoulder were shattered. One bullet hit the side of Terrell's head and another his hip. Captain Berry received two slight wounds. Union Lieutenant Thompson helped Terrell. Captain Berry charged and chased Terrell's men to Chaplin Hills. This was Captain Berry's last battle.[277]

CHAPTER TWENTY-TWO

Captain Sam Berry Surrenders

On December 8, 1865, Sam Berry, along with the rest of his gang, surrendered to Union Major Cyrus Wilson's detachment of mounted infantry and taken to Louisville and tried before a military court. According to Joseph Cox, who was a clerk in Taylorsville, he had a meeting between Major Cyrus Wilson and Berry. Mr. Hoke, who was the lawyer for Berry, stated that General John Palmer offered Berry a parole on the condition that he and his guerillas would give up the guerilla Texas. Berry and Dick Mitchell found Texas and delivered him to Wilson in Taylorsville. Berry and Mitchell got their parole and the parole was drawn up by Berry and signed by Major Wilson who said to Berry: "You are now a paroled Confederate soldier and may go about your business." Wilson told the *Louisville Journal* that Berry and Mitchell "should go free for any offenses they had committed, provided they had murdered no person for money or Union sentiments, and that, if I should find they were accused of any murder, I would retake them, if possible."[278] Union soldiers had afterwards met him and respected him and since the parole was signed there was no proof that he has been acting as a guerilla. Previous to the parole Berry would have come in and surrendered himself, only had given him such an exaggerated bad name. Major Wilson commanded a squad of soldiers sent out by General Palmer. Berry was sure that Palmer would keep his promise. Berry surrendered himself and was led to believe that if he ever was to be tried, he would be tried by a jury of his fellow citizens, not a military court. The Judge Advocate stated that the statements were untrue. The Judge Advocate stated that no one has the authority to pardon until the party is charged and tried. The Judge Advocate stated that no one has ever left a military prison when there was sufficient evidence to prove he was a murderer.[279]

Thomas Green was a farmer and lived in Spencer County and was present during the meeting between Berry and Wilson for the surrender. The meeting took place at his house. He knew Berry for eighteen months. Alex Thomas was a farmer in Spencer County and knew Berry and stated that Berry was a peaceable man and no Union man was afraid of him. Samuel Russell was a farmer and lived in Nelson County. He knew about the meeting between Berry and Wilson. Russell stated that Berry was a good neighbor. He was never looked upon as a murderer or robber in the community. He stated that the meeting took place at his father's place. Major Russell was a farmer and lived in Bloomfield. He saw the African Americans being taken out of the jail by the guerillas. His father tried to prevent the guerillas from shooting the African American prisoners and Mundy threatened to kill him. Berry rode up and told Clarke if he shot Russell's father, he would shoot him. He saw Berry let a prisoner go free and he made his escape.[280]

Major Wilson stated he was employed by General Palmer. He had no commission, but Palmer gave him a gang of men to hunt down guerillas. Wilson stated that he signed the parole for Berry on June 2. He wanted Berry to come to Louisville and General Palmer told him to get the guerilla Texas. Wilson reported to General Palmer and he approved of his conduct. Wilson received a letter from Berry stating he understood Palmer did not recognize it. Wilson showed the note to General Palmer and he said he did approve the parole. Wilson agreed to parole Mitchell and Berry if they gave up Texas. They did, which made the parole would not shield a man who committed murder, rape, or was instrumental in stopping trains. Wilson gave Berry the understanding that the parole only shielded him from acts committed as a Confederate soldier not as a guerilla. Wilson advised Berry to leave the state. Wilson stated that Mitchell was in business and doing well. Wilson stated he never had the power to offer Berry a pardon. General Palmer told Wilson to apprehend Texas at all hazards and to come to terms with Berry and Mitchell was the only way he could take Texas. Berry said to Wilson that he will not catch him without giving him notice. Wilson could not get Berry to come to Louisville and would rather go to hell. Berry told Wilson that he was not to be arrested for any crimes committed, prior to the signing of the parole. Wilson gave Berry his parole solely for the purpose of catching Texas. Wilson stated that the parole was his only strategy and without the authority of General Palmer. Wilson stated he did not know Berry had committed murder. Wilson stated that the parole was only for a Confederate soldier, not a guerilla. His orders were to capture Texas. Wilson did not explain to Berry that the parole was only for a Confederate soldier. Palmer did not give Wilson orders to capture Berry.[281]

According to General Palmer, Mr. Kirk from Taylorsville stated that he was sent by Berry or whether he claimed to act from his own views of the interests of the public, Palmer could not remember; but Kirk came to Palmer and attempted to arrange for the surrender of Berry, Mitchell, and perhaps some other persons. Berry stated he wanted to surrender as a solider. Berry was hoping for the same terms that the United States government gave to Confederate General

Portrait of Jerome Clarke (Courtesy of Octagon Hall Museum, Franklin County, Kentucky)

Robert E. Lee and Confederate General Joseph Johnson. Palmer stated that Berry knew that he had offered a reward and Palmer refused to accept the surrender of any Rebel soldier or guerilla in Nelson County or who had been in Nelson County before a certain period because of the rape of a woman in Nelson County. Berry knew that Palmer had made a condition that two men by the name of Brothers and Texas should be either killed or captured. Palmer stated that in strong language that he would pay any price to have them killed or captured. Captain Young sent Palmer a list of the names of the guerillas who were killed. Palmer forwarded the list to President Lincoln, with the recommendation that he pardon the whole lot. Texas made his escape while Quantrill's band killed Brothers. Texas was still at large until Berry and Mitchell surrendered him. Major Wilson brought Texas to town and he was put in jail until Colonel Coyl, who was the Post Commander for Kentucky, reported to Palmer that there was not sufficient evidence that Texas was connected to the rape. Texas was kept in prison for four or five months. Palmer stated that he received letters from Berry and Mitchell stating they would kill him if he had Sue Mundy, aka M. Jerome Clarke hung.[282]

Palmer received a letter from Berry complaining the way he had been treated by the military authorities in Kentucky. He gave a justification for his actions. Berry claimed to be a Confederate soldier. Palmer paid no attention to the letter. Palmer remembered that from February 19, 1865, when he took command of Kentucky to June 1865, the guerillas that wanted to surrender grew stronger. He heard that Berry wanted to surrender when the Confederate rebellion collapsed. He heard of Berry's desire to surrender. Berry had a lot of friends in Spencer and Nelson County that called upon Palmer to see how he felt about what he planned to do with Berry. Palmer did not hear anymore from Berry until he made the deal with Wilson. General Lovell Rousseau visited Palmer and told him that Mrs. Merriman, was the sister of Berry. Rousseau stated Mrs. Merriman and Berry wanted to negotiate for the surrender of her brother. Berry sent a letter to General Palmer complaining that his parole had been taken away from him by a party of Union soldiers. Palmer claimed that he never gave Wilson orders to pardon Berry for any murders, rapes, or flagrant outrages. Palmer stated he never authorized anyone to negotiate with any Confederate soldier or guerillas to promise that he would pardon or remit for murder, rape, or for the specific act of throwing passenger trains, with women and children in, off the track. Palmer stated that Wilson was an exception. Wilson was the only agent for Palmer that accepted a surrender and Palmer approved the surrender. Anyone that was not guilty of any of these crimes could come to his office and that the men that were guilty of murder of killing not in battle, should be punished.[283]

Cyrus Wilson stated that he had no commission and was employed by Palmer. Palmer gave him a gang of men to hunt guerillas. When confronted with the parole he gave Berry on June 2, Wilson claimed he did not know whether he signed the pardon or not by the authority of General Palmer. Wilson wanted Berry to come to Louisville. General Palmer told Wilson to get Texas and Wilson thought the best way to take Texas was to have Berry sign the pardon. Wilson reported to General Palmer and he said he did approve of Wilson's conduct. Wilson got a letter from Berry saying he understood General Palmer did not recognize the pardon. Wilson showed the note to Palmer and he said he did approve the pardon. Wilson agreed to parole Dick Mitchell and Berry if they gave up Texas. Berry and Mitchell gave up Texas. Wilson made Berry understand that the parole would not shield a man who committed murder, rape, or was instrumental in upsetting railroad trains. Wilson also made Berry understand that the parole only shielded him from acts committed as a Confederate soldier not a guerilla. Wilson advised Berry to leave the state. Wilson stated Mitchell was in business and doing well. Wilson stated he never had to power to pardon Berry. General Palmer told Wilson to get Texas at all hazards and by coming to terms with Berry and Mitchell was his only chance. Wilson stated that Berry told him that he would not go to Louisville and that he had committed no murder. Wilson stated that Berry may have understood from Wilson that he was not to be arrested for any crimes committed before the parole. Wilson resorted to giving Berry the parole, solely for the purpose of catching Texas. The parole was only a piece of strategy of his own and without authority of General Palmer. Wilson stated that he did not know that Berry had committed murder. Wilson stated that that the parole was specifically given, only for a Confederate soldier and not for a guerilla. Wilson stated that he was not sure if he told Berry that his orders were to capture Texas. Palmer did not give him orders to capture Berry. Berry told Wilson that Texas was the man that committed the rape against a lady.[284]

On January 16, 1866, Berry's trial began in Louisville. The members of the commission to try Berry were General Jefferson Davis, presiding judge, Lieutenant Colonel U. S. Babcock, of the 12th United States Colored Heavy Artillery, Lieutenant Colonel T.R. Weaver, 119th United States Colored Infantry, Brevet Lieutenant Colonel U.T. Drum, 2nd U.S. Infantry, Major J. B. Collins, 2nd U.S. Infantry, Captain J.W. Parker, 119th U.S. Colored Infantry, Lieutenant Thomas Byrne, 2nd U.S. Infantry, Brevet Lieutenant Colonel W.H. Coyle, Major and Judge Advocate Department of Kentucky, Judge Advocate of the Commission. Former Judge W.B. Hoke and R.H. Cockrell were Berry's counsel for the defense. Berry entered the courtroom wearing high boots. He was very pale and had lost weight since being incarcerated. He was heavily ironed with shackles. When the court asked if he would like to have his chains removed, he declined. The judge proceeded to read the charges. He was charged with being a guerilla, robbery, rape, and murder. After each charge, Berry replied that he was not guilty and at one point seemed to smile.

During the conclusion of the trial R. H. Cockrell gave his concluding remarks. He stated that he was not given much time to prepare his defense and the charges were so general and the testimony was unlimited that Cockrell did not know where or how to begin his defense. He objected to the proceedings of the trial as being contrary to all law, both civil, military, human, "and divine." He stated that the charges against Berry were too unlimited and according to all laws both civil and military that the accused had the right to know what he was being charged, with sufficient accuracy as to time, place, and circumstances, so as to be able to make his own defense without being informed by the witnesses for the prosecution. Cockrell stated his client had charges of murder, robberies, etc., which he had never heard of before and some of the crimes were not even committed by Berry.[285]

In the charge of murder, Cockrell stated that he had to defend murder by shooting or drowning and in other cases, he had to defend murder by hanging or shooting. He stated that Berry was charged with robbery in Jefferson County, when evidence proved that the robbery was in Spencer County. Cockrell stated that the charges were not specific enough or sufficient in time or place to afford him time to prepare the rebuttal.[286]

Cockrell stated that Berry took the amnesty oath and he was the first citizen tried in a military court since the revocation of martial law by the President of the United States. Cockrell stated that the Judge Advocate stated that although martial law had been removed, military law still existed, but there was a great difference between military and martial law. The former applied to officers and soldiers of the army and not to any members of any specific body politic. The Code is the rules and articles of war. He stated that martial law is entirely different than military law. The best definition of martial law is "the will of the general commanding the army." Martial law is sometimes declared by the president of the United States and only during war and in a hostile country. Although Lincoln declared martial law in July of 1861, President Andrew Johnson ceased martial law on October 15, 1865. Cockrell stated that the trial of Berry was illegal because Berry was now a citizen and being tried in a military court.[287]

Cockrell also brought up the parole that Berry received by Major Wilson. Cockrell pointed out that the parole was more of an amnesty oath than a parole. He asked the court to look at where Mr. Kirke asked General Palmer on what terms he would receive the surrender of a certain company of partisans. Palmer informed Berry that in consequence of an outrage committed on a lady by some of the parties there would be no more pardons until the guilty parties were handed over and that General Palmer would pardon any six guerillas who would turn over the perpetrator. Berry received a description of the guilty parties which described Texas and Brothers, who were already suspected of the crime of rape and sent Kirke again to General Palmer, who said he would go to Taylorsville with an escort in a few days and receive the surrender of Texas and parole Berry and Mitchell. Palmer did not come, but sent Major Wilson, who was a guerilla catcher to complete the negotiations and receive the surrender of Texas.[288]

Cockrell argued that through the "anxiety" of General Palmer and Wilson to arrest Texas Berry and Mitchell got the best of the bargain that was not their fault. Cockrell stated: "A bargain is a bargain" and if the General was deceived, he has a remedy in "equity" and not at common law.[289]

The counsel referred to the evidence that General Palmer and supposed that Kirk and Russell and the other parties were mistaken as to their understanding of the terms of the surrender and that Wilson reported to Palmer correctly. Cockrell stated: "What is the inevitable conclusion? It is this: First, that the prisoner is exempt from cold blooded murder, rape, and throwing railroad cars off the track. You have no right, then, to try Berry under the general charge of being a guerilla." Cockrell stated that the military tribunal had no right to try Berry with a half dozen specifications of robbery. He stated the tribunal had no right to try Berry for manslaughter or arson. Cockrell stated that the tribunal must confine to the crimes which were specifications, which were rape, murder, and throwing railway cars off the track.[290]

Cockrell stated that the rule of law is that parole testimony is admissible to explain a written instrument. Kirk and Russell understood that the parole to be a pardon. Kirk and other witnesses stated that the parole written by Cox required Berry to leave the state of Kentucky in fifteen days. Berry objected to that clause and Wilson agreed to leave out the condition. Cockrell stated: "Why did Major Wilson want Berry to leave the state in fifteen days if he intended to hold him answerable to the military authorities?" Cockrell argued that Wilson inferred that Berry was to be held responsible to the civilian authority for his own individual acts as a citizen, but not as a guerilla and if so what advantage was the parole or amnesty oath to him? Cockrell stated that Berry was not to be held responsible for offenses committed in the capacity of a guerilla not for violation of the laws of war. Berry looked upon the parole as the "children of Israel looked upon the brazen serpent-it was to heal him from the bite and stigma of guerilla."[291]

Cockrell stated there was a big difference between crimes committed in the capacity of a guerilla and those committed in the capacity of a citizen or soldier. Killing, which might be murder in a guerilla, would be manslaughter or justifiable homicide in a citizen or soldier. Cockrell stated that General

Palmer stated that with the exception of certain offenses, Berry was under his protection. Cockrell asked the commission to not look on Berry's conduct as a guerilla because his parole or amnesty oath, his crimes were compromised or waived.[292]

He asked the commission to "discard from your minds, then, all the prejudices which naturally attend the charge of guerilla; let not public opinion influence you, remembering that it was public opinion that released Barabbas and crucified Christ." He stated that the commission did not have a "scintilla of evidence to establish either of the three crimes specified. Cockrell told the commission that under military law and laws of nations, is that "An amnesty is a perfect oblivion of the past."[293]

Cockrell failed to realize the fact that both Palmer and Wilson stated that they wanted Texas by any means and to persuade Berry and Mitchell to give up Texas through a parole, which only pardoned a soldier and not a guerilla, was a means to an end. Certainly Berry was guilty of numerous crimes, and should have been punished. Through Palmer and Wilson's written testimony, they never intended to honor the parole. Berry was found guilty in early February of 1866 and was convicted of seven murders and the charge of being a guerilla. On February 28, 1866, the sentence of the military court was approved by Military District Commander Union General John Palmer. On March 3,

Capt. S.O. Berry, Sr. (center bottom row) and Messmates at Camp Douglas. (Photograph courtesy of Thomas Berry's Four Years with Morgan Forrest)

1866, Berry was to be executed in the yard of the military prison on the corner of 10th and Broadway Streets.[294] According to Palmer, before Berry was to be executed two ladies visited his office and introduced themselves as Mrs. Smith and Miss Bailey and requested to see Berry. Palmer said to the ladies if they were related to Berry. The ladies said they were not related and Palmer told the ladies he had a rule that no one can see prisoners, who are under the sentence of death, other clergymen or the prisoner's relatives. Palmer asked if the ladies were religious teachers. The ladies told Palmer they were spiritualists. Palmer told the ladies that they will not tell Berry that he will not be hanged on Friday. The ladies agreed.[295]

In the afternoon the ladies came to Palmer's headquarters and told Palmer they "had seen Berry's mother with a rainbow about her head and that she had told them, that Berry would not die on the day of his execution. Palmer told the ladies that Berry will be hanged on the appointed day and said the ladies treated him badly. Several days later the ladies returned again and asked to see Berry. Palmer again refused their request and sent them out of his office. Soon afterwards a prison guard came to Palmer with a written request from Berry that he might be allowed to see Miss Bailey and Mrs. Smith. Palmer agreed and the ladies came to Palmer's office and after seeing Berry told Palmer that Berry would not die.[296]

On February 26, 1866 an order was issued from the adjutant general's office commuting the sentence of Harvey Welles, aka William Henry, aka Jim Davis to ten year's confinement at hard labor in the penitentiary at Albany, New York. Palmer stated Davis was worse than Berry and thought that he owned the commutation of Berry's sentence due to interference from influential friends and insistent that Berry not be executed. Palmer felt that Berry deserved death. From the direction of the president, the War Department issued to following order:

On March 7, 1866, under General Court Martials No. 21, the death sentence in the case of Sam Berry, under Court Martial Orders Number 11, February 10, 1866, was commuted to a ten-year sentence with hard labor in the penitentiary at Albany, New York.[297]

Palmer sent both Berry and Jim Davis to the prison in Albany. Palmer insisted that both men should have been executed. The spiritualists returned to his officer and told Palmer that "the spirits knew much more" than Palmer did. On February 19, 1866, Palmer resigned as major general of volunteers and on April 1, 1866, he resigned as commander of the Department of Kentucky.

Only seven years into his sentence, Sam Berry died on July 4, 1873. He was only thirty-four years old. There are varying reports on how Berry died while in prison. One report stated he was punished by being placed beneath a small and constant stream of cold water, which poured over his head and down his spinal column and he died from his torture.[298] Another report stated he died of tuberculous. He was buried in the prisoner's section of the Albany Rural Cemetery.

Sam Berry's grave marker. Photo courtesy of Mark Bodnar

CHAPTER TWENTY-THREE

Conclusion

What happened to the Union guerilla hunters Captain Edwin Terrell and Colonel James Bridgewater? On May 24, 1865, with the war over and the threat of guerilla attacks over, the Union army disbanded Terrell and his men and a month later the Shelbyville trustees stopped paying Terrell's room and board. Terrell refused to disband.

On August 25, 1865, Terrell killed an Illinois cattle trader by the name of William R. Johnson. Johnson rode from Frankfort to Anderson County to buy stock and he carried a large sum of money. After passing through Anderson County, he rode into Nelson County. In Bloomfield, Terrell and Terrell's Lieutenant, Harry Thompson, arrested Johnson and took him to Shelbyville, where Johnson remained for a day or two. The people of Shelbyville did not know if Johnson was a prisoner or one of Terrell's men. Johnson was last seen alive while walking in the direction of the Mount Eden turnpike toward Clear Creek Bridge. Two weeks later his body was found in the creek. His money was gone and a large rock tied to neck and stones in his pocket. He also had a bullet hole in the back of his head. Terrell and his men were arrested and tried for the murder of Johnson. Terrell and his men were brought to jail in Jefferson County for safe keeping, because the authorities feared that Terrell would be lynched by the citizens of Shelby County or Terrell's men would rescue him. The result of the trial was a hung jury.[299]

After staying in jail for a couple days, the prisoners were taken to the Spencer County jail for trial on an indictment of murder of Enos Oughten (Wooden). While in the jail at Taylorsville, Terrell and two of his men escaped. Everyone hoped that Terrell would leave the State, but instead Terrell and his men began attacking Shelby County and the surrounding counties, doing whatever he pleased.

On April 26, 1866 the Louisville Courier-Journal reported that Captain Terrell and John Withers were released from the Spencer County jail and gathered up a posse and rode to Shelbyville. The citizens of Shelby County and surrounding counties feared Terrell. The paper reported on Terrell's men who were wanted for murder in Shelby and Spencer County. Terrell stated that he was determined to hunt down and kill several of the jurors in Spencer County, who expressed their opinion that Terrell should be hung. The paper stated that Governor Thomas Bramlette "owes it to cause of human safety and to the honor of the Commonwealth to bring these outlaws to speedy justice." The paper stated the multiple rewards to capture Terrell were not enough. The paper suggested that the Governor should call out the militia and arm a company of men to "capture or exterminate the highwaymen." The paper stated the citizens of Shelby County will not give information that would help in punishing Terrell, Withers, or other men for fear of retribution.

On May 26, 1866, Terrell and his uncle John Baker, who was a former member of the 15th Kentucky Union Infantry, rode into Shelbyville around sundown and rode up to the Armstrong Hotel and called for a boy to hold the reins of their horses while they could get a drink. Terrell asked for Sheriff Harbeson and Deputy Sheriff Waters, and said he had a settlement with them. He informed the citizens that he was Captain Terrell and that there were not enough men in Shelbyville to take him. He asked about town marshal George Caplinger and his guard and wanted to know if they would like to get five hundred dollar's reward which had been offered for him. Terrell was abusive towards the citizens of Shelbyville. Terrell dismounted and walked into the hotel armed with six pistols and a Henry rifle and registered his name and came out and re-mounted his horse.

Fifteen minutes later Marshal Caplinger formed a posse of either six or eight men and started in the direction of the hotel around the same time that Terrell and his men left the hotel and rode up the street. Terrell met the posse about midway up the block. One of the men in the posse told Terrell to halt, but Terrell fired one of his pistols and put his spurs to the horse. In less than a minute, twenty-five shots were fired and Terrell's horse fell on the street, but the horse rose up and rode off without Terrell. Terrell's men rode down the street with gunfire coming from every door in town for more than a block. Terrell received four buckshot in the abdomen and one carbine bullet through the breast. The surgeon removed seven pieces of buckshot and his leg was paralyzed.

After the shootout, the citizens of town ran to Terrell in the streets and he begged the townsfolk not to kill him. He was taken to the Redding Hotel, where he again asked the citizens not to murder him and asked for a preacher. During the hail of gunfire, innocent citizens were killed. William Randolph, a young clerk standing in the door of Gorham & Schooler, was shot in the hand and the second bullet hit his collar, cutting his collar in half. He would later die from his wounds. Merritt Redding, Sr. was standing in front of his door when a bullet entered his mouth and back of the head. Also killed during the gunfire was John Baker.

Terrell was taken to the jail in Louisville, Kentucky where he remained for several months and later taken to Shelbyville for trial. He never recovered from his injuries and he was released on bond and went to go live with his brother in Mount Eden. On November 4, 1868 he was taken to City Hospital in Louisville. He was to undergo a surgical procedure to help relieve his suffering from the wounds he received in the shootout in Shelbyville. He thought that some of the buckshot was still in his body and lodged in his spine. The operation was performed by the surgeons, but the operation did not find any buckshot. The surgery did not relieve Terrell's pain and he rapidly went into decline. His doctors knew that he did not have long to live. His nurse was the only person in the room when he died on December 13, 1868 at the age of twenty-two. His body was taken from the City Hospital and buried in St. Mary's Catholic Cemetery in Louisville. He still had a grandfather, brother, sister, and uncle living in Spencer or Shelby County.[300]

After the Civil War, Major James Bridgewater ran for the State House of Representatives, but lost. He obtained a job working for the Freedman's Bureau. The role of the Freedman's Bureau was to protect the rights of the former slaves. Although Bridgewater's Home Guard unit, the Hall's Gap Battalion, was mustered out of military service after the Civil War, Bridgewater and about twelve men decided that the area needed to be guarded. Bridgewater would tell the citizens that he was guarding their property so he needed food, money, or horses and then he would take what he wanted. In May 1867, Bridgewater turned in a list of regulators who were in the area who were allegedly terrorizing the former slaves and Union supporters to the Military District Commander in Louisville. Walter Saunders of Crab Orchard, Kentucky, lived near Crab Creek, was plowing next to the road and found a pistol. Saunders tied the pistol to him as Bridgewater rode by. He demanded that Saunders turn over the pistol to him. As Saunders gave Bridgewater the pistol, Bridgewater noticed a nice ring on Saunders' left hand. Bridgewater said: "Give me that ring." Saunders pleaded with Bridgewater not to take his ring, since the ring belonged to his dead mother. Bridgewater shot Saunders in the shoulder, took the ring, and left Saunders for dead. An eye witness watched the incident and brought Saunders a doctor who saved his life. Saunders decided to take revenge and kill Bridgewater. Saunders told the doctor: "Doc, save that bullet from my shoulder. I'm going to remold it and kill him with it."[301] Saunders came to Stanford, Kentucky in an attempt to kill Bridgewater. Saunders changed his mind when he saw Bridgewater, his brothers, brothers-in-law, and nephews in the streets armed with Spencer Carbines.[302]

On another occasion in 1867, Bridgewater ambushed Saunders and his men where the Louisville & Nashville Railroad used to cross the Danville Avenue in Stanford.

Many of Bridgewater's men and relatives were afraid of retribution and moved to Missouri. Just before Bridgewater and one other member of his gang were about to leave for Missouri, Saunders made a third attempt to kill Bridgewater. On July 17, 1867, while in a saloon in downtown Stanford, Saunders and four other men came into town to kill Bridgewater. Bridgewater's gang member saw Saunders approaching and tried to warn Bridgewater, but he was too focused on his card game. The gang member said to Bridgewater: "Major, Major, I need to talk to you," but Bridgewater said: "I'm busy now." Bridgewater's Spencer carbine was in the corner of the room, while he was playing cards. When Bridgewater saw Saunders and his men, he immediately reached for his Spencer, but Saunders fired and killed Bridgewater first. Dink Farmer, Sr., who was one of the men with Saunders, ended up with the Spencer. Saunders and the four men were tried the following week for murder in Crab Orchard, but were acquitted when the prosecution's witnesses did not show up in court to testify. Saunders was elected sheriff, but was later shot and killed in a gun battle with the town marshal in Richmond, Kentucky.

Bridgewater was buried in the Logan's Creek Cemetery at the foot of Hall's Gap. After her husband's death, Susan Dawes Bridgewater moved to Vernon County, Missouri along with her five children.

In 1899, E.S. Brainerd gave an advance review in the *Louisville Courier-Journal* newspaper of General Palmer's published his memoirs entitled: *Personal Recollections of John Palmer: The Story of an Ernest Life*. After the Civil War, Palmer became Governor of Illinois, United States Senator, and candidate for the president of the United States. In his book he stated that the state of Kentucky was "cursed at the time I assumed command of the department by the presence of "Sue Mundy" (Jerome Clark) Marion, Magruder, and

Quantrell, who finally came into the state." He stated that his predecessor military district commander Union General Stephen Gano Burbridge tried to terrify the guerillas by "hanging their friends." Under Order Number 59, Burbridge would select four prisoners from military prison and took them to the nearest scene of the crime and hang them. They were retaliator executions. In his book, Palmer wrote that he chose a different route and took the war personally to the guerillas. In the advance review, Brainerd stated that Sam Berry and Harvey Wells were tried and convicted to hang on the same day and were confined in the prison in Louisville. Brainerd wrote that in Palmer's book, he wrote that although Berry's crimes were many, Harvey Wells' crimes were atrocious in method that Palmer denounced Wells. Both men were to be executed on Friday, but the preceding Monday, Brainerd mentions the case of the two spiritualists who came into Palmer's office. Brainerd wrote that Palmer had in no way any sympathy or patience with spiritualist beliefs and firmly decided to both Wells and Berry should hang. Only five days were left until the execution. Brainerd wrote about the story in Palmer's book where the spiritualists returned that Berry would not hang. On that Thursday, Palmer received a notice from the president commuting the sentence for Wells to ten years imprisonment. Brainerd wrote that if Wells could escape death and his crimes were even worse than Berry's, then Berry's sentence should be commuted also. Brainerd stated that both men were sent to Albany penitentiary. Brainerd wrote that Palmer verified the prophecy of the spiritualists.[303] In his book, Palmer felt that Berry still "deserved death."[304]

When Palmer's book was writing his book in 1899, Dr. Thomas Berry, who was a corner in Louisville and Sam Berry's brother, wrote to The *Louisville Courier-Journal* newspaper on April 30, 1899, defending his brother. Thomas Berry served in the Confederate army and wrote a book entitled: *Four Years in the Saddle*. He stated that Palmer's book contained "misleading and slanderous" statements. Berry stated that the animosities that occurred during the Civil War should be forgotten. Berry stated that the past cannot be forgotten because of men like Palmer that wore the United States Military uniform continued to make "false, vicious, and uncalled for attacks upon Southern soldiers, dead or alive. As long as men like Palmer, treacherous and inhumane to their victims during life, with ghoulish instincts assail them in their graves, so long will the old wounds be torn afresh."[305]

Berry stated that Palmer was "conscience haunted" by the memory of a "plighted faith betrayed." He stated that Palmer made up the story of the

prophecy of the spiritualists. Berry said that Palmer sought to "blacken" Sam
Berry's memory and Palmer sought praise for himself. Tom Berry stated that
his brother was a commissioned captain in the Confederacy and was sent by
Confederate authorities to recruit in the fall of 1863. He stated that during the
remainder of the war Sam Berry raised three companies for the Confederate
army and while he was recruiting, he was defending himself from numerous bands of marauding Federal soldiers. The Federal soldiers were always
searching for rebels. In a sarcastic tone, Tom Berry said the Federal looked for
Rebels in wardrobes, bandboxes, and bureau drawers. Tom Berry called the
Federal soldiers "land pirates" and showed no quarter and expected none. He
stated that Palmer raised the black flag himself. His captains were instructed
to bring in any and all Confederates found with arms in Kentucky dead or
alive. Thomas stated that Henry Magruder, Sam Berry, Jerome Clarke, Dick
Mitchell, and Tom Henry were the special objects of Palmer's wrath. After
the surrender of Confederate General Robert E. Lee to General Ulysses S.
Grant at Appomattox in April of 1865, various small units of Confederate in
Kentucky surrendered. Berry, seeing that further resistance to the power of
the United States was useless, asked to be allowed to surrender on the same
terms as that had been granted to the men in General Lee's army, which was
a parole and pardon for all offenses, real or imaginary, done during the period
of warfare. Thomas Berry pointed out that William Quantrill's men received
the same terms as Lee. The request for Berry was granted and he surrendered
under the above terms, which were fixed by General Palmer by Major Cyrus
Wilson, acting under Palmer's orders. Major Wilson handed Berry his parole,
assuring him of perfect safety and protection. Thomas Berry stated that what
followed was *"one of the dark and bloody chapters in the history of Federal
military rule in the border states, chapters that ex-Confederates, for the honor of
humanity and their reunited country, would gladly desire forgotten if it were not
necessary to record them in defense of memory of their mistreated and murdered
comrades and friends."*

Thomas Berry stated that Sam Berry surrendered at Mrs. Green's house
in Spencer County, near Smileytown. On receiving his parole, Berry went
to West Point, Kentucky, near the mouth of the Salt River, and arranged to
teach school as a means of earning a living. Sam Berry traveled to Nelson
County for a visit, but on the public highway he was met by a party of Federal
soldiers who had been sent by Palmer to arrest him. The Federal soldiers took
his parole papers and informed him that he was to be tried by a "drumhead"

court martial. Berry escaped from the Federal soldiers and wrote to Palmer asking for his parole and claimed protection under the terms of the surrender. Palmer refused to return the parole and according to Thomas Berry, Palmer "falsely charged his brother with crimes and misdeeds. In making his escape, Sam Berry was severely wounded and had to go into hiding. A Confederate deserter told the Major Wilson and his company of men where Sam Berry was hiding. Berry was arrested and taken to Louisville and placed in jail on Tenth and Broadway.

Thomas stated that in his brother's trial, Sam Berry was not allowed to have defense witnesses. Thomas Berry also stated that his brother's life depended on the testimony of "ignorant" African Americans and women, which was not true. Berry had multiple white male witnesses. According to Thomas Berry, Sam Berry was approached three times by members of the military court and told Berry that they would release him if he managed to raise a sufficient sum of money could be raised. First they wanted fifty thousand dollars, then thirty-five thousand dollars, and finally the military court wanted twenty-five thousand dollars. The court refused to allow the parole as evidence and General Palmer testified against Berry. Thomas Berry stated that Palmer's claim of commuting Berry's sentence after Harvey Wells sentence had been commuted was false. Thomas Berry stated that Palmer had no power to commute Berry's sentence. The president of the United States was the only person who could commute a sentence. Thomas Berry stated that his father, three brothers, a sister, five uncles, and twelve cousins suffered under Union General Burbridge and General Palmer's cruelty. Thomas Berry stated that his brother never betrayed a trust or broke "plighted faith." His friends in various counties throughout Kentucky testified to Berry's "noble and generous" qualities.[306]

Thomas Berry stated that Harvey Wells and his brother's cases were brought to the president's attention by the friends of both men. The sentences were commuted by the president not by Palmer. Wells was sent to a prison in Columbus, Ohio and Berry was sent to Albany. Thomas Berry claimed that Palmer was "seriously at fault or seeks to cover up the true facts of notable acts of cruel injustice to Capt. Berry." Thomas Berry stated that he remembered the betrayal of Henry Magruder and Jerome Clarke. He stated that "these two gallant young soldiers lost their lives by listening to the faithless promises of one of Palmer's Captains, who promised them if they would be protected and receive the same treatment accorded to prisoners of war." Thomas Berry stated that the treachery of the Union commanders in Kentucky cruelly treated the two men. Berry wrote: "They must be sacrificed at any cost or hazard, to satisfy the insatiable thirst for blood." Berry stated that the Union officials would not take the two men by a direct fight, but cajoling or flattering the men with false promises. He said his brother made the mistake of listening. Thomas Berry said that the men were tried and condemned before captured.[307]

Thomas Berry wrote that he was told to forgive and forget. He wrote that he would like to, but "the memory of those bloody days still remains, ground into my bones and flesh. The innocent blood of all my near relatives was dashed; as it were into my very face." Thomas Berry stated that he is told to keep silent and keep his peace. He stated that for his

Capt. T.F. Berry in Ball and Chain at a Louisville prison. (Photograph from Thomas Berry Four Years with Morgan and Forrest)

part "I have no apology nor excuse to offer for myself nor my brother; he and all comrades did their duty as they saw it. I am heartily tired of his enemies constantly making and uttering garbled and false statements about him." Thomas stated that both he and his brother were given the choice, they would do it all over again. He believed that he had the right to defend their lives, their homes, and their honor. He stated that sacred privilege is more valuable than lives and that defending their sacred privilege is not a crime. He stated that most of the Kentuckians believed in self-defense.[308]

On May 14, 1899, the Berry-Palmer controversy, E.S. Brainerd wrote to the *Louisville Courier-Journal* newspaper and stated that Thomas Berry assailed Palmer in the most "bitter and denunciatory language." Brainerd spoke on behalf of General Palmer and wrote that the article was written as a matter of history that he is no way wished to bring sorrow or bitter remembrance to the minds of those who knew and loved "One-armed" Berry. Palmer did not mind the personal attacks on him, but his authority in commuting the sentence was indisputable. Palmer referenced the records of the Office the Secretary of War. Palmer stated that Berry had the right to protect his family and his the reputation of his brother, but Brainerd wrote that if Dr. Berry re-read Palmer's article which Berry denounced, he would find Palmer had written about Sam Berry from a 'purely historic standpoint and with no stroke of the pen has he attempted to "stir up afresh the animosities and wounds of the Civil War. Brainerd stated that the records will show that Palmer, as military governor of Kentucky, had the authority to commute the death sentence of Sam Berry to ten years in prison at Albany, New York.[309]

Thomas Berry became a practicing physician in Louisville and corner at one point for the city. A few years before his death he left Louisville for Oklahoma, where in 1914 he published his book *Four Years in the Saddle with Forrest and Morgan*. He died on December 23, 1917 in Oklahoma City, Oklahoma and was buried in the United Confederate Veterans section at Fairlawn Cemetery, in Oklahoma.

Built in 1847 in Franklin, Kentucky, Octagon Hall stands today as a monument to a bygone era. The hall has been a residence, Masonic meeting lodge, a hospital, and even served as a safe house for soldiers during the Civil War.

Endnotes

1 Sutherland, **A Savage Conflict**, xi.
2 Sutherland, **A Savage Conflict**, xii.
3 James Martin, Black Flag Over the Bluegrass: Guerilla Warfare in Kentucky, 1863-1865, *The Register of the Kentucky Historical Society*, Autumn 1988, Vol. 86, No. 4, 353.
4 Martin, 357.
5 Martin, 354.
6 Martin, 375.
7 Sutherland, **A Savage Conflict**, xi.
8 Thomas Berry, **Four Years with Morgan and Forrest**, 1
9 Thomas Berry, 2-3.
10 Thomas Berry, 4.
11 Thomas Berry, 6.
12 One-Armed Sam Berry: Many Incidents of his Raid on Perryville in 1864 Never Before Published, *The Danville News*, Danville, Kentucky, December 22, 1905,
13 Game Guerillas: Quantrell, Sam Berry, Magruder, Marion, and Others, *The Louisville Courier-Journal*, August 27, 1882, 4.
14 Howard Swiggett, **The Rebel Raider**, 14.
15 Thomas Berry, **Four Years in the Saddle**, 100-101.
16 Ibid. 100
17 Thomas Berry, **Four Years in the Saddle**, 101.
18 Berry, 104-105.
19 Berry, 104.
20 Berry, 106
21 Berry, 107
22 Trial of Henry Magruder, First Day's proceedings, *The Louisville Courier-Journal*, 9-15-1865, 1.
23 Cruel Guerillas: The Hitherto Unwritten History of Their Hellish Deeds in Nelson County, *The Louisville Courier-Journal*, September 9, 1882, 3.
24 Tom Berry, **Four Years with Morgan and Forrest**, 399.

[25] Henry Magruder, **Three Years In The Saddle: The Life and Confession of Henry C. Magruder, the Original "Sue Munday"**, published by his captor, Major Cyrus Wilson, Louisville, Kentucky, 1865, 10-18.

[26] Berry, 109.

[27] Berry, 113.

[28] Berry, 113.

[29] Allison Young, Sue Munday: An Account Of The Terrible Kentucky Guerilla of War Times, *The Louisville Courier-Journal*, February 6, 1887, 16.

[30] Allison Young, Sue Munday: An Account Of The Terrible Kentucky Guerilla of War Times, *The Louisville Courier-Journal*, February 6, 1887, 16.

[31] About Sue Munday: Dr. T. F. Berry Declares Him Not As Black as Painted, *The Louisville Courier-Journal*, June 6, 1890, 8.

[32] Berry, Ibid.

[33] Thomas Shelby Watson, **Confederate Guerilla Sue Mundy**, 44.

[34] Thomas Berry, **Four Years with Morgan and Forrest**, 114.

[35] Tom Berry, **Four Years with Morgan and Forrest**, 116.

[36] Berry, 116.

[37] Berry, 121.

[38] Berry, 127.

[39] Berry, 128.

[40] Berry, 131.

[41] Berry, 133.

[42] Berry, `135.

[43] Berry, 136.

[44] Berry 146.

[45] Berry, 146.

[46] Berry, 183

[47] Berry, 157.

[48] Berry, 173.

[49] Berry, 174.

[50] Berry, 175.

[51] Berry, 177.

[52] Berry, 177.

[53] Berry, 179.

[54] Berry, 183

[55] Edwin Bearss, The Battle of Hartsville and Morgan's Second Kentucky

Raid, *The Register of the Kentucky Historical Society*, April 1967, Vol. 65, No.2, 12-133.

56 Edwin Bearss, The Battle of Hartsville and Morgan's Second Kentucky Raid, *The Register of the Kentucky Historical Society*, April 1967, Vol. 65, No.2, 12-133.

57 Edwin Bearss, The Battle of Hartsville and Morgan's Second Kentucky Raid, *The Register of the Kentucky Historical Society*, April 1967, Vol. 65, No.2, 12-133.

58 Edwin Bearss, The Battle of Hartsville and Morgan's Second Kentucky Raid, *The Register of the Kentucky Historical Society*, July 1967, Vol. 65, No. 3, 239-252.

59 Edwin C. Bearss, GENERAL JOHN HUNT MORGAN'S SECOND KENTUCKY RAID (DECEMBER, 1862): Part Two: MORGAN ATTACKS ELIZABETHTOWN, *The Register of the Kentucky Historical Society*, Vol. 71, No. 2 (April, 1973), pp. 177-188.

60 Game Guerillas: Quantrell, Sam Berry, Magruder, Bill Marion, and Others, *The Louisville Courier-Journal*, August 27, 1882, 4.

61 Edwin C. Bearss, GENERAL JOHN HUNT MORGAN'S SECOND KENTUCKY RAID (DECEMBER, 1862): Part Two: MORGAN ATTACKS ELIZABETHTOWN, *The Register of the Kentucky Historical Society*, Vol. 71, No. 2 (April, 1973), pp. 177-188.

62 Edwin C. Bearss, GENERAL JOHN HUNT MORGAN'S SECOND KENTUCKY RAID (DECEMBER, 1862): Part Two: MORGAN ATTACKS ELIZABETHTOWN, *The Register of the Kentucky Historical Society*, Vol. 71, No. 2 (April, 1973), pp. 177-188.

63 Edwin C. Bearss, GENERAL JOHN HUNT MORGAN'S SECOND KENTUCKY RAID (DECEMBER, 1862): Part Two: MORGAN ATTACKS ELIZABETHTOWN, *The Register of the Kentucky Historical Society*, Vol. 71, No. 2 (April, 1973), pp. 177-188.

64 Edwin C. Bearss, GENERAL JOHN HUNT MORGAN'S SECOND KENTUCKY RAID (DECEMBER, 1862): Part Three: MORGAN Beings His Return To Middle Tennessee, *The Register of the Kentucky Historical Society*, Vol. 71, No. 4 (October, 1973), pp. 426-438.

65 Edwin C. Bearss, GENERAL JOHN HUNT MORGAN'S SECOND KENTUCKY RAID (DECEMBER, 1862): Part Four: MORGAN, In A Hard Night March, Eludes the Trap, *The Register of the Kentucky Historical Society*, Vol. 72, No. 1 (January 1974), pp. 20-37.

66 Berry, **Four Years With Morgan and Forrest**, 207.

67 Berry, **Four Years With Morgan and Forrest**, 207.

68 Howard Swiggett, **The Rebel Raider**, 113-114.

69 Ibid., 115.

70 Ibid., 121.

71 Ibid., 123,125.

72 Thomas Berry, **Four Years With Morgan and Forrest**, 214-215.

73 Berry, 215-216.

74 Howard Swiggett, **The Rebel Raider**, 130.

75 Howard Swiggett, **The Rebel Raider**, 131.

76 Ibid., 132.

77 Ibid., 133.

78 Ibid., 132, 134, 135.

79 Swiggett, 137;

80 Ibid., 138-139.

81 Taylor Bishop, Morgan's Great Raid of 1863, War Beyond the Ohio River, https://www.battlefields.org/learn/articles/morgans-great-raid-1863

82 The Military Department of Kentucky, Military *History of Kentucky*, (The American Guide Series, Works Projects Administration, 1939), 203.

83 Bryan Bush, **Butcher Burbridge**, 71.

84 Ibid. 71.

85 Ibid., 73.

86 Ibid., 73.

87 Ibid., 73.

88 Ibid., 73-74.

89 Ibid., 74.

90 Ibid., 74.

91 Ibid., 74-75.

92 Ibid., 77.

93 Ibid., 78.

94 Ibid., 78.

95 Ibid., 79.

96 Ibid., 80.

97 Ibid., 82.

98 Ibid., 82.

99 Ibid., 83.

100 Ibid., 83.

[101] O.R. Series I, Vol. XXXII/3 Union Correspondence, Orders, and Returns Relating to Operations in Kentucky, Southwest Va, Tennessee, Mississippi, Alabama, and North Georgia, from March 1, 1864 to April 30, 1864. [#59]

[102] Swiggett, **The Rebel Raider**, 219.

[103] Tom Berry, **Four Years With Morgan and Forrest**, 286.

[104] Bush, Bryan, **Butcher Burbridge**, 86-87.

[105] Ibid., 87.

[106] Ibid., 87.

[107] Ibid., 87-88.

[108] Ibid., 88.

[109] Ibid., 88.

[110] Ibid. 88-89.

[111] Ibid., 90.

[112] Ibid., 90.

[113] Ibid., 91.

[114] Ibid., 91.

[115] Ibid., 91.

[116] Ibid., 92-93.

[117] Ibid., 93-94.

[118] Ibid., 94.

[119] Ibid., 94.

[120] Ibid., 95.

[121] Ibid., 95-96.

[122] Ibid., 96.

[123] Myers, William, Cochran, Albert, Trail of One-Armed Berry, The Guerilla: Tenth Day's Trial, *The Louisville Daily Journal*, Jan. 31, 1866, 1.

[124] Move Made To Remove Remains, *The Lexington Herald*, Lexington, Kentucky, February 8, 1906.

[125] Thomas Berry, **Four Years With Morgan and Forrest**, 291.

[126] Bush, Bryan, **Butcher Burbridge**, 114.

[127] Ibid., 115.

[128] Ibid., 115.

[129] Ibid., 115.

[130] Ibid., 115-116.

[131] Ibid., 117.

[132] Ibid., 117.

133 Thomas Shelby Watson & Perry Brantley, **Confederate Guerillas Sue Mundy**, 39.

134 *The Daily Dispatch*, July 13, 1864, Richmond, Virginia. "News From Kentucky."

135 O.R.--SERIES I--VOLUME XXXIX/2 [S# 78] UNION CORRESPONDENCE, ORDERS, AND RETURNS RELATING TO OPERATIONS IN KENTUCKY, SOUTHWEST VIRGINIA, TENNESSEE, MISSISSIPPI, ALABAMA, AND NORTH GEORGIA (THE ATLANTA CAMPAIGN EXCEPTED), FROM MAY 1, 1864, TO SEPTEMBER 30, 1864.(*)--#7, General Order Number 59, General Stephen Gano Burbridge, HDQRS. DISTRICT OF KENTUCKY, AND 5TH DIVISION, 23rd ARMY CORPS, Lexington, Ky., July 16, 1864, 174.

136 *Louisville Daily Journal*, July 20, 1864, Military Order.

137 O.R.--SERIES I--VOLUME XXXIX/2 [S# 78] UNION CORRESPONDENCE, ORDERS, AND RETURNS RELATING TO OPERATIONS IN KENTUCKY, SOUTHWEST VIRGINIA, TENNESSEE, MISSISSIPPI, ALABAMA, AND NORTH GEORGIA (THE ATLANTA CAMPAIGN EXCEPTED), FROM MAY 1, 1864, TO SEPTEMBER 30, 1864.(*)--#9, General Order Number 61, 205.

138 O.R.--SERIES I--VOLUME XXXIX/2 [S# 78]UNION CORRESPONDENCE, ORDERS, AND RETURNS RELATING TO OPERATIONS IN KENTUCKY, SOUTHWEST VIRGINIA, TENNESSEE, MISSISSIPPI, ALABAMA, AND NORTH GEORGIA (THE ATLANTA CAMPAIGN EXCEPTED), FROM MAY 1, 1864, TO SEPTEMBER 30, 1864.(*)--#9, 215.

139 Ibid.

140 Ibid.

141 Ibid.

142 Ibid.

143 Joshua Flood Cook, **Old Kentucky**, 1908, 226.

144 Captain W. H. Davidson-The Guerilla, *The Louisville Courier-Journal*, Louisville, Kentucky, February 11, 1865, 1

145 Trail of Henry Magruder, First Day's Proceedings, *The Louisville Courier-Journal*, 9-15-1865, 1.

146 Ibid.

147 Myers, William, Cochran, Albert, Trail of One-Armed Berry, The Guerilla: Third Day's Trial, *The Louisville Daily Journal*, Jan. 18, 186

148 Jesse Gang Dispensed, *The Louisville Daily Courier*, Louisville, Kentucky, September 7, 1864, 1

149 Col. Craddock After Jesse, *The Louisville Daily Courier*, Louisville, Kentucky, September 6, 1864, 3.

150 Thomas Berry, **Four Years With Morgan and Forrest**, 314-315.

151 Ibid., 315-316.

152 Ibid., 317.

153 Ibid., 319.

154 Trial of Henry C. Magruder, Second Day's Proceedings-Continued, *The Louisville Courier-Journal*, September 16, 1865, 3.

155 Myers, William, Cochran, Albert, Trail of One-Armed Berry, The Guerilla: Third Day's Trial, *The Louisville Daily Journal*, Jan. 18, 1865, 3.

156 Myers, William L; Cochran, Albert E, Sam One Arm Berry, the Guerilla: Fourth Day's Proceedings, *The Louisville Daily Courier*, January 19, 1866, 2.

157 Myers, William L; Cochran, Albert E, Sam One Arm Berry, the Guerilla: Fourth Day's Proceedings Concluded, *The Louisville Daily Courier*, January 20, 1866, 3.

158 Historic Bank Building at Harrodsburg Razed: Scene of Attempted Raid by Celebrated Guerilla Band in October 8, 1864, *The Louisville Courier-Journal*, June 29, 1917, 7.

159 Myers, William L; Cochran, Albert E, Sam One Arm Berry, the Guerilla: Fourth Day's Proceedings, *The Louisville Daily Courier*, January 20, 1866, 3.

160 Body of Famous Raider Moved To New Location, *The Bourbon News*, Paris, Kentucky, August 11, 1914, 2.

161 Myers, William L; Cochran, Albert E, Sam One Arm Berry, the Guerilla: Fourth Day's Proceedings, *The Louisville Daily Courier*, January 20, 1866, 3.

162 Myers, William, Cochran, Albert, Trail of One-Armed Berry, The Guerilla: Third Day's Trial, *The Louisville Daily Journal*, Jan. 18, 1865, 3.

163 Ibid.

164 Myers, William L; Cochran, Albert E, Sam One Arm Berry, the Guerilla: Fourth Day's Proceedings, *The Louisville Daily Courier*, January 19, 1866, 1.

165 Ibid.

166 Ibid.

167 Order No. 8, October 26, 1864, O.R. Series I, Vol. XXXIX/2 [#79] Union Correspondence, Orders, and Returns to Operations in Kentucky, Southwest Virginia, Tennessee, Mississippi, Alabama, and North Georgia (the Atlanta Campaign excepted) from October 1, 1864 to November 13, 1864, 457.

168 Thomas Shelby Watson & Perry Brantley, **Confederate Guerillas Sue Mundy**, 81

169 Myers, William L; Cochran, Albert E, Sam One Arm Berry, the Guerilla: Second Day's Proceedings, *The Louisville Daily Courier*, January 17, 1866, 1.

170 Ibid.

171 Ibid.

172 Ibid.

173 Ibid.

174 Myers, William L; Cochran, Albert E, Sam One Arm Berry, the Guerilla: Second Day's Proceedings, *The Louisville Daily Courier*, January 17, 1866, 1.

175 Trial of One Armed Berry, Reported Exclusively for the *Louisville Courier, Daily Courier*, Jan. 24, 1866, 2.

176 Trial of One Armed Berry, Reported Exclusively for the *Louisville Courier, Daily Courier*, Jan. 16, 1866, 1.

177 Trial of Henry Magruder, First Day's Testimony, *The Louisville Courier-Journal*, September 15, 1865, 1.

178 Ibid.

179 Trial of Henry C. Magruder, Second Day's Proceedings, Continued, *The Louisville Courier-Journal*, September 9, 1865, 3.

180 James Head, 205; Collins, 146.

181 James Head, *The Atonement of John Brooks*, 205-206.

182 Myers, William L; Cochran, Albert E, Sam One Arm Berry, the Guerilla: Second Day's Proceedings, *The Louisville Daily Courier*, January 17, 1866, 1.

183 Myers, William L; Cochran, Albert E, Sam One Arm Berry, the Guerilla: Second Day's Proceedings, *The Louisville Daily Courier*, January 17, 1866, 1.

184 Myers, William L; Cochran, Albert E, Sam One Arm Berry, the Guerilla: Second Day's Proceedings, *The Louisville Daily Courier*, January 17, 1866, 1.

185 Guerilla Murders and Robbery in Washington County, *The Louisville Courier-Journal*, Louisville, Kentucky, December 3, 1864, 3.

186 Myers, William, Cochran, Albert, Trail of One-Armed Berry, The Guerilla: Third Day's Trial, *The Louisville Daily Journal*, Jan. 18, 1865, 3.

187 Ibid.

188 Myers, William L; Cochran, Albert E, Sam One Arm Berry, the Guerilla: Fourth Day's Proceedings Concluded, *The Louisville Daily Courier*, January 20, 1866, 3.

189 Richard J. Browne to Thomas E. Bramlette, 29 November 1864, Guerilla Letters, Document Box 1, Folder G. L. 1864, Kentucky Department of Military Affairs, Frankfort, KY. Accessed via the Civil War Governors of Kentucky Digital Documentary Edition, discovery.civilwargovernors.org/document/KYR-0002-225-0060, (accessed January 28, 2024).

190 Myers, William L; Cochran, Albert E, Sam One Arm Berry, the Guerilla: Second Day's Proceedings, *The Louisville Daily Courier*, January 17, 1866, 1.

191 Ibid.

192 Myers, William, Cochran, Albert, Trail of One-Armed Berry, The Guerilla: Tenth Day's Trial, *The Louisville Daily Journal*, Jan. 31, 1866, 1.

193 Ibid.

194 Myers, William, Cochran, Albert, Trail of One-Armed Berry, The Guerilla: Third Day's Trial, *The Louisville Daily Journal*, Jan. 18, 1866, 3.

195 Ibid.

196 Ibid.

197 Myers, William L; Cochran, Albert E, Sam One Arm Berry, the Guerilla: Fourth Day's Proceedings Concluded, *The Louisville Daily Courier*, January 20, 1866, 3.

198 Myers, William L; Cochran, Albert E, Sam One Arm Berry, the Guerilla: Fourth Day's Proceedings Concluded, *The Louisville Daily Courier*, January 20, 1866, 3.

199 Myers, William L; Cochran, Albert E, Sam One Arm Berry, the Guerilla: Fifth Day's Proceedings Concluded, *The Louisville Daily Courier*, January 20, 1866, 1.

200 Myers, William, Cochran, Albert, Trail of One-Armed Berry, The Guerilla: Third Day's Trial, *The Louisville Daily Journal*, Jan. 18, 1865, 3.

201 Myers, William, Cochran, Albert, Trail of One-Armed Berry, The Guerilla: Third Day's Trial, *The Louisville Daily Journal*, Jan. 18, 1865, 3.

202 Myers, William, Cochran, Albert, Trail of One-Armed Berry, The Guerilla: Tenth Day's Trial, *The Louisville Daily Journal*, Jan. 31, 1866, 1.

203 Myers, William, Cochran, Albert, Trail of One-Armed Berry, The Guerilla: Third Day's Trial, *The Louisville Daily Journal*, Jan. 18, 1866, 3.

204 Trail of Henry C. Magruder, Eighth's Days Proceedings, *The Louisville Courier-Journal*, September 23, 1865, 3

205 Trail of Henry C. Magruder, Eight's Days Proceedings, *The Louisville Courier-Journal*, September 23, 1865, 3.

206 Myers, William, Cochran, Albert, Trail of One-Armed Berry, The Guerilla: Third Day's Trial, *The Louisville Daily Journal*, Jan. 18, 1866, 3.

207 Myers, William, Cochran, Albert, Trail of One-Armed Berry, The Guerilla: Third Day's Trial, *The Louisville Daily Journal*, Jan. 18, 1866, 3.

208 Trial of Henry C. Magruder, Eighth's Days Proceedings, *The Louisville Courier-Journal*, September 23, 1865, 3.

209 Myers, William, Cochran, Albert, Trail of One-Arme Berry, The Guerilla: Third Day's Trial, *The Louisville Daily Journal*, Jan. 18, 1866, 3.

210 Sue Mundy's Gang, *The Louisville Journal*, Louisville, Kentucky, December 8, 1864, 1.

211 One Armed Sam Berry, *The Danville News*, Danville, Kentucky, December 22, 1905, 1

212 Ibid.

213 Henry Magruder, **Three Years in the Saddle**, 95-98.

214 We have been handed the following, *The Louisville Daily Journal*, Louisville, Kentucky, January 24, 1865, 3.

215 Thomas Berry, **Four Years With Morgan and Forrest**, 334-335.

216 Ibid., 336.

217 Ibid., 336-337.

218 Ibid., 338.

219 Thomas Shelby Watson & Perry A. Brantley, **Confederate Guerilla Sue Mundy**, 108.

220 Magruder's Operations, *The Louisville Courier-Journal*, January 4, 1865, 3.

221 Henry Magruder, **Three Years in the Saddle**, 104.

222 Trial of Henry C. Magruder, Second Day's Proceedings Continued, *The Louisville Courier-Journal*, September 15, 1865, 3.

223 Game Guerillas: Quantrell, Sam Berry, Magruder, Marion, and Others, *The Louisville Courier-Journal*, August 27, 1882, 2.

[224] Trial of Henry C. Magruder, First Day's Proceedings, *The Louisville Courier-Journal*, September 15, 1865, 1.

[225] Ibid.

[226] Trial of Henry C. Magruder, First Day's Proceedings Concluded, *The Louisville Courier-Journal*, September 15, 1865, 3.

[227] Ibid.

[228] Ibid.

[229] Ibid.

[230] Trail of Henry C. Magruder, Fourth Day's Proceedings, *The Louisville Courier-Journal*, September 18, 1865, 3

[231] Myers, William L; Cochran, Albert E, Sam One Arm Berry, the Guerilla: Second Day's Proceedings, *The Louisville Daily Courier*, January 17, 1866, 1.

[232] William Elsey Connelley, **Quantrill and the Border Wars**, 461.

[233] Tom Berry, **Four Years With Morgan and Forrest**, 325-326.

[234] Henry Magruder, **Three Years in the Saddle**, 112.

[235] Horrible Butchery-Negro Soldiers Murdered by Guerillas, *The Louisville Daily Journal*, January 26, 1865, 3.

[236] Tom Berry, **Four Years with Morgan and Forrest**, 327-328.

[237] Yeatman, Ted, **Frank and Jesse James: The Story Behind the Legend**, Nashville, Tennessee, Cumberland Publishing House, 2000, 66.

[238] Lewis Witherspoon McKee & Lydia Kennedy Bone, **A History of Anderson County**, Regional Publishing Company, 1975, ; **Official Records of the War of the Rebellion**, D.W Lindsey, Inspector and Adjuatnt General of the Kentucky Volunteers, to General Edward Hobson, January 28, 1865

[239] "Eulogies and Flowers for Dead Confederate Veterans," *Louisville Courier-Journal*, June 4, 1904.

[240] Gerry Fischer, Hunt for guerilla fighter Big Zay Coalter ended at remote Anderson Cemetery, *The Kentucky Bugle*, April-June 2016, Vol. 10, No. 2

[241] Berry, **Four Years With Morgan and Forrest**, 420.

[242] Late Guerilla Operations, *The Louisville Courier-Journal*, April 16, 1865, 3.

[243] O.R. Series I, Vol. XLVI/2 [#96] Letter from Secretary of War Edwin Stanton to Major General John Palmer.

[244] William Elsey Connelley, **Quantrell and the Border Wars**, 462.

[245] Henry Magruder, **Three Years in the Saddle**, 114-155.

[246] Henry Magruder, **Three Years in the Saddle**, 116-117.

[247] Ibid., 118-119.

[248] Ibid. 121.

[249] Myers, William L; Cochran, Albert E, The Trial of One-Armed Berry, the Guerilla: Second Day's Proceedings, *The Louisville Daily Journal*, January 17, 1866, 1

[250] Berry, **Fours Years With Morgan and Forrest**, 373.

[251] Ibid., 425.

[252] Ibid., 426.

[253] Ibid., 333

[254] Myers, William L; Cochran, Albert E, Sam One Arm Berry, the Guerilla: Fifth Day's Proceedings, *The Louisville Daily Courier*, January 20, 1866, 1.

[255] Berry, **Four Years With Morgan and Forrest**, 416-417.

[256] Ibid., 419.

[257] US, Compiled Service Records of Volunteer Union Soldiers Who Served in Organizations from the State of Kentucky, 1861-1865, The National Archives, May 1, 1864, Letter from Cyrus Wilson to J.A. Campbell, A.A. General.

[258] Allison, Young, Sue Mundy: An Account of the Terrible Kentucky Guerilla of War Times, *The Louisville Courier-Journal*, Feb. 6, 1887, 16.

[259] Ibid.

[260] Allison Young, Sue Mundy: An Account Of The Terrible Kentucky Guerilla of War Times, *The Louisville Courier-Journal*, February 6, 1887, 16.

[261] A Curiosity, *The Louisville Courier-Journal*, March 25, 1865, 1.

[262] Execution of Henry Magruder, *The Cincinnati Daily Enquirer*, October 24, 1865, *The Louisville Courier-Journal*, 1.

[263] Myers, William L; Cochran, Albert E, Sam One Arm Berry, the Guerilla: Second Day's Proceedings, *The Louisville Daily Courier*, January 17, 1866, 1.

[264] Myers, William L; Cochran, Albert E, Sam One Arm Berry, the Guerilla: Second Day's Proceedings, *The Louisville Daily Courier*, January 17, 1866, 1.

[265] Myers, William L; Cochran, Albert E, Sam One Arm Berry, the Guerilla: Second Day's Proceedings, *The Louisville Daily Courier*, January 17, 1866, 1.

[266] A Union Man Executed By Guerillas, *The Louisville Courier-Journal*, April 3, 1865, 1.

267 Myers, William L; Cochran, Albert E, Sam One Arm Berry, the Guerilla: Second Day's Proceedings, *The Louisville Daily Courier*, January 17, 1866, 1.

268 Myers, William L; Cochran, Albert E, Sam One Arm Berry, the Guerilla: Second Day's Proceedings, *The Louisville Daily Courier*, January 17, 1866, 1.

269 Gen. Palmer and the Guerilla Marion, *The Louisville Courier-Journal*, April 12, 1865, 3.

270 Thomas Shelby Watson, **Confederate Guerilla Sue Mundy**, 179-180

271 William Elsey Connelley, **Quantrill and the Border Wars**, Cedar Rapids, Iowa, The Torch Press Publishers, 1910, 465.

272 Berry, **Four Years With Morgan and Forrest**, 433.

273 Ibid., 433-434.; Thomas Watson, **Confederate Guerilla Sue Mundy**, 181.

274 Berry, **Four Years With Morgan and Forrest**, 435-436.

275 Ibid., 396.

276 **The Courier-Journal**, July 31, 1865, 3.

277 Berry, **Four Years With Morgan and Forrest**, 456.

278 *The Louisville Courier-Journal*, June 15, 1865, 1; "Texas" The Guerilla, *The Louisville Courier-Journal*, June 6, 1865, 3.

279 Myers, William L; Cochran, Albert E, Sam One Arm Berry, the Guerilla: Sixth Day's Proceedings, *The Louisville Daily Courier*, January 22, 1866, 1.

280 Myers, William L; Cochran, Albert E, Sam One Arm Berry, the Guerilla: Sixth Day's Proceedings, *The Louisville Daily Courier*, January 22, 1866, 1.

281 Myers, William L; Cochran, Albert E, Sam One Arm Berry, the Guerilla: Eighth Day's Proceedings, *The Louisville Daily Courier*, January 24, 1866, 2.

282 Ibid.

283 Myers, William L; Cochran, Albert E, Sam One Arm Berry, the Guerilla: Ninth Day's Proceedings, *The Louisville Daily Courier*, January 25, 1866, 3.

284 Trial of One Armed-Berry, Eighth Day's Proceedings, *The Louisville Daily Journal*, January 24, 1866, 2

285 Trial of One Armed Berry, *The Louisville Daily Courier*, February 7, 1866, 1.

286 Ibid.

287 Ibid.

288 Ibid.,

289 Ibid.,

290 Ibid.

291 Ibid.

292 Ibid.

293 Trail of One Arm Berry, *The Louisville Daily Courier*, Louisville, Kentucky, February 7, 1866, 1.

294 One-Armed Berry Sentenced To Be Hanged, *The Louisville Daily Journal*, February 14, 1866, 3.

295 John Palmer, **Personal Recollections of John M. Palmer: The Story of An Earnest Life**, The Robert Clarke Company, Cincinnati, Ohio, 1901, 276-277.

296 Ibid.

297 Sentences of One-Armed Berry and J.A. Wells Commuted, *The Louisville Daily Courier*, March 8, 1866, 2

298 One Armed Sam Berry, *The Danville News*, Danville, Kentucky, December 22, 1905, 1.

299 Terrell: Death of a Notorious Guerilla, *The Louisville Courier-Journal*, December 14, 1868, 4.

300 Terrell: Death of a Notorious Guerilla, *The Louisville Courier-Journal*, December 14, 1868, 4.

301 David Gambrel, Story of outlaw's killing passed through the family, *The Advocate Messenger*, August 8, 1996, 18.

302 David Gambrel, Monument To Be Dedicated to colorful Civil War figure, **The Interior Journal**, June 14, 2007, 9A

303 E. S. Brainerd, Story of An Earnest Life: Memoirs of a Noted General and Statesman-Advance Review of Gen. John M. Palmer's book, *The Louisville Courier-Journal*, Louisville, Kentucky, April 9, 1899, 22.

304 John Palmer, **Personal Recollections of John M. Palmer: The Story of An Earnest Life**, The Robert Clarke Company, Cincinnati, Ohio, 1901, 276.

305 Thomas Berry, "One-Armed Berry" Defended by His Brother: Statements in Gen. Palmer's Forthcoming Book Controverted by Ex-Corner Berry, *The Louisville Courier-Journal*, April 30, 1899, B8.

306 Thomas Berry, "One-Armed Berry" Defended by His Brother: Statements

in Gen. Palmer's Forthcoming Book Controverted by Ex-Corner Berry, *The Louisville Courier-Journal*, April 30, 1899, B8.

[307] Ibid.

[308] Ibid.

[309] The Palmer-Berry Controversy, *The Louisville Courier-Journal*, May 14, 1899, 24.

Bibliography

Berry, Thomas, **Four Years With Morgan And Forrest**, The Harlow-Ratliff Company, Oklahoma City, Oklahoma, 1914.

Bush, Bryan, **Butcher Burbridge: Union General Stephen Gano Burbridge and His Reign of Terror Over Kentucky**, Acclaim Press, Morley, Missouri, 2007.

Connelley, William Elsey, **Quantrill and the Border Wars**, Cedar Rapids, Iowa, The Torch Press Publishers, 1910,

Fischer, Gerald, **Guerilla Warfare in Civil War Kentucky**, Acclaim Press, Morley, Missouri, 2014.

McKnight, Brian & Myers, Barton, **The Guerilla Hunters: Irregular Conflicts during the Civil War (Conflicting Worlds: New Dimensions of the American Civil War)** Louisiana Press University, Louisiana, 2017.

Magruder, Henry, **Three Years in the Saddle: The Life and Confession of Henry Magruder, The Original "Sue Munday" The Scourge of Kentucky,** Published by his Captor, Maj. Cyrus J. Wilson, Louisville, Kentucky, 1865.

Mellish, Gordon, Guerilla War in Kentucky: Burbridge and the Berrys, Trafford Publishing, Victoria, BC, Canada, 2008

Sickles, John, **The Legends of Sue Mundy** and **One Armed Berry: Confederate Guerillas**, Heritage Press, Merrillville, Indiana, 1999.

Sutherland, Daniel E., **A Savage Conflict: The Decisive Role of Guerrillas in the American Civil War**. Civil War America Series. Chapel Hill: University of North Carolina Press, 2009.

Swiggett, Howard. **The Rebel Raider: A Life of John Hunt Morgan**, The Garden City Publishing Company, Inc., Garden City, New York, 1934.

Watson, Shelby Thomas & Brantley, Perry, Confederate Guerilla **Sue Mundy: A Biography of Kentucky Solider Jerome Clarke**, McGarland & Company, Inc. Publishers, Jefferson, North Carolina & London, 2008.

Watson, Thomas Shelby, **The Silent Riders**, Beechmont Press, Louisville, Kentucky, 1971.

United States War Department, **The War of the Rebellion: A Compilation of The Official Records of the Union and Confederate Armies**, Government Printing Office, Washington, D.C., 1880-1901.

Articles

Bearss, Edwin, The Battle of Hartsville And Morgan's Second Kentucky Raid, *The Register of the Kentucky Historical Society*, April 1967. Vol. 65, No. 2, Kentucky Historical Society, 120-133.

Beilein, Joseph, Jr., The Terror of Kentucky: Sue Mundy's Highly Gendered War Against Convention, *The Register of the Kentucky Historical Society*, Vol. 116, No. 2, Irregular Violence and Trauma In Civil War Kentucky, (Spring 2018), 157-181.

Bush, Bryan, A Look Back at Civil War History in Kentucky-Part I Guerilla fighter William Quantrill Visits Kentucky, October 10, 2023, *The Middlesboro News*, Middlesboro, Kentucky

Bush, Bryan, A Look Back at Civil War History in Kentucky-Part II Guerillas Fighter fought his way around Kentucky, *The Danville Advocate-Messenger*, Danville, Kentucky, October 28, 2023

Martin, James, Third War: Irregular Warfare on the Western Border 1861-1865, Combat Studies Institute Press, US Army Combined Arms Center, Fort Leavenworth, Kansas, 2012.

Martin, James, Black Flag Over the Bluegrass: Guerilla Warfare in Kentucky: 1863-1865, *The Register of the Kentucky Historical Society*, Kentucky Historical Society, Autumn 1988, Vol. 86, No. 4, 352-375.

Valentine, L. L., Sue Mundy of Kentucky, Part I, *The Register of the Kentucky Historical Society*, Vol. 62, No. 3, (July 1964) 175-205.

Valentine, L. L., Sue Mundy of Kentucky, Part II, *The Register of the Kentucky Historical Society*, Vol. 62, No. 4, (October 1964), 278-306.

Young, Allison, Sue Mundy: "An Account of the Terrible Kentucky Guerilla of Civil War Times," *The Register of the Kentucky Historical Society*, Vol. 57, No. 4 (October 1959, 295-316.

Newspapers

The Louisville Courier-Journal.

About the Author

Bryan Bush was born in 1966 in Louisville, Kentucky and has been a native of that city ever since. He graduated with honors from Murray State University with a degree in History and Psychology, and received his Master's Degree from the University of Louisville in 2005.

Bryan has always had a passion for history, especially the Civil War. He has been a member of many different Civil War historical preservation societies and roundtables. He has consulted for movie companies and other authors, coordinated with other museums on displays of various museum articles and

Bryan Bush

artifacts, has written for magazines, such as *Kentucky Civil War Magazine, North/South Trader, The Kentucky Civil War Bugle, The Kentucky Explorer* and *Back Home in Kentucky,* and worked for many different historical sites.

In 1999, Bryan published his first work: *"The Civil War Battles of the Western Theater."* Since then, Mr. Bush has had published over fourteen books on the Civil War and Louisville history, including several titles for The History Press, including *Louisville During the Civil War: A History and Guide* and *Louisville's Southern Exposition, Favorite Sons of Civil War Kentucky,* and *The Men Who Built The City of Progress: Louisville During The Gilded Age.*

Bryan Bush has been a Civil War re-enactor for fifteen years, portraying an artillerist. For five years Bryan was on the Board of Directors and curator for the Old Bardstown Civil War Museum and Village, The Battles of the Western Theater Museum in Bardstown, Kentucky, was a board member for the Louisville Historical League, and is the official Civil War tour guide for Cave Hill Cemetery.

In December of 2019, Bryan Bush became the park manager for the Perryville State Historic Site.

Index

Numerical

1st Kentucky Cavalry 38, 102
1st Kentucky Confederate Infantry Regiment 131
2nd Indiana Cavalry 42-43
2nd Kentucky 44, 49, 52-53
2nd Kentucky Cavalry 19, 26, 131
2nd Kentucky Infantry 43
3rd Kentucky Cavalry 122-123
3rd Kentucky Infantry 32
4th Kentucky Cavalry 67
4th Kentucky Infantry 31
4th Missouri Cavalry 127
4th Ohio Cavalry 38
5th United States Colored Cavalry 123-124
6th Kentucky Cavalry 11, 35
6th Kentucky Infantry 144
7th Kentucky Cavalry 44
7th Ohio Cavalry 70
7th Pennsylvania Cavalry 115
8th Kentucky 46
8th Kentucky Cavalry 43, 107
8th Texas Cavalry 19, 50
9th Kentucky Cavalry 28, 47
9th Kentucky Infantry 42-44, 131
9th Michigan Cavalry 34, 37
9th Tennessee 53
10th Kentucky 53
10th Kentucky Union Infantry 115
11th Kentucky Cavalry 43
11th Kentucky Infantry 87-88
11th Kentucky Union Infantry 89
11th Michigan 61-62
11th Michigan Cavalry 65
12th Ohio Cavalry 65

13th Indiana Battery 42
15th Kentucky Union Infantry 118, 133, 160
20th Kentucky 52
22nd Kentucky Infantry 66
25th Michigan Cavalry 51
26th Kentucky Infantry 122, 138
32nd Indiana Infantry 19
33rd Kentucky Union Volunteer Infantry 138
37th Kentucky 64-65
37th Kentucky Infantry 98
37th Kentucky Mounted Infantry 132
39th Kentucky 63, 65
40th Kentucky 64-65
40th Kentucky Mounted Infantry 56
41st Georgia Infantry 129
44th Indiana Volunteers 76
45th Kentucky 63, 65
47th Kentucky 68
52nd Kentucky 64, 70
54th Kentucky Mounted Infantry 37, 112, 127
71st Indiana 47
78th Illinois 47
80th Illinois 49
91st Illinois 46
101st Indiana 49
104th Illinois 43-44
105th Ohio Infantry 49
106th Ohio 43-44
108th Ohio 43-44
123rd Illinois 49
168th Ohio 68
171st Ohio National Guard 68-69

A

Abington, Virginia 62, 71-72
Adams, Benjamin 145
Adams, N. 97
Alexandria, Tennessee 45, 126
Alice Dean 53

Allen, Ben 30
Allen, Jack 25, 73, 103, 139
Alston, R.A. 72
Ammen, Jacob 56-57
Anderson, (Bloody) Bill 121
Anderson, Henry 30
Ashbrook, Private 30
Asper, Joel F. 68-69
Averell, William 62-63
Avery, Sam 30
Axton, Isaac H. 122-123

B

Babcock, U.S. 153
Bailey, Miss 157
Baker, Captain 148
Baker, John 160, 161
Baker, Thomas 130
Ball, J. P. 113
Ball, Pat 112
Bardstown, Kentucky 45, 48, 52, 78, 92-94, 98, 112, 115, 186
Barker, Captain 84
Barker, John 127-129
Barnett, Andrew M. 122-123
Barnett, Charles 117-118
Barnett, Dick 119
Barnett, Doc. 118
Barnett, Joe 118, 120-123
Battle of Perryville 37, 41, 129
Battle of Shiloh 20, 26
Battle of Stone's River 49
Beard, Perry 17
Bell *(guerilla)* 33
Berry, Alex 16
Berry, George W. (G.W.) 69-70
Berry, Jim 17
Berry, Lewis 17
Berry, Louis 123
Berry, Minnie 11, 16
Berry, Rose 18
Berry, Samuel Oscar *(father)* 16, 156

Berry, Samuel (Sam) Oscar (One-Arm) 7, 9, 11, 16, 23, 35, 73, 80-84, 86-95, 98-106, 108, 110-113, 115, 117, 121-126, 130, 132-137, 143-145, 147-158, 163-165, 167
Berry, Susan 16
Berry, Thomas (Tom) 7, 9, 11-12, 16-17, 19-21, 23-31, 34-39, 41, 47, 49, 55, 62, 66, 73, 81-84, 112-115, 123-126, 132, 135, 137, 147-148, 163-167
Berry, William (uncle) 16
Berry, William W. (brother) 16-17
Berry, Younger 17
Biddle, W. H. 144-145
Bird, James 119-120
Black, Captain 144
Blakely, Mr. 121
Blant (guerilla) 121
Bloomfield, Kentucky 73, 91-93, 98, 103-104, 113, 115, 120, 126, 136, 146, 150, 159
Bodnar, Mark 158
Boone, William 40
Booth, John Wilkes 146
Bosley, Charles 99-101
Bosley, G.J. 110
Botto, Anthony 120
Bowles, Jim 36, 49
Bowling Green, Kentucky 19-20, 25
Boyle, Jeremiah 56, 132
Brady, Father 142
Bragg, Braxton 36-37, 41, 45, 49-50, 109, 131
Brainerd, E.S. 162-163, 166-167
Bramlette, Thomas 56-57, 74, 78, 160
Brandenburg, Kentucky 53, 138
Breckinridge, John C. 20, 25, 42, 61
Breckinridge, R.C. 128
Breckinridge, Robert J. 7, 17
Breckinridge, William Campbell Preston (W.C.P.) 46
Brenner, Frank 120

Brent, Major 51
Bridgewater, Henry 32
Bridgewater, James 13, 32-33, 114, 126-127, 130, 133-134, 136-137, 159, 161-162
Bridgewater, John 32
Bridgewater, Mary Hamlet 32
Bridgewater, Susan Dawes 162
Bristow, Major 132-133
Brothers, John 30, 135, 151, 154
Brown, John 63-65, 70-71
Brown, Lorenzo 127
Brown, Mrs. 99
Bruce, Sanders 52
Buchanan, James 30
Buckley, Harvey 37, 81-82, 137
Buckner, Simon B. 13, 25, 62
Buell, Don Carlos 37, 41
Buford, Abraham 60
Buford, Absalom 35
Burbridge, Stephen Gano 12-13, 56-57, 59-61, 63-67, 70-71, 73-79, 82, 90-91, 132, 163, 165
Burkesville, Kentucky 50, 115
Burns, Captain 101
Bush, Bryan 186
Bushnell, John 137
Butler, C.B. 107
Butler, J.S. 68
Butner, Isaac 102
Byers, Joseph G. 143
Byrne, Thomas 153

C

Cager, Jesse 87-88
Calahan, Pat 30
Camp Burnett 31
Camp Charity 19, 25, 34
Camp Denson 54
Camp Dick Robinson 21, 26
Camp Douglas 156
Camp Morton 31
Camp Nelson 23, 56, 123
Campbell, Captain 73
Campbell, James 17
Caplinger, George 160
Cardwell, J.W. 88-89
Cardwell, Sue 89

Carter, John 21, 23, 82-83
Carter, Mrs. 88
Cassell, Captain 51
Castalian Springs, Tennessee 41
Catlin, Al 32
Cave Hill Cemetery 186
Cecil, R.W. 87-88
Chaplintown, Kentucky 126, 130, 135-136
Chenault, David 42-44, 51-52
Chenoweth, Major 65, 69
Cincinnati, Ohio 36, 55
Clark, Colonel 42
Clarke, Beverly 30
Clarke, Branch 30
Clarke, Hector M. 30
Clarke, Marcellus Jerome (see Mundy, Sue) 7, 9, 11-12, 30-31, 33-34, 37, 39, 52, 73, 79, 81, 84, 86, 88-97, 106, 112-114, 117-120, 122, 125-126, 129, 132-133, 135, 137-141, 143, 148, 150-152, 162, 164-165
Clarke, Pauline 52
Clarke, Tandy 30
Claunch, D.C. 17
Clement, Mr. 106
Cluke, Roy 43-44, 46, 52
Cobb, Robert 43-44
Cockrell, R.H. 153-156
Collins, J. B. 153
Columbia, Kentucky 50, 115
Conn, John 34
Connolly, Mr. 134
Connolly, Mrs. 134
Conrad, James 30
Cook, Captain 82-83
Cook, John 126
Cooper, Captain 66, 69
Cooper, Eli 104
Cooper, Wickliffe 67
Corbett, Lieutenant 46-47
Corinth, Mississippi 20, 25-26
Corydon, Indiana 53
Coulter, Isaiah (Big Zay) 79, 81, 86, 88, 93, 98-101, 125, 129, 137, 144, 147
Cowan, Captain 51

Cox, Joseph 149, 155
Coyle, W.H. 151, 153
Craddock, Jesse 82
Crittenden, Thomas 42
Crook, George 62-63
Cruickshank, Stewart 98
Cunningham, John 30
Cunningham, Mrs. 109
Cynthiana, Kentucky 68-71, 73

D

David, Jim 30
Davis, Jefferson 76, 153
Davis, Jim *(see Henry, William and Wells (Welles), Harvey)* 95, 104-106, 109-110, 115, 157
Davis, Jonathan 115, 146
Davis, Jonathon 73
Dawes, Susan 32
Demaree 101
Derr, Mr. 81
Desha, Joe 40
Devine, James 98-99
Dickson, J. Bates 66-67, 71
Diehl, Henry 134
Drake, Jim 147
Drum, U.T. 153
Dugan, Elijah 91, 93
Dugan, James 91
Duke, Basil 42-44, 46-48, 50-51, 54
Duncan, James C. 144
Dupont, Indiana 54
Durham, William 96-97

E

Edges, Arch 83, 84
Edwards, J. D. 143
Edwards, Major 129
Elizabethtown, Kentucky 45-47, 120
Ellsworth, George A. (Lightening) 52, 54
Engle, Anne 117
Engle, James 117-119
Enloe, George 23-24, 26-27, 30, 33-34, 73
Enloe, John 147
Ennis, John 136
Evans, Dr. 45, 73, 112-113
Evans, Jim 73, 81-84, 135, 147-148

Everett, Captain 69
Everett, Peter 65
Ewing, Hugh 78

F

Fairleigh, Colonel 78
Falmouth, Kentucky 69
Farmer, Dink, Sr. 162
Ferguson, Lieutenant Colonel 51, 60
Fiddler, Captain 112
Finley, Colonel 102
Finley, Willis 144
First National Bank 88
Fischer, Gerald 146
Fitch, Graham 76
Flowers (guerilla) 93
Forrest, Nathan Bedford 59-61, 108, 115, 145
Foster, David 98-99
Foster, John 102
Four Years in the Saddle with Forrest and Morgan 163, 167
Fox, Mrs. 97
Fox, William 96
Franklin, Kentucky 30, 141, 167
Franks, Tom 51-52
Froman, Abe 105
Froman *(guerilla)* 86, 93, 125

G

Gallatin, Tennessee 38-41
Gallop, Colonel 61
Gano, Richard 38, 41-42, 50
Garrard, Israel 67, 70-71
General Lytle 114
Georgetown, Kentucky 66
Giltner, Colonel 62, 65, 69
Gist 91, 93
Glasgow, Kentucky 37, 45
Glasscock, Richard 147
Glendale, Ohio 54
Grant, Ulysses S. 56-57, 61, 145, 164
Gray, T. W. 35
Green, Ezekiel 42, 44
Green, John 91
Green, Mrs. 164
Green, Sam 102
Green, Thomas 149
Green, Wallace 111
Greeneville, Tennessee 9
Greg *(guerilla)* 121

Grider, Colonel 64
Grier, James 91
Grier, Milton 91
Grier, Thomas 91
Grigsby, Colonel 49, 52, 104
Grigsby, Mrs. William R. 115-116
Grisby, Alex 147
Guthrie, Dick 111

H

Hackett, Warren 144
Hagerstown, Maryland 121
Hail, Mary 30
Halee (guerilla) 135, 147
Haley, Dennis 88
Hall, Albert S. 49
Hall, Jacob 101
Hall, Martha 102
Hall, Thomas 102
Halleck, Henry 75-76
Halloway, Lieutenant 51
Hamilton, Mrs. 72
Hammon, Amelia 32
Hanson, Charles 52, 65, 71, 132
Hapeman, Douglas 43
Harbeson, Sheriff 160
Harlan, John 42, 48
Harper, Adam 97
Harrington, Alfred 91, 93
Harris, Mr. 142
Harrodsburg, Kentucky 20, 87-90, 128
Hartford, Kentucky 122
Hartsville, Tennessee 41-44
Hawes, Captain 66
Hawes, Richard 72
Hawkins, Frank 30
Hays, John 30
Head, James 98
Heady, Squire 129
Heath, Henry 36-37
Heintzelman, Samuel 69, 76
Helm, Ben Hardin 131
Henry, Bill 95
Henry, Captain 109
Henry, Jim 134-135
Henry, John 91
Henry, Tom 30, 73, 76, 93, 117, 143, 145, 164
Henry, William *(see Wells (Welles), Harvey and Davis, Jim)* 157

Herbert *(guerilla)* 33
Hester, Francis 91
Hicks, Stephen 60
Hill, James D. 118
Hill, William 118-119
Hilton, Dave 147
Hindman, Thomas 19
Hines, Thomas 53
Hinkle, Mr. 132
Hobson, Edward 50, 54-55, 61-63, 68-70
Hockersmith, Clark 147
Hockersmith, James 147
Hodge, George B. 60-61
Hoke, W.B. 149, 153
Holmes *(guerilla)* 91
Holms, Widow 104
Holt, Joseph 78-79
Houston, Sam 17
Howell, Mr. 143
Hudgins, John 73
Hughes, Billy 112, 125
Hughes, James 108
Hulse, Bill 121, 135, 147
Hunt, Thomas 42-44, 131
Huntsville, Alabama 19
Hurlbut, Stephen 61
Hutchinson, Clarence 30, 33, 36, 49
Hutton, Dave 147

I
Indianapolis, Indiana 31

J
Jackson, J. 97
Jackson, M. 97
Jacob, Richard 24, 28
James, Frank 121, 127, 129, 137
James, Jesse 121, 135
James Pratt 113
James, Private 128-129
Jenkins, Captain 65, 69
Jesse, George 82, 105
Johnson, Adam Rankin (Stovepipe) 8-9, 49-50, 53, 55, 62
Johnson, Albert (Stovepipe) 11
Johnson, Andrew 154
Johnson, Bill 30
Johnson *(guerilla)* 125
Johnson, Henry 30
Johnson, Joseph 151
Johnson, Richard 41
Johnson, William R. 159

Johnston, Albert Sidney 20, 25
Johnston, Andrew 146
Johnston, Joseph 145
Jones, Elijah 96
Jones, Jimmy 125
Jones, Oscar 30, 33
Jones, Peg Leg 111
Jones, Sam 112
Jones, William 62
Jordan, Lewis 53
Judah, Henry 50

K
Kentucky State Normal School 7, 17
Key, Foster 128-129
Kirk, Alphonso 116
Kirk, Mr. 151
Kirke, Mr. 154
Knott, Mrs. 106

L
Lancaster, Captain 113
Lawrence, Kansas 121-122
Lawrence Massacre 122
Lawson, John 111
Lawton, Walter B. 122-123
Lebanon, Kentucky 51-52, 60
Lebanon, Tennessee 39
Lee, Mrs. 108
Lee, Robert E. 145, 151, 164
Lee, Thornton 108, 110
Lee, T.W. 106-107
Lester, Richard 111
Lewis, A. L. 80
Lewis, Caroline 80
Lexington, Kentucky 7, 16-17, 19, 35, 38, 61, 65-67, 71, 127
Liberty, Tennessee 49-50
Lincoln, Abraham 76, 78, 132, 147, 151, 154
Little, Richard (Dick) 88
Llewellyn, D. H. 47
Long, Silas 30
Longstreet, James 61
Louisville Courier-Journal, The 45, 141, 162-163, 166
Louisville Daily Journal 77, 81, 82, 113
Louisville Journal 125, 149

Louisville, Kentucky 36, 146, 161, 186
Love, George 54

M
Mack, Captain 109
Mackey, John 113
Magoffin, Beriah 89
Magruder, Amy 24
Magruder, Archibald 24
Magruder, Bill 148
Magruder, Ezekiel 24
Magruder, Henry 7, 9-12, 21, 23-26, 30, 33-34, 73, 79-80, 84-85, 88, 93, 95-96, 101, 104, 108-109, 112, 114-120, 122, 124-125, 129, 132-133, 135, 138-139, 142-143, 146, 148, 162, 164-165
Manton, Kentucky 130-131
Marattay, Mr. 107
Marion, Bill *(see Catlin, Al; Oliver, John and Young, Stanley)* 7, 12, 30, 32, 45, 93, 95, 115, 117, 123, 125-126, 139, 141, 144, 146, 162
Marity, J.J. 110
Marsh, William 32
Marshall, Humphrey 17, 36-37
Martin, James 8-10
Martin, Robert (R.M.) 49-50, 65
Martin, Samuel 98
Matson, Courtland 47
Mayfield, W. H. 118
McCann, Major 50
McCay, F. H. 120
McCloskey, John 114-115, 130, 135
McCluskey, Doctor 102
McComb 53
McCormack, Charles 115
McCormick, Robert 115-116
McElroy, A.C. 107-108
McElroy, Charles 108
McElroy, Hugh 108-109
McGraw, Elizabeth 16
McGraw, Henry 111
McGraw, John 16-17, 123
McKay, F.H. 121
McKnight, Brian 7

McMinnville, Tennessee 50
McMurty, Lee 137, 147
Medkiff, Henry 120, 138-139, 146
Memphis, Tennessee 61
Merriman, Bill (Billy) 73, 104, 112, 115-120, 125, 147
Merriman, Mrs. 152
Merriwether, Captain 53
Merryfield *(guerilla)* 125
Metcalf, Henry 117
Midway, Kentucky 97, 130
Milam, John 16
Miller, Joe 79, 80
Miller, Montgomery 146
Milton, William 88, 91
Minty, Robert 50, 115
Mires, Colonel 63
Mitchell, Captain 50, 109
Mitchell, Dick 99, 106-108, 110, 115, 120, 124-125, 134, 149-153, 155-156, 164
Mitchell, Squire 100
Monroe, George W. 66
Moore, Absalom 42-44
Moore, James F. 93
Moore, Orlando 51
Moore, W.T. 128
Morehead, James T. 43
Morgan, Calvin 52
Morgan, John Hunt 7-11, 17, 19-21, 26, 34-55, 60-72, 126, 131
Morgan, John *(student)* 84-85
Morgan, Rebecca 52
Morgan, Thomas 52
Morrison, Bill 73
Mosby, John S. 8, 30, 64
Mount Sterling, Kentucky 60, 62, 64-66, 72-73
Muir, Mr. 133
Mundy, Sue *(see Clarke, Marcellus Jerome)* 9-10, 31-32, 73, 91, 94, 97-98, 106, 111, 113, 126, 135, 139, 152, 162
Murphy, Captain 52

N

Nashville, Tennessee 20
Neal, J. P. 142
New Albany Daily Ledger 76
Newton, James 148

Noland, Henry 128-129
Noland, William 128

O

Octagon Hall 167
Oklahoma City, Oklahoma 167
Oliver, John *(see Catlin, Al; Marion, Bill and Young, Stanley)* 32
Oughten, Enos 159

P

Paducah, Kentucky 60
Palmer, Allen 137, 147
Palmer, Baylor 46-47
Palmer, John 13, 132, 141, 146, 149-157, 162-165, 167
Parker, J.W. 153
Parkhurst *(guerilla)* 93, 98
Parks, W. H. 111
Parmer, Allen 127
Patterson, John 30-31
Pence, Bud 137, 147
Pence, Denny 137
Penn, George W. 146
Perkins, Jacob 81, 98, 100-101
Perryville, Kentucky 17, 86, 111
Perryville State Historic Site 186
Personal Recollections of John Palmer: The Story of an Ernest Life. After the Civil War 162
Peyton, Jim 30
Phillips, Captain 114
Piepho, Carlo 43
Pogniard, D. R. 121
Pratt, James 112, 115
Pratt, Thomas 115
Prentice, George 31
Price, Sterling 121-122

Q

Quantrill, William 121-122, 126-127, 132-133, 137, 146-148, 164
Quirk, Captain Tom 50

R

Randolph, William 161
Ratliff, Colonel 65
Ready, Martha 50
Redding, Merritt, Sr. 161

Renick, Chat 129
Renick, Chatham (Chad) 127-128
Reynold, Joseph 48
Richmond Daily Dispatch, The 76
Richmond, Kentucky 162
Richmond, Virginia 62
Riddle, Captain 25
Riley, William 98-99
Rissinger, G. 97
Robinson, George 110
Robinson, G. S. 106
Robinson, William 86-90
Rosecrans, William 41, 45, 49
Ross, John 147
Rousseau, Lovell 152
Rude (guerilla) 114
Rusk, John 106
Russel, John 105-106
Russell, Captain 93-95
Russell, Henry 91-92
Russell, John Bedford 147
Russell, Mitch 92
Russell, Samuel 150
Rutland, Ohio 54

S

Salem, Indiana 54
Sanders, Burke 30
Saunders, Walter 161-162
Savage Conflict, A 7
Sawyer, R.M. 60
Sawyers, Thomas 76
Scarce, Captain 17
Schofield, John 57, 60-61
Scott *(guerilla)* 121
Scott, Joseph 42, 43
Searcy, Captain 137
Shelby, Joseph 121
Shelbyville, Kentucky 123, 159-160
Sheldon, Ralph 41
Sherman, William T. 10, 12, 17-18, 20- 22, 24, 26-31, 33-34, 36-38, 41, 45-46, 49, 56, 60-62, 66-67, 73-75, 145
Shirk, John L. 115-116
Shouse, Private 128
Sidell, Major 78
Simms, R.J. 110
Simpsonville, Kentucky 124-125, 143, 145
Simpsonville Massacre 126

Sims, Henry 30
Singleton, Jake 147
Sissol, R.H. 136, 137
Smedler, J. M. 90
Smith, Edmund Kirby 35-37, 146
Smith, Harry 46-47
Smith, Jake 30
Smith, Mrs. 157
Smith, Rough 30
Smithville, Tennessee 48
Snyder, Eli 91
Snyder, Samuel 104, 123
Spalding, Charles 115
Spencer, Herbert 30, 33
Spencer, Willie 135
Spieback, Golightly 121
Springfield, Kentucky 106-108, 110-111
Stagg, Thomas 88
Stanton, Secretary of War Edwin 75, 78, 132
Stearn, Colonel 42
Stokes, William B. 42
Stone, Colonel 92
Stoneman, George 67
Stoner, Robert 46
Stower, Colonel 34
Sturgis, Samuel 60-61
Suder, John 73
Sutherland, Daniel 7-8, 10
Sutherland, John 91, 93
Sutherland, Mrs. 91, 93
Sutherland, Tom 93
Sweeney, Mr. 81
Symes (Simms), Robert 107

T
Tafel, Gustavus 43-44
Talbot, Reverend 139-140
Tandall (guerilla) 91
Taylor, Bob 30
Taylor, Captain 53, 112, 114
Taylor, Dick 127-128
Taylor, Grayson 127
Taylor (guerilla) 93
Taylor, Richard 145
Taylorsville, Kentucky 104, 123
Taylor, W. R. 128
Techener, James 117
Temlinson, James 89-90

Terrell, Edwin (Ed) 13, 129-130, 132, 134-136, 146-148, 159-161
Terrell, William 136
Terrill, Edwin 123, 131
Terry, Benjamin 19
Terry's Texas Rangers 50
Texas (guerilla) 30, 33, 73, 114, 135, 143, 145, 149-156
Thomas, Alex 149
Thomas, Butler 93
Thomas, George 132
Thomasson, John 94
Thomasson, Mollie 94
Thompson, Harry 148, 159
Thompson, Mitchell 99
Tibbs, Mary 30
Tinsley, Henry 91-93, 95
Todd (guerilla) 121
Todd, Henry 30
Todd, Miss 72
Toler, Jim 30, 33
Tompkinsville, Kentucky 45
Townsley, James Wisley 123
Trabue, James 30
Treble, Captain 51
True, C. J. 56, 64
Turner, Henry 106, 109-110, 112, 123
Tyler, Major 70

U
Upton, H. 147

V
Vance, William 88
Vanderipe, David 18
Vanderipe, James 18
Violet, John 91-92

W
Wainwright, Captain 81-83
Wakefield, Captain 147
Walch, Bill 73
Walker, Harvey 111
Walker, Kirk 136
Walker, Mr. 100
Warford, Harvey 91-93, 98
Warren, Enoch 99

Waters, Deputy Sheriff 160
Watson, Benjamin 105
Watson, Joseph 104-105
Wayne, Mad Anthony 21
Weatherford, Colonel 132-133
Weatherton, John 110
Weaver, T.R. 153
Webb, H. H. 143
Wells (Welles), Harvey (see Henry, William and Davis, Jim) 157, 163, 165
Wells, Harvey (hotel keeper) 119
Wells, Sarah 32
West, Howard 147
Wetherton, Mr. 106-108
Wharton, Captain 112
Whitaker, General 142
White, King 91-93, 114, 135
Whitesides (guerilla) 125
Wigginton, James 32
Wilkinson, William 87
Williamson, William 86
Wilson, Bill (Billy) 30, 34
Wilson, Captain 68
Wilson, Cyrus 138, 146, 148-150, 152-156, 164-165
Wilson, James 101
Winstead, Jake 118, 120
Withers, John 159-160
Wright (guerilla) 94
Wright, John 128

Y
Yager (guerilla) 121
Young, Bennett 42
Young, Captain 151
Young, Joe 137
Young, John 90
Young, Robert 112
Young, Stanley (see Catlin, Al; Marion, Bill and Oliver, John) 7, 12, 32
Young, St. Clair 32
Younger, Jim 127
Younger Brothers 121